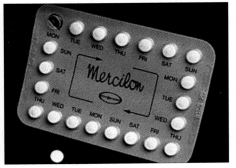

Human hormones

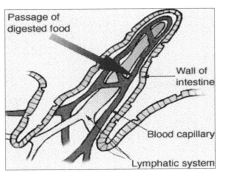

Passage of
digested food

Wall of
intestine

Blood capillary

Lymphatic system

Human digestion

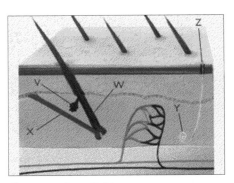

Z

V W

X Y

Cross-section of skin

Introduction

This book will help you to study and to revise biology for GCSE Science. You can use it to test your knowledge and understanding of the subjects covered in your syllabus.

Structure of the book

This book is divided into five sections that correspond to the main subject areas in biology. These are further divided into chapters. Each chapter contains key facts, questions, and answers.

At the end of the book, there is a quickfire questions section, which will help you to identify any gaps in your knowledge of the syllabus.

• Key facts

The key facts are a brief summary of the important ideas that relate to specific topics within a section. Read them carefully as they provide a basic introduction to subject areas, as well as a quick reminder of important facts.

• Questions

Most of the questions are multiple choice. Use the tick boxes to make your selection (there is only one correct answer for each question). Some questions are easy; others are more difficult. Make sure you study the questions carefully, because it is often just one word that makes the difference between a right answer and a wrong one.

If you cannot pick the correct answer straight away, think very carefully. Even if you have not studied the specific point that is being tested, you may be able to work out the answer using your general understanding of biology.

• Answers

In many ways, this is the most important part of the book. Check whether your answer is correct or not. If it is, tick the box next to the appropriate answer. Make sure you fully understand why the answer you chose was the right one. Don't worry if your answer is incorrect. Make sure you understand how and why you made a mistake by reading the comprehensive explanation provided with each answer. These explanations will provide you with all the information that you need to answer the questions correctly.

You will learn a lot by reading over this section carefully, and you may want to test yourself on any new information learnt by answering the questions again at a later revision session.

• Quickfire Questions

These are organised into the same chapters as those found in the book. Some questions require one word answers; others need to be answered as fully as you can. Check your answers after each chapter. If you have a wrong answer, you should go back to check the whole of the relevant chapter in the book.

Syllabuses

Check the content of your syllabus carefully because there are several different GCSE Science syllabuses and they vary slightly in their content. They cover a lot of the same material, but you will find that this book includes some areas of biology that are not on your syllabus, and that there may be a few topics that you will need to look at separately.

GCSE Science options

There are four options available for the candidate studying biology for GCSE Science. They are as follows (attainable grades are in brackets):

Single Science Foundation Level (grades G to C)

Single Science Higher Level (grades D to A*)

Double Science Foundation Level (grades GG to CC)

Double Science Higher Level (grades DD to A*A*)

This books caters for all four options. The contents pages highlight the chapters that relate to both Single and Double Science Awards, and those that relate to Double Awards only. The chapters include questions for both the Foundation and the Higher Level candidate, and may include some that relate to the Higher Level candidate only. You need only study the chapters that relate to you. However, you may find it both interesting and useful to read through some of the other chapters.

GCSE Science coursework

Science coursework makes up 25% of the overall marks of your GCSE Science grade. The coursework is split into four skill areas as follows:

• Planning experimental procedures

• Obtaining evidence

• Analysing evidence and drawing conclusions

• Evaluating evidence

You will need to check with your school or college that you have provided all the coursework required for each skill area.

Marking system

Evaluate your biology knowledge and determine which subject areas need the most revision and practice by using this marking system. Add up your correct answers and enter the scores into the boxes below (the totals are cumulative, so higher candidates need only fill in the last column).

Compare results for each section by converting your score into a percentage by using this equation: (100 ÷ [maximum score]) x your score = % score e.g., (100 ÷ 46) x 30 = 65 %
Use the key at the bottom of the page to assess your results.

SECTIONS		Single and Double Awards	Double Award only	Foundation Level	Foundation and Higher
LIFE PROCESSES:	Cell activity			/19 = %	/20 = %
	Organs working together			/14 = %	/14 = %
	Cell division			/3 = %	/8 = %
	Transport between cells			/2 = %	/11 = %
HUMANS AS ORGANISMS:	Human diet			/12 = %	/12 = %
	Human digestion			/40 = %	/43 = %
	Human circulation			/25 = %	/25 = %
	Composition and function of blood			/14 = %	/14 = %
	Human breathing			/24 = %	/28 = %
	Human respiration			/12 = %	/20 = %
	Human nervous system			/16 = %	/26 = %
	Human eye			/18 = %	/22 = %
	Human hormones			/8 = %	/30 = %
	Importance of homeostasis			/28 = %	/30 = %
	Excretion in the kidneys			/6 = %	/25 = %
	Defence against disease			/12 = %	/17 = %
	Use and abuse of drugs			/19 = %	/19 = %
GREEN PLANTS AS ORGANISMS:	Plant structure			/12 = %	/12 = %
	Plant nutrition			/23 = %	/29 = %
	Plant hormones			/3 = %	/9 = %
	Transport systems inside plants			/16 = %	/21 = %
VARIATION, INHERITANCE AND EVOLUTION:	Variation			/25 = %	/29 = %
	Genetics			/19 = %	/45 = %
	Scientific uses of genetics			/8 = %	/27 = %
	DNA			/0 = %	/7 = %
	Evolution			/9 = %	/23 = %
LIVING THINGS IN THEIR ENVIRONMENT:	Adaptation, competition and predation			/32 = %	/32 = %
	Human impact on the environment			/24 = %	/39 = %
	Energy and nutrient transfer			/30 = %	/39 = %
	Carbon and nitrogen cycles			/23 = %	/29 = %
	Food production			/0 = %	/19 = %

0–25 % Long way to go!	26–50 % Keep going!	51–75 % Nearly there!	76–100 % Excellent!	Average Score
				/496 = % /724 = %

5

Revision tips

General tips

Set yourself a reasonable revision timetable and try to stick to it. When you're not revising, relax and do things that you enjoy.

Find a quiet area in which to revise. You will take in much more if you have no distractions, such as the television or music.

Try to revise at a regular time each day. For example, in the holidays you might decide to revise from 10:00 am to 12 noon and from 5:00 pm to 7:00 pm every day.

When you return to your revision after a break, spend a few minutes thinking about the material covered in the last session. This will help you to consolidate what you have already revised.

In an ideal world, you should aim to complete your revision two weeks before the exam. In the final two weeks you should try plenty of past exam questions.

Try to stay fit and healthy – this means you should get plenty of sleep, eat properly, and take regular exercise.

There are lots of people who want you to do well – friends, parents, relatives, and teachers. These people will always be happy to help you.

Your revision sessions

Try to make each revision session about 35 minutes long. A common mistake is to concentrate hard for the first five minutes, daydream for the next 25 minutes, and then to resume a high level of concentration for only the last five minutes. You think that you've done 35 minutes of hard work, but really you have done only ten! The secret of good revision is making the most of these 35 minute sessions. The following tips should help you do this.

• The sessions must be varied. In any one session you should aim to read, answer questions, highlight key words, and possibly produce labelled diagrams. You may find it useful to write your notes onto revision cards to use as a reminder of important facts.

• Before you start, make sure that you have everything that you need.

• The first thing you must do is to make sure that you understand what you are revising. There is no point learning something that you don't understand. Do not be afraid to ask your teachers any questions that you might have – they are there to help you. Make sure you ask at a sensible time, and not at the very last minute.

• Once you understand a topic, make notes on it in your own words. If possible, draw a diagram. It is easier to remember things as pictures rather than as words.

• Test yourself at regular intervals by using the questions in this book. Start by looking at questions that address just one topic, and progress to those that address a wider range of topics.

• As you revise a topic, use a highlighter pen to pick out the key words and points. After going through your notes several times, you will be able to fit enough basic information on to one revision card to remind you of a whole topic. Remember to use these cards often to test yourself on the information you have already learnt.

• Keep your notes and cards organised! This is very important but often forgotten – you will lose much of the benefit of your revision if you lose your notes.

• As the exam gets closer, try past questions from your exam board. When you first start answering questions you may have to use your notes to produce a full answer. As your knowledge improves, you will need to refer to your notes less. If you cannot find an answer in a text book or in your notes, ask your teacher. Don't just ignore it – a similar type of question may come up in your exam. Be aware of the time taken to answer a question; your answering speed will increase as your knowledge improves.

The night before the exam

There are several different views as to what to do the night before the exam, ranging from working all night to having the afternoon off school the day before in order to relax. The best solution lies between these two.

We have consulted doctors and examiners to come up with this simple list. It is incredibly easy to follow and will give you the best chance of success in your exam.

• Have a good meal.

Variation

DNA

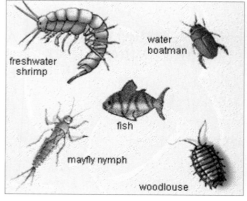
Adaptation

• Go over your revision cards for about an hour early in the evening.

• If you have any questions, ask someone rather than remain silent and worry about it.

• In the hour before your regular bedtime, try to relax. Many people relax by watching television or by listening to music.

• Go to bed at your regular bedtime and try to get a good night's sleep.

The exam

Arrive at least 15 minutes before the exam starts.

Make sure you have everything you need – pens, a pencil, a rubber, a watch, a ruler, coloured pencils, and a calculator.

Read all the instructions for the exam carefully and note the time allocated for the exam. Check whether or not you have to answer all the questions. If you do not, make sure that you understand all the instructions attached to the questions that you do need to answer.

Plan your time carefully. Look at the marks available for the question and determine what proportion they are of the total marks. You should spend a similar proportion of the time available on that question. For example, if a question is allocated 20% of the overall marks, you should spend 20% of the exam period on that question.

The marks available for each question give you a guide as to how much information the examiners are after. For example, a 2-mark question generally requires two separate points or one fully explained point as an answer.

Look out for key words in the question. For example, "calculate" means show your calculations.

Always read the question at least twice.

If your exam contains multiple choice questions, make sure that you answer them all. In multiple choice questions, if you are unsure of an answer, first eliminate the answers that you know are wrong, then make an educated guess between the options that remain. For the extended questions (generally worth 6 marks), the examiner requires several key points. You may wish to briefly plan your answer.

Make sure that all your answers stick to the point. Consider carefully what the question is asking and try not to waffle!

Exam presentation

There is more to doing exam questions than getting the right answer. How you present your answer can gain or lose you valuable points. In GCSE Science there are some rules that will help you pick up as many points as possible.

• If a question requires a calculation, always show your working and use the correct units.

• In a calculation, work with more decimal places than the question requires and then reduce your final answer to the required number of decimal places. This will ensure that your answer is accurate. For example, if the question asks for your answer to 2 decimal places, do the calculation working to at least 3 decimal places. When you have your final answer reduce it to 2 decimal figures.

• If a diagram will aid your answer, use one. Make sure that it is neat, and properly labelled.

• When including graphs, make sure that they have a title and that both axes are labelled. Plot the points on the graph accurately and clearly, and draw the best line of fit with a sharp pencil. If the graph line is straight, use a ruler and position it symmetrically between the points in order to draw the line. If the graph line is not straight, draw a smooth curve that best fits the plotted points.

• If you have any time remaining at the end of the exam, read over all your answers. First check that your answers are correct, and then check your spelling, punctuation, and grammar. (In some exams, 5% of the marks are awarded for correct spelling, punctuation, and grammar.)

And finally...GOOD LUCK!

Energy and nutrient transfer

Plant nutrition

Competition

Life Processes

Cell activity *(Single and Double Awards)*

'What is the meaning of Life?' This is a frequently asked question that has been answered in many ways – from comedy to religion. Biologists point to the life processes that are common to all living things – both plants and animals. The more we learn about how plants and animals live, the more we realise that they have a great deal in common. Some of these processes are remarkably similar, such as respiration, whilst others are less so, for example, movement in plants, which is difficult to see.

Not only do plants and animals have many life processes in common, but they also have cells that are remarkably similar in structure. Both plants and animals can exist as single cells, small groups of cells, or large multicellular organisms, yet virtually all of their cells have a basic structure that includes a nucleus, cytoplasm and a cell membrane. (A notable exception is the red blood cell, which does not have a nucleus.) The nucleus contains the most remarkable molecules known. They form the DNA, which can reproduce itself and carries all the information needed to produce a new organism.

KEY FACTS

• **Life processes** There are seven life processes common to plants and animals. The easy way to remember them is by the acronym 'MRS GREN', where each letter stands for one of the processes.

• **Movement** Although it might not be obvious that plants can move, if they are observed under a microscope, movement can be seen within their cells.

• **Respiration** The release of energy from food occurs in all living cells and the released energy is used in all the other life processes.

• **Sensitivity** This is the ability to react to the environment. Plants react more slowly than animals.

• **Growth** This is the development of offspring to adult size.

• **Reproduction** This is the production of offspring.

• **Excretion** This is the release of waste products. Plants turn wastes into harmless products, which they store.

• **Nutrition** Plants use light energy to make food; animals eat plants and other animals.

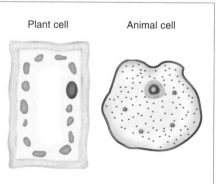

Plant cell   Animal cell

Animal and plant cells

• **Cells** These are the tiny building blocks that make up plants and animals. Plant and animal cells have some similarities in structure. Animal and plant cells both have a cell membrane, cytoplasm and a nucleus. Only plant cells have a cell wall, chloroplasts and a large central vacuole.

• **Cell membrane** This is the thin sheet that runs around the outside of the cell. It controls which substances go in and out of a cell.

• **Cytoplasm** This is the fluid inside the cell where most of the cell's chemical reactions take place.

• **Nucleus** This controls the actions of the cell. The nucleus contains chromosomes that carry the hereditary material in units called

genes. Genes determine many of a living thing's characteristics, such as the eye colour of an animal. The genes are strung together in long chains that are coiled up many times to form chromosomes. A human has twenty-three pairs of chromosomes. One of each pair of chromosomes comes from the mother, the other from the father.

• **Cell wall** This strengthens the cell.

• **Chloroplasts** These are needed for the process of photosynthesis.

• **Large central vacuole** This large central sac contains a liquid called the cell sap that stores food and minerals.

QUESTIONS

1 Respiration is a characteristic of all living things. Which of the following is the best definition of respiration?

☐ (a) Releasing energy from food
☐ (b) Making energy by food
☐ (c) Using energy to contract a muscle
☐ (d) Animals eating plants
☐ (e) Breathing

2 Which of the following is the term used for the release of waste products made by a living organism?

☐ (a) Movement
☐ (b) Sensitivity
☐ (c) Excretion
☐ (d) Digestion
☐ (e) Peristalsis

3 Which of the following is not a characteristic of both plants and animals?

☐ (a) Respiration
☐ (b) Photosynthesis
☐ (c) Growth
☐ (d) Movement
☐ (e) Nutrition

4 Which letter labels the cell membrane of the cell shown in the following diagram?

☐ (a) V
☐ (b) W
☐ (c) X
☐ (d) Y
☐ (e) None

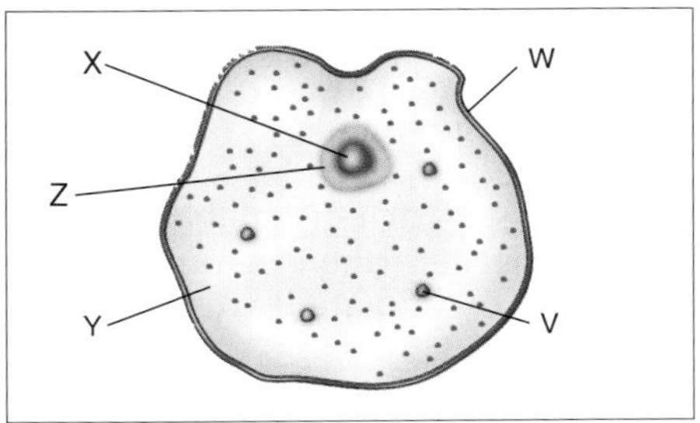

Q4, 5

5 Which letter labels the nucleus of the cell shown in the diagram above?

☐ (a) V
☐ (b) W
☐ (c) X
☐ (d) Y
☐ (e) None

6 Which letter identifies the vacuole of the cell shown in the following diagram?

☐ (a) V
☐ (b) W
☐ (c) X
☐ (d) Y
☐ (e) None

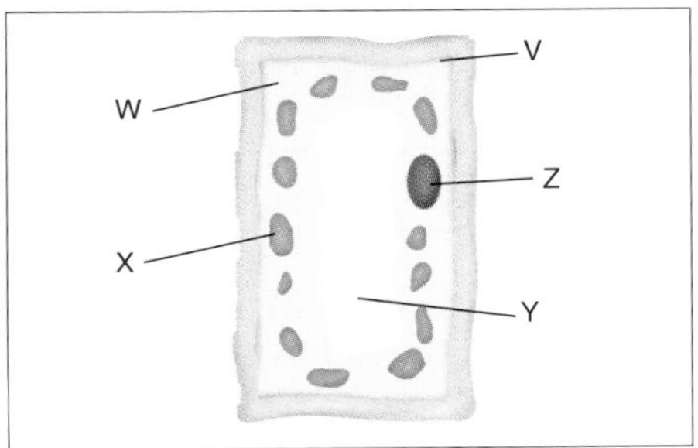

Q6, 7, 8

7 Which letter labels a chloroplast in the cell shown in the diagram above?

☐ (a) V
☐ (b) W
☐ (c) X
☐ (d) Y
☐ (e) None

8 Which letter labels the cytoplasm of the cell shown in the diagram above?

☐ (a) V
☐ (b) W
☐ (c) X
☐ (d) Y
☐ (e) None

9 What is the function of the cell membrane?

☐ (a) To stop anything entering or leaving the cell
☐ (b) To control all the functions of a cell
☐ (c) To act as a matrix for the reactions of a cell
☐ (d) To release energy from food
☐ (e) To control what enters or leaves the cell

10 What structure within a cell controls all the actions of that cell?

☐ (a) Chloroplast
☐ (b) Nucleus
☐ (c) Cell membrane
☐ (d) Vacuole
☐ (e) Cytoplasm

11 Which part of a cell is the location of most of the cell's chemical reactions?

☐ (a) Nucleus
☐ (b) Chloroplast
☐ (c) Membrane
☐ (d) Cytoplasm
☐ (e) Vacuole

12 What is the function of a chloroplast?

☐ (a) To act as the control centre for the cell
☐ (b) To release energy from foods in the cell
☐ (c) To produce sugars by photosynthesis
☐ (d) To control what enters and leaves the cell
☐ (e) To dissolve the cell enzymes in water

13 Which of the following is a function of the vacuole of a plant cell?

☐ (a) To maintain the turgidity of the cell
☐ (b) To contain the genes and chromosomes
☐ (c) To store air when stomata are closed
☐ (d) To act as part of the plant immune system
☐ (e) To store starch during rapid photosynthesis

14 True ☐ or false ☐ ?
Both plant and animal cells have a sap vacuole.

15 Which activity in the following list is something a living animal or plant would not be able to do?

☐ (a) Reproduce its own kind
☐ (b) Excrete wastes from the body
☐ (c) Harness energy to fuel work
☐ (d) Harness materials to fuel growth
☐ (e) Exist without a supply of energy

16 Which of the following statements about plant and animal nutrition are true? X: Plants are able to synthesise their own food substances by photosynthesis. Y: Animals must eat organic material, which they then respire to release energy. Z: Photosynthesis and respiration both involve breaking down molecules of carbohydrate.

☐ (a) X, Y and Z
☐ (b) X and Y
☐ (c) X and Z
☐ (d) Y and Z
☐ (e) X only

17 True ☐ or false ☐ ?
Both plants and animals carry out respiration but only plants photosynthesise.

18 True ☐ or false ☐ ?
Only animals are capable of movement, but both plants and animals are sensitive to their surroundings.

19 True ☐ or false ☐ ?
Plant and animal cells both have cell membranes.

Higher Level only

20 All organisms are made up of cells and the cells found within a single organism, for example, in a human, vary in both size and shape. Why does this variation occur?

☐ (a) Due to the random mutation of cells within the lifetime of an individual organism, producing various random types
☐ (b) Because it is the only way possible to fit all the cells into the body of a typical organism
☐ (c) Because some cells take their genetic instructions from the mother and some from the father
☐ (d) Because cells are designed to suit their function, and different functions require different shapes and sizes
☐ (e) Because some cells are sex cells (gametes) and therefore contain different chromosomes from other cells

9

Organs working together *(Single and Double Awards)*

In larger plants and animals, groups of organs work together to carry out many of the essential functions. The digestive system is a good example. In humans, the system is about ten metres long and uses several distinct organs, each one playing a different role in the process of digestion. It is interesting to consider how a single-celled animal can carry out all of these processes essential to life with just one cell!

KEY FACTS

• **Organ Systems** Cells are adapted to carry out specialist jobs. Groups of specialised cells form a tissue. Different tissues do different but related jobs in an organ. Groups of organs work together in an organ system. Organ systems each have a job to do and are adapted for their roles in the life processes.

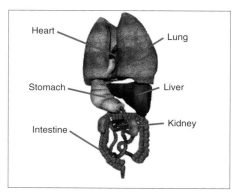

Human organs

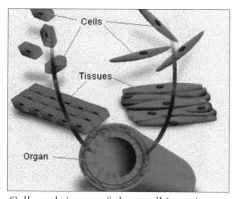

Cells and tissues of the small intestine

• **Digestive system** This breaks down food so that it is small enough to be absorbed into the bloodstream.

• **Breathing system** The large surface area of the breathing system allows the absorption of oxygen into the blood, and the excretion of carbon dioxide from the blood.

• **Circulatory system** This pumps blood round the body, transporting substances and fighting infection.

• **Urinary system** This removes the poisonous waste, called urea, and balances the water and mineral content of the blood.

• **Nervous system** This enables an animal to react to its surroundings and then co-ordinate its response.

• **Root system** This anchors a plant and also absorbs water and minerals from the soil.

• **Shoot system** Stems connect all the parts of a plant above ground. They hold the leaves in the right places for photosynthesis, and the flowers in the best place for reproduction.

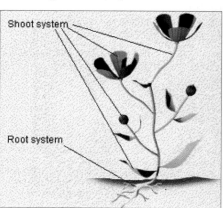

Plant systems

QUESTIONS

21 Which type of cell is shown in the following diagram?

☐ (a) Human sperm cell
☐ (b) Human cheek cell
☐ (c) Human red blood cell
☐ (d) Plant leaf cell
☐ (e) Plant root hair cell

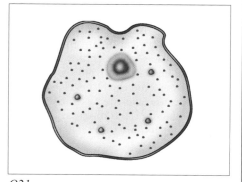

Q21

22 Which type of cell is pictured in the following diagram?

☐ (a) Human sperm cell
☐ (b) Red blood cell
☐ (c) Nettle stinging cell
☐ (d) Palisade cell of a leaf
☐ (e) Root hair cell

Q22

23 Which type of animal cell is illustrated in the following diagram?

☐ (a) Sperm cell
☐ (b) Cheek cell
☐ (c) Egg cell
☐ (d) Muscle cell
☐ (e) Nerve cell

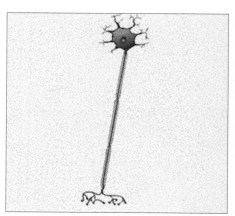

Q23

24 What is the identity of the group of cells shown in the following diagram?

☐ (a) Muscle cells
☐ (b) Nerve cells
☐ (c) Palisade cells
☐ (d) Phloem cells
☐ (e) Red blood cells

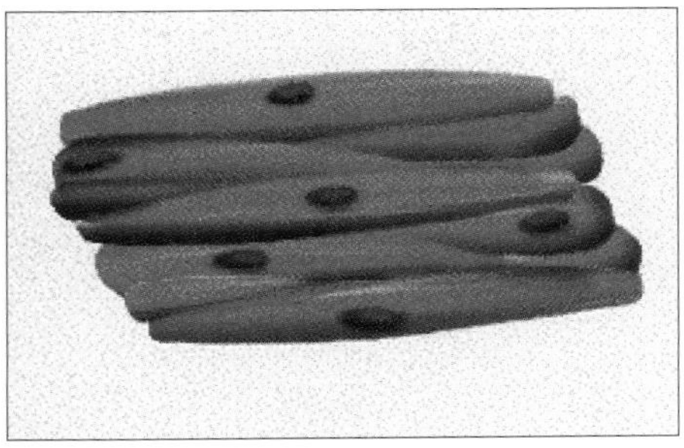

Q24

25 Most cells are specialised. Which of the following cells is specialised to carry genetic information from a father to his child?

☐ (a) Egg cell
☐ (b) Sperm cell
☐ (c) Palisade cell
☐ (d) Nerve cell
☐ (e) Red blood cell

26 Tissues are also specialised for their functions. What function is glandular tissue specialised for?

☐ (a) To produce waste materials
☐ (b) To produce substances the body needs
☐ (c) To contract to move the body
☐ (d) To carry water
☐ (e) To respire

27 What is the name given to a group of cells, of a similar type and function, joined together in large masses within the body of a living organism?

☐ (a) Cytoplasm
☐ (b) Organ
☐ (c) Organism
☐ (d) Pathogen
☐ (e) Tissue

28 Which of the following best defines a 'tissue'?

☐ (a) A thin sheet of transparent cells used to hold organs in position
☐ (b) A section of the digestive tract involved with the digestion of cellulose
☐ (c) A group of similar cells with a common function
☐ (d) A group of cells responsible for secreting mucous in the nasal passages
☐ (e) A group of bacteria cultured in an artificial nutrient jelly in a petri dish

29 Organs are made of different tissues working together. Which of the following is not an organ?

☐ (a) Brain
☐ (b) Heart
☐ (c) Kidney
☐ (d) Lung
☐ (e) Sperm

30 Which of the following is the name given to any collection of joined tissues, acting together to carry out a series of functions?

☐ (a) Hernia
☐ (b) Liver
☐ (c) Organ
☐ (d) Organism
☐ (e) Orgasm

31 Which of the following items can properly be described by the term 'organ'?

☐ (a) Stomach of a human being

☐ (b) Head of a human being
☐ (c) Carpel of a flowering plant
☐ (d) Digestive system of a worm
☐ (e) Guard cells of a plant stoma

32 Which of the following best describes an organ system?

☐ (a) It is made of different cells which work together
☐ (b) It is several different tissues with a common function
☐ (c) It is made up of different organs which work together
☐ (d) It is the muscles and glands that carry out digestion
☐ (e) It is how the body co-ordinates its actions

33 Which of the following is not an organ system?

☐ (a) Circulatory
☐ (b) Lungs
☐ (c) Nervous
☐ (d) Shoot
☐ (e) Urinary

34 Which of the following is a correct sequence in the way that organisms are constructed?

☐ (a) Organ makes cell makes tissue
☐ (b) Organ makes tissue makes cell
☐ (c) Tissue makes organ makes cell
☐ (d) Cell makes tissue makes organ
☐ (e) Cell makes organ makes tissue

11

Cell division (*Single and Double Awards*)

Every cell in your body contains an exact copy of the DNA given to you by your parents nine months before you were born. The remarkable process of cell division is even more staggering when you consider that each cell has nearly two metres of DNA in its nucleus and you have at least 50 trillion cells in your body. Cells divide by mitosis so that growth takes place, and by meiosis to produce gametes.

 ## KEY FACTS

• **Mitosis** This takes place wherever growth is occurring. Copies of the chromosomes are made first and then the cell divides to produce two genetically identical cells.

• **Meiosis** This takes place in the reproductive organs, the testes or the ovaries, where gametes are produced. First the chromosomes make copies of themselves, then the cells divide twice to produce four gametes each with only one set of chromosomes.

• **Fertilisation** When fertilisation occurs, an egg cell, the female gamete, fuses with a sperm cell, the male gamete. The original number of chromosomes is restored and the cell produced now has chromosomes in pairs again. The new individual will then develop from this one cell, which divides many times by mitosis.

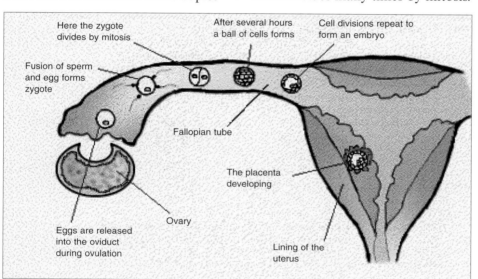

Cell division

Here the zygote divides by mitosis
After several hours a ball of cells forms
Cell divisions repeat to form an embryo
Fusion of sperm and egg forms zygote
Fallopian tube
The placenta developing
Eggs are released into the oviduct during ovulation
Ovary
Lining of the uterus

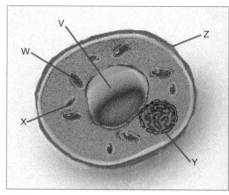

Q37

- [ ] (a) V
- [ ] (b) W
- [ ] (c) X
- [ ] (d) Y
- [ ] (e) Z

QUESTIONS

35 Where are the genes found in a cell?

- [ ] (a) In the cytoplasm
- [ ] (b) On the chromosomes
- [ ] (c) On the Golgi body
- [ ] (d) Within the cell membrane
- [ ] (e) Within the nuclear membrane

36 What is the function of the nucleus in a human egg cell?

- [ ] (a) To contain the genetic information that will be passed onto the next generation
- [ ] (b) To provide a food store for the developing embryo
- [ ] (c) To provide energy via respiration for the egg to move down the Fallopian tube
- [ ] (d) To provide a mechanism for the sperm to find the egg, by creating a type of 'perfume' that attracts the sperm
- [ ] (e) To provide enzymes that will be used to break down the sperm's membrane, enabling the nuclei of the egg and the sperm to fuse

37 Which letter on the following diagram of a plant cell best labels the structure within which the genetic material of the plant would be found?

Higher Level only

38 The following diagram shows some of the stages of mitosis in a cell with two pairs of chromosomes. In which sequence do these stages happen?

- [ ] (a) W - X - Y - Z
- [ ] (b) W - Y - Z - X
- [ ] (c) X - Y - W - Z
- [ ] (d) X - W - Y - Z
- [ ] (e) Y - Z - W - X

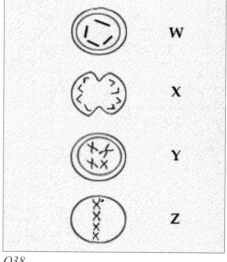

W

X

Y

Z

Q38

39 What is produced when cells undergo mitosis?

- [ ] (a) 2 genetically identical cells
- [ ] (b) 2 genetically different cells
- [ ] (c) 4 genetically identical cells
- [ ] (d) 4 genetically different cells
- [ ] (e) 8 genetically identical cells

40 Which of the following processes does not rely on mitosis?

- ☐ (a) Growth in mammals after birth
- ☐ (b) Repair
- ☐ (c) Asexual reproduction
- ☐ (d) Production of gametes
- ☐ (e) Growth in mammals before birth

41 In which of the following processes are the cells produced by meiosis?

- ☐ (a) Growth in mammals after birth
- ☐ (b) Repair of tissues as mammals age
- ☐ (c) Asexual reproduction in plants
- ☐ (d) Production of gametes in amphibians
- ☐ (e) Growth in mammal embryos before birth

42 What is the name for the process by which the cell divides after fertilisation?

- ☐ (a) Implantation
- ☐ (b) Meiosis
- ☐ (c) Mitosis
- ☐ (d) Binary fission
- ☐ (e) Nuclear fission

Transport between cells *(Double Award only)*

Cells require materials so that they can carry out the life processes essential to their survival. Many cells manufacture materials for other cells. Cells also make waste materials. The movement of these substances into and out of cells is carried out by diffusion, osmosis and active transport.

KEY FACTS

• **Diffusion** This is the spreading of a substance from an area of high concentration to an area of low concentration until the concentration of the substance is evenly spread. Examples of diffusion include oxygen diffusing into the blood in the lungs and carbon dioxide diffusing out of the blood in the lungs. Both oxygen and carbon dioxide diffuse in and out of leaves and leaf cells.

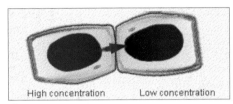

High concentration   Low concentration

Osmosis

• **Osmosis** This is the diffusion of water molecules across a partially permeable membrane that will only allow water molecules across it from an area of high water molecule concentration to an area of low water molecule concentration. An

example of a partially permeable membrane is the cell membrane.

• **Active transport** This is the movement of a substance against its concentration gradient. This requires energy from respiration. An example of active transport is the movement of mineral ions from the soil into the root hair cells.

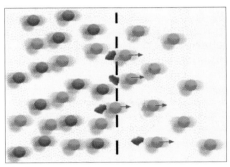

Active transport

QUESTIONS

43 Which liquid compound makes up the majority of a cell's contents?

- ☐ (a) Ethanol
- ☐ (b) Oxygen
- ☐ (c) DNA
- ☐ (d) Chlorophyll
- ☐ (e) Water

44 Which of the following best defines diffusion?

- ☐ (a) The net movement of molecules from a high concentration to a low concentration
- ☐ (b) The movement of water molecules from a high concentration to a low concentration
- ☐ (c) The movement of water molecules from a low concentration to a high concentration
- ☐ (d) The movement of gaseous molecules from a high concentration to a low concentration
- ☐ (e) The movement of liquid molecules from a low concentration to a high concentration

Higher Level only

45 What is the name of the process by which water moves from cell to cell through the tissues of the plant?

- ☐ (a) Active transport
- ☐ (b) Cyclic flow
- ☐ (c) Osmosis
- ☐ (d) Perspiration
- ☐ (e) Respiration

46 Which of the following best defines osmosis?

- ☐ (a) The movement of water molecules from a low concentration to a high concentration through a partially permeable membrane
- ☐ (b) The net movement of water molecules from a high concentration to a low concentration, through a partially permeable membrane
- ☐ (c) The movement of water molecules from a high concentration to a low concentration into the tissues of a root
- ☐ (d) The net movement of gas molecules from a high concentration to a low concentration, through the stomata of a leaf
- ☐ (e) The movement of water molecules, in gaseous state, from a high concentration to a low concentration

47 Substances can be absorbed against a diffusion gradient. Which of the following is required for this to happen?

- ☐ (a) Diffusion
- ☐ (b) Energy
- ☐ (c) Sugar
- ☐ (d) Photosynthesis
- ☐ (e) Osmosis

48 The following diagram shows an experiment in osmosis. After setting up the apparatus as shown, the experiment is left for 15 minutes. Which letter would represent the level of the sugar solution in the tube after 15 minutes?

☐ (a) V
☐ (b) W
☐ (c) X
☐ (d) Y
☐ (e) Z

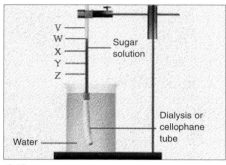

Q48

49 In the osmosis experiment shown in the following diagram, which letter would represent the level of liquid in the tube after 15 minutes?

☐ (a) V
☐ (b) W
☐ (c) X
☐ (d) Y
☐ (e) Z

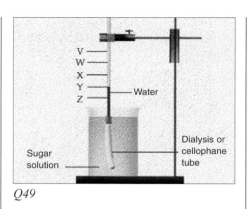

Q49

50 A potato cylinder was taken from the heart of a potato, using a cork borer. The cylinder was found to weigh 0.5 g, and was then submerged in a petri dish containing a strong sugar solution for 30 minutes. After this time it was taken out and weighed again. In which range do you think this new weight would most likely be?

☐ (a) 0.00 - 0.05 g
☐ (b) 0.05 - 0.10 g
☐ (c) 0.40 - 0.45 g
☐ (d) 0.50 - 0.55 g
☐ (e) 0.55 - 0.60 g

51 A potato cylinder was taken from the heart of a potato, using a cork borer. The cylinder was found to weigh 0.5 g, and was then submerged in a petri dish containing distilled water for 30 minutes. After

this time it was taken out and weighed again. In which range do you think this new weight would be?

☐ (a) 0.00 - 0.05 g
☐ (b) 0.25 - 0.30 g
☐ (c) 0.35 - 0.40 g
☐ (d) 0.65 - 0.70 g
☐ (e) 1.95 - 2.0 g

52 Which of the following is an example of active uptake?

☐ (a) Carbon dioxide being excreted from the lungs
☐ (b) Oxygen uptake in the lungs
☐ (c) Water passing into a root hair cell
☐ (d) Water evaporating from the stomata of a leaf
☐ (e) Plant roots absorbing ions from dilute soil solutions

53 Which of the following statements are true? X: All mineral ions enter the root of a plant by diffusion. Y: Mineral ions enter the root of a plant by active transport. Z: Water enters the root of a plant by diffusion.

☐ (a) X and Z
☐ (b) X and Y
☐ (c) Y and Z
☐ (d) X, Y and Z
☐ (e) Z only

 ANSWERS

Cell activity

☐ **1** *(a)*
Respiration happens in plants and animals and is the chemical process that releases energy from food. Breathing in provides oxygen for respiration in some animals. When animals eat plants they are getting the food they need for respiration. Muscles use the energy released from food.

☐ **2** *(c)*
Excretion describes how waste products, made by a living organism, are removed from its body. Movement and sensitivity are also characteristics of living things. Peristalsis describes how food is moved through the gut (alimentary canal).

☐ **3** *(b)*
Photosynthesis is only carried out by plants. Plants use sunlight energy to make energy rich sugars from carbon dioxide and water. Respiration, growth,

movement and sensitivity are common to both plants and animals, and are dependent upon the energy in foods made by the plants.

☐ **4** *(b)*
The cell membrane, a thin sheet made of fats and proteins, runs around the outside of the cell and controls what substances enter and leave the cell.

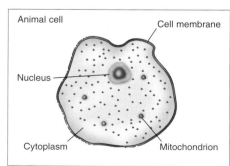

A4, 5, 21

☐ **5** *(c)*
The nucleus is the control centre for the cell. It contains the genetic information

by which the cell runs its chemical processes (metabolism) from moment to moment.

☐ **6** *(d)*
The vacuole occupies a large area of a plant cell and contains cell sap, a liquid that acts as a food and mineral store.

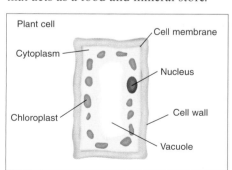

A6, 7, 8, 22

☐ **7** *(c)*
Chloroplasts are present in green plant cells and are where photosynthesis takes place. Photosynthesis is the process by which plants produce sugars by

combining elements from carbon dioxide and water, using the energy of sunlight to power the reactions.

☐ **8** *(b)*
The cytoplasm is the liquid matrix present in all cells.

☐ **9** *(e)*
The cell membrane controls what enters and leaves the cell. In a plant cell, the cell membrane lies just inside the cell wall and so is more difficult to see than in an animal cell. The cell wall is completely permeable and only performs a structural function.

☐ **10** *(b)*
The nucleus contains all the genetic information necessary to run the chemistry of the cell, and this information can be passed on to descendent cells if it divides. This provides a way by which the next generation of cells will have all the information they require to carry out their functions in the organism.

☐ **11** *(d)*
The cytoplasm is where the organelles outside of the nucleus are located and where most of the chemical reactions happen.

☐ **12** *(c)*
Chloroplasts are present only in green plant cells and are where the process of photosynthesis, the making of carbohydrate from water and carbon dioxide, takes place.

☐ **13** *(a)*
The main role of the cell sap in plant vacuoles is to keep the concentration of the vacuole salts high enough so that water continues to diffuse into the cell down its concentration gradient. As long as the direction of diffusion is into the vacuole from the environment, the cell will remain rigid (turgid) and the plant will not wilt.

☐ **14** *False*
Only plant cells have a sap vacuole, which is a large central sac filled with a fluid that contains mineral salts and sugars amongst other things.

☐ **15** *(e)*
No living organisms can live without a source of energy, though some may be able to slow down for considerable periods, such as when bacteria form spores. Even the parasitic viruses cannot reproduce without a supply of the host cell's energy.

☐ **16** *(b)*
The first two statements are true. They summarise the fundamental difference between animal and plant nutrition. The third is correct only of animal nutrition, because in photosynthesis, molecules of carbon dioxide and water are built up to produce carbohydrate, which may then be broken down later in respiration to release energy.

☐ **17** *True*
Respiration is the process by which organisms release energy from carbohydrates, such as glucose, for use in other processes, such as movement or uptake of minerals by the roots. Animals get their carbohydrates from the food they eat. Plants make their own food molecules during the process called photosynthesis, which uses simple molecules from the plants' surroundings and the sun's energy.

☐ **18** *False*
Whilst movement in animals is obvious, movement still goes on within plant cells; for example, chloroplasts are capable of moving nearer to light. Both plants and animals can respond to their environment because they are sensitive to it. It is important that they respond to the environment in order to survive: for example, plant shoots grow away from gravity, animals run away from predators.

☐ **19** *True*
Both plant and animal cells have cell membranes that surround the cell and control which substances enter or leave the cell. Plant cells also have a cell wall outside the cell membrane, which gives the plant cell extra support.

☐ **20** *(d)*
Cells within a single organism vary in size and shape as they are designed to suit their function. For example, in humans, a sperm cell is mobile, shaped like a tadpole and about 0.05 mm in length, whilst a nerve cell is long, thin and can be up to a metre in length.

Organs working together

☐ **21** *(b)*
A human cheek cell is a good example of a typical animal cell. It cannot be a plant cell for it does not have a cell wall, a vacuole, or any chloroplasts. It is the wrong shape to be a sperm cell, and a red blood cell would have a different shape and no nucleus.

☐ **22** *(d)*
The diagram shown must be of a plant cell because it has a cell wall, vacuole and some chloroplasts. It is the wrong shape to be a root hair cell, which would also have no chloroplasts, and does not have any obvious stinging apparatus, so it must be a leaf palisade cell. These cells are the main photosynthetic cells of the leaf, making sugars by combining the elements contained in water and carbon dioxide, using the energy of sunlight.

☐ **23** *(e)*
Nerve cells are specialised for conducting nervous messages, in the form of electrical impulses, along their length. The cells have special features that enable them to carry these electrical impulses efficiently and quickly. They can also be very long; in humans they are up to one metre in length, and can be even longer in some other mammals.

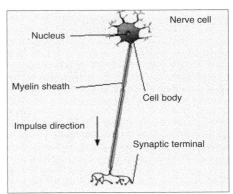

A17, 23

☐ **24** *(a)*
Muscle cells are tapered at either end and fit tightly together in your muscles. Unlike other types of cell they are able to contract when stimulated by a nerve impulse.

☐ **25** *(b)*
The sperm and the egg cells carry half of each parent's genetic information into their offspring. The sperm is specialised by having a 'tail' and being able to swim.

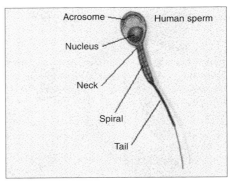

A17, 25

26 *(b)*
Glandular tissue, like any other tissue, will produce waste and respire, but it is not specialised to do this. Glandular tissue produces useful substances in the body, such as enzymes.

27 *(e)*
A tissue is made up of cells of a similar type. For example, the bones in our bodies are grown and maintained by a specialised set of bone cells, which occur nowhere else in the body.

28 *(c)*
A tissue is made up of cells, which due to their similar structures, have a particular function in the body. Muscle tissue, for example, is able to contract and relax to move bones and other parts of the body.

29 *(e)*
A sperm is a cell that carries the male genetic information to an egg cell. As a single cell it cannot be an organ.

30 *(c)*
Tissues are often grouped together in complicated arrangements to form an entire co-ordinated structure, called an organ, with a specific function or set of functions. For instance, the kidney is a typical organ containing several different types of tissue, arranged to regulate water and salts, and to excrete urea.

31 *(a)*
Organs are collections of tissues, perhaps of several different types, that together perform a similar function. The human stomach has muscular tissue to mix up the food, and glandular tissue to produce enzymes, which digest the food.

32 *(c)*
An organ system is a group of organs that work together and have a common purpose. For example, the function of the digestive system is to digest and absorb food. There are several organs that combine to do this including the stomach and the intestines.

33 *(b)*
The lungs are an organ and part of the breathing system. They are not a system but an organ within a system. All the others are organ systems. The shoot of a plant has stems, leaves and flowers.

34 *(d)*
Cells of similar types grouped together make tissues, and collections of joined tissues make organs. Collections of organs make organisms.

Cell division

35 *(b)*
The genes, the fundamental units of inheritance, are found on the chromosomes within the nucleus of the cell.

36 *(a)*
The egg's nucleus contains half the normal genetic information and the sperm's nucleus contains half also. When they fuse at fertilisation, the embryo will have the full genetic complement with half of the genetic make-up of the embryo coming from the mother and half from the father.

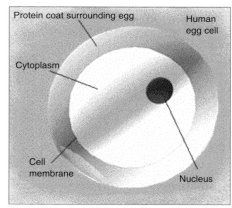

A36

37 *(d)*
The genes are part of the chromosomes that are located within the cell nucleus. They are the fundamental units of inheritance and strongly influence many of the physical characteristics of the cell and organism.

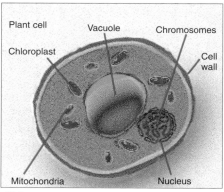

A37

38 *(b)*
Mitosis results in two identical 'daughter' cells from a single 'parent' cell. The chromosomes first become visible, and then reveal that each chromosome has already been duplicated into two identical chromatids. Next, the chromosomes line up across the middle of the nucleus, before the chromatids are pulled to

opposite ends of the cell by a 'spindle'. Finally, the cytoplasm splits and two genetically identical cells are produced.

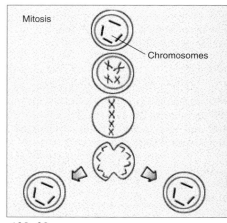

A38, 39

39 *(a)*
If a cell undergoes mitosis, it will produce two genetically identical cells after replicating its chromosomes to form two copies. The two cells produced are sometimes called 'daughter' cells.

40 *(d)*
Mitosis is the type of cell division used in growth, in repair of damaged tissue, and in asexual reproduction. Gametes are produced by meiosis, a type of cell division that produces cells with half the genetic information of the parent cell.

41 *(d)*
Gametes in all vertebrates are produced by meiosis, a type of cell division that produces cells with half the genetic information of the parent cell, so that at fertilisation the full number of chromosomes is restored.

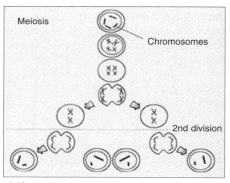

A41

42 *(c)*
After fertilisation the cell must divide many times if it is to successfully grow into an embryo. Mitosis is the type of cell division that will eventually result in a ball of many hundreds of genetically identical cells. They must be genetically identical because all cells must carry all the genetic information if there is to be

successful 'building' of an embryo from the first cell.

Transport between cells

☐ **43** *(e)*
Water is a liquid in which all the substances that have to be transported around the body can be dissolved. It also provides a medium for all the chemical reactions of a cell to occur, and is a raw material for photosynthesis in plant cells.

☐ **44** *(a)*
Diffusion is the overall (or 'net') movement of any molecule from a high concentration to a low concentration, until the two concentrations are equal. For example, if a crystal of purple potassium permanganate is left in a beaker of water, the permanganate diffuses until all the water is purple.

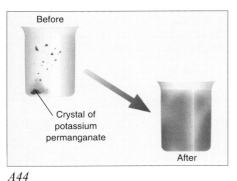

A44

☐ **45** *(c)*
Water moves between cells in a plant by osmosis, which is the net movement of water from a high water concentration to a low water concentration. The plant can control these flows by controlling the concentration of salts within the cytoplasm of cells. A high concentration of salts will cause water to flow into cells by osmosis.

☐ **46** *(b)*
Osmosis is the net movement of water molecules from a high concentration to a low concentration, through a partially permeable membrane. Osmosis is the mechanism by which water is transported around plants, with water moving from a cell with a high water concentration to a cell with a low water concentration.

☐ **47** *(b)*
The uptake of substances against a diffusion gradient is called active uptake. Osmosis and diffusion rely on the random movement of molecules along a diffusion gradient. Photosynthesis produces sugars that are used in respiration to produce energy in a form that can be used for active uptake.

☐ **48** *(a)*
The water column moves because of osmosis. In this experiment, the higher concentration of water is outside the tube, so the water moves into the tube from outside, and the water column rises.

☐ **49** *(e)*
In this experiment, water moves via osmosis. The higher concentration of water is inside the tube, and so water moves out of the tube and the level falls.

☐ **50** *(c)*
The potato cylinder loses water, and weight, due to osmosis. The water moves from the potato to the sugar solution, as the sugar solution has a lower concentration of water molecules. A great deal of the potato is made from cellulose and starches so the weight would not fall to below 0.10 g.

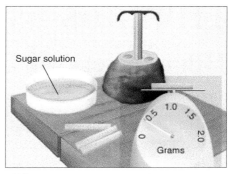

A50

☐ **51** *(d)*
The potato cylinder gains water, and weight, due to osmosis. The water moves into the potato, as it has a lower concentration of water molecules than the pure water outside. However, not enough water would move to quadruple the weight because the cells become full of water.

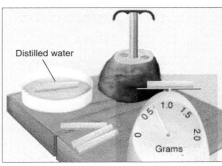

A51

☐ **52** *(e)*
The uptake of ions by a root hair cell is the only example of substances being moved against a diffusion gradient, so requiring energy.

☐ **53** *(c)*
Mineral ions can enter the roots of a plant by active transport, using energy from respiration, whilst water enters the roots by diffusion.

Humans as Organisms

Human diet *(Single and Double Awards)*

Stomach cells live for only a couple of days and red blood cells for about four months. The cells need to be constantly replaced. Food is digested and then changed into the molecules that are used to construct these cells, so it is essential that the food you eat contains the correct chemicals for rebuilding these cells. A balanced diet includes proteins, fats, carbohydrates, vitamins, mineral ions, dietary fibre, and water.

 KEY FACTS

Examples of food for a balanced diet

• **Protein** Most protein is used to maintain and repair tissues. Too little protein stunts growth.

• **Carbohydrates and fats** These are the main sources of energy. More active people require more carbohydrate and fat for extra energy. These energy-giving foods can be stored as fat. Saturated fats can block blood vessels.

• **Vitamins and mineral ions** A shortage of these causes deficiency diseases.

• **Dietary fibre** This helps to move faeces easily through the large intestine.

Recommended daily intake of energy according to age, activity and sex				
Age/years	Average body weight/kg	Degree of activity circumstances	Energy requirement Kj	
			Male	Female
1	7	Average	3200	3200
5	20	Average	7500	7500
10	30	Average	9500	9500
15	45	Average	11500	11500
		Sedentary	11300	9000
25	65 (male)	Moderately active	12500	9500
	55 (female)	Very active	15000	10500
		Sedentary	11000	9000
50	65 (male)	Moderately active	12000	9500
	55 (female)	Very active	15000	10500
75	63 (male)	Sedentary	9000	8000
Any		During pregnancy		10000
Any		Breast feeding		11500

Recommended daily intake

QUESTIONS

1 Which of the following need not be included in a balanced human diet?

☐ (a) Alcohol
☐ (b) Fat
☐ (c) Protein
☐ (d) Minerals
☐ (e) Water

2 What else, other than protein, carbohydrate, vegetable fibre and water, should be part of a balanced human diet?

☐ (a) Minerals and vitamins
☐ (b) Minerals, vitamins and sugars
☐ (c) Minerals, vitamins and fats
☐ (d) Minerals, sugars and fats
☐ (e) Vitamins, sugars and fats

3 Vegetable fibre is an important part of a balanced diet. Which problem may occur if too little fibre is included in the diet?

☐ (a) Appendicitis
☐ (b) Constipation
☐ (c) Diarrhoea
☐ (d) Indigestion
☐ (e) Stomach cramps

4 Which of the following parts of our diet provides a source of energy?

☐ (a) Minerals
☐ (b) Vitamins
☐ (c) Fibre
☐ (d) Carbohydrate
☐ (e) Water

5 True ☐ or false ☐ ?
In an iodine test, the iodine turns a light brown colour if starch is present.

6 Which of the following portions of food and drink contains the most energy?

☐ (a) 100 g baked beans
☐ (b) 100 g cooked cabbage
☐ (c) 100 g fried potato
☐ (d) 100 g white fish
☐ (e) 100 g water

7 Which of the following foodstuffs contains the most energy?

☐ (a) 50 g cabbage
☐ (b) 50 g cheese
☐ (c) 50 g roast turkey
☐ (d) 50 g peas
☐ (e) 50 g carrots

8 Which of the following is most likely to lead to an increase in body weight, and poor health?

☐ (a) A balanced diet but with more starch than recommended
☐ (b) A balanced diet but with more fat than recommended
☐ (c) A balanced diet but with more fibre than recommended
☐ (d) A balanced diet but with more vitamins than recommended
☐ (e) A balanced diet but with more water than recommended

9 Which of the following statements are true? W: Too little protein in the diet stunts growth. X: A lack of fibre in the diet can lead to constipation. Y: A lack of fibre in the diet can increase the chances of developing lung cancer. Z: A lack of fibre in the diet can increase the chances of developing bowel cancer.

☐ (a) W, X, Y and Z
☐ (b) W, X and Y
☐ (c) W, Y and Z
☐ (d) W, X and Z
☐ (e) X, Y and Z

10 Lack of fibre in a human diet seems to cause many problems, but which common cancer is more common among people with a shortage of fibre in their diet?

☐ (a) Bowel cancer
☐ (b) Breast cancer
☐ (c) Lung cancer
☐ (d) Throat cancer
☐ (e) Testicular cancer

11 Which two types of food usually provide most of the energy required to maintain your body temperature at 37°C?

☐ (a) Carbohydrates and vitamins
☐ (b) Carbohydrates and proteins
☐ (c) Carbohydrates and fats
☐ (d) Fats and proteins
☐ (e) Proteins and vitamins

12 Which of the following statements about the fats we eat as part of our diet is/are true? X: Fats are needed to produce energy. Y: Fats are needed to produce cell membranes. Z: Cheese acts as a major source of fats.

☐ (a) X, Y and Z
☐ (b) X and Y
☐ (c) X and Z
☐ (d) Y and Z
☐ (e) X only

Human digestion *(Single and Double Awards)*

The digestive system is essentially a long muscular tube running from the mouth, through the body to the anus. It has different sections where different digestive jobs take place. It has various organs attached to it, such as the liver and the pancreas. The long muscular tube is the alimentary canal, which squeezes the food through it, giving time for enzymes to digest the food. For example, the stomach can hold nearly two litres of food for up to five hours.

Dr. Beaumont was the first person to study directly the process of digestion. He helped a young fur trapper called Alexis St. Martin, who had been shot in the stomach. Alexis' wound healed in such a way that the doctor could look directly into his stomach. He put food, attached to string, through the hole into his stomach. He timed how long the food took to be digested. Today, we can use x-rays and fibre optics to directly observe what is going on in the digestive system.

 KEY FACTS

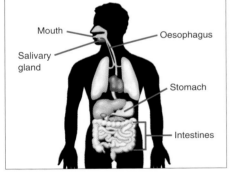

Human digestive system

• **Mouth** Food is chewed into small lumps by the teeth and is mixed with saliva, which contains an enzyme.

• **Oesophagus** This connects the mouth to the stomach. Food moves down it by peristalsis, which is rhythmic contractions of circular and longitudinal muscles.

• **Stomach** Food is stored here after being ingested. The food is mixed with more enzymes, and with acid to kill germs, and becomes a thick liquid.

• **Small intestine** Food is mixed with more enzymes and bile, and useful products of digestion are absorbed through villi into the bloodstream.

• **Large intestine** Water is absorbed from the undigested food that is passing through.

• **Rectum** Faeces are stored here before being egested out of the body via the anus.

• **Anus** This is the end of the digestive tube surrounded by muscle that shuts off the digestive system and opens the anus during egestion.

• **Physical digestion** This is one of two types of digestion. It occurs in the mouth as the teeth chew up the food, and in the stomach where the muscular walls of the digestive system churn the food. The food is given a larger surface area for the enzymes involved in chemical digestion to work on.

• **Bile** This contributes to physical digestion. It breaks up large fat drops into small fat droplets. This is called emulsification. Bile is made in the liver, stored in the gall bladder and released into the small intestine via the bile duct.

• **Chemical digestion** This is the other type of digestion. It occurs whenever enzymes come into contact with food. Stomach acid kills any bacteria entering the stomach and helps the enzymes in the stomach.

• **Enzymes** These break down large food molecules into small molecules, which can be absorbed into the bloodstream. Different enzymes are produced in different parts of the digestive system and work on different types of food. Carbohydrases break down carbohydrates, such as starch, until they eventually become sugars. Lipases break down fats until they eventually become fatty acids and glycerol components. Proteases break down proteins until they eventually become amino acids. Each enzyme works best at a different, specific pH.

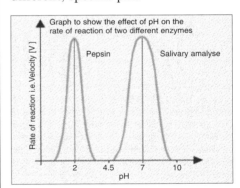

Rate of enzyme reaction

QUESTIONS

13 Which letter labels the gullet, or oesophagus, in the following diagram?

- ☐ (a) V
- ☐ (b) W
- ☐ (c) X
- ☐ (d) Y
- ☐ (e) Z

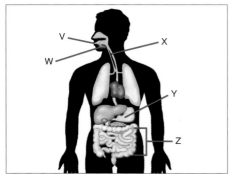

Q13, 14, 15, 16, 17

14 Which structure is labelled X in the diagram above?

- ☐ (a) Nasal cavity
- ☐ (b) Oesophagus
- ☐ (c) Oral cavity
- ☐ (d) Pancreas
- ☐ (e) Stomach

15 Which letter labels the stomach in the diagram above?

- ☐ (a) V
- ☐ (b) W
- ☐ (c) X
- ☐ (d) Y
- ☐ (e) Z

16 Which structure is labelled Y in the diagram above?

- ☐ (a) Pancreas
- ☐ (b) Oesophagus
- ☐ (c) Liver
- ☐ (d) Kidney
- ☐ (e) Stomach

17 Which structure is labelled Z in the diagram above?

- ☐ (a) Intestines
- ☐ (b) Kidney
- ☐ (c) Liver
- ☐ (d) Stomach
- ☐ (e) Testes

18 The following diagram shows the major internal organs of a typical mammal. Which letter labels the intestine?

- ☐ (a) V
- ☐ (b) W
- ☐ (c) X
- ☐ (d) Y
- ☐ (e) Z

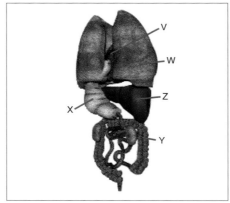

Q18

19 Which letter correctly labels the large intestine in the following diagram?

- ☐ (a) V
- ☐ (b) W
- ☐ (c) X
- ☐ (d) Y
- ☐ (e) Z

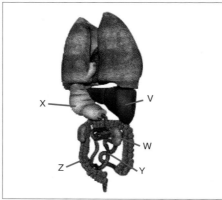

Q21

20 Which of the following is the name given to an infolding of the wall of the mammalian small intestine?

- ☐ (a) Ileum
- ☐ (b) Lacteal
- ☐ (c) Ventricle
- ☐ (d) Villus
- ☐ (e) Vulva

21 Why is the wall of the small intestine folded into so many small villi?

- ☐ (a) To increase the surface area of the wall
- ☐ (b) To decrease the surface area of the wall

- ☐ (c) To trap small food particles in the wall
- ☐ (d) To filter the food particles between the villi
- ☐ (e) To form a furry and insulating surface

22 What is the name of the structure through which undigested waste food is expelled from the alimentary canal?

- ☐ (a) Anus
- ☐ (b) Appendix
- ☐ (c) Duodenum
- ☐ (d) Ileum
- ☐ (e) Oesophagus

23 What is structure X on the following diagram?

- ☐ (a) Adrenal gland
- ☐ (b) Appendix
- ☐ (c) Diaphragm
- ☐ (d) Ileum
- ☐ (e) Pancreas

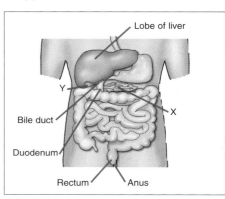

Q23, 24

24 What is structure Y on the diagram above?

- ☐ (a) Adrenal gland
- ☐ (b) Diaphragm
- ☐ (c) Gall bladder
- ☐ (d) Ileum
- ☐ (e) Pancreas

25 Fleur, a student at Cass College, Cambridge, has been set the task of finding out whether a food solution she has been given contains protein. She decides to carry out the Biuret test on the solution. What colour would the solution go if there was protein present in it?

- ☐ (a) Clear
- ☐ (b) Light blue
- ☐ (c) Orange
- ☐ (d) Purple
- ☐ (e) Yellow

20

26 Which of the following can be added to a food solution to see if it contains fat?

- ☐ (a) Benedict's reagent
- ☐ (b) Biuret's solution
- ☐ (c) Cholesterol
- ☐ (d) Ethane
- ☐ (e) Ethanol then water

27 Which of the following has the function of increasing the surface area of food once it has been ingested (entered the body)?

- ☐ (a) Amylase
- ☐ (b) Enzymes
- ☐ (c) Saliva
- ☐ (d) Teeth
- ☐ (e) Villi

28 Which of the following terms describes the rhythmical contraction of muscles in the wall of the oesophagus, leading to food being transported from the mouth to the stomach?

- ☐ (a) Ciliary motion
- ☐ (b) Peristalsis
- ☐ (c) Perimason
- ☐ (d) Periwinkle
- ☐ (e) Regurgitation

29 True ☐ or false ☐ ?
Peristalsis is the movement of food down the gullet by the contraction of circular muscles in front of the food.

30 What are the two types of muscle present in the oesophagus that enable peristalsis to occur?

- ☐ (a) Circular and cardiac
- ☐ (b) Circular and intestinal
- ☐ (c) Circular and longitudinal
- ☐ (d) Longitudinal and intestinal
- ☐ (e) Cardiac and longitudinal

31 Which of the following best defines 'digestion'?

- ☐ (a) The breaking down of complex foodstuffs into smaller molecules
- ☐ (b) The absorption of simple molecules into the blood
- ☐ (c) The entry of food into the body of a consuming organism
- ☐ (d) The chemical oxidation of food to liberate energy
- ☐ (e) The manufacture of large molecules from smaller molecules

32 Which of the following is defined as a 'biological catalyst'?

- ☐ (a) Carbohydrate
- ☐ (b) Enzyme
- ☐ (c) Fat
- ☐ (d) Lipid
- ☐ (e) Membrane

33 Digestion uses special chemicals that break down large food molecules. What is the name given to these chemicals?

- ☐ (a) Amino acids
- ☐ (b) Enzymes
- ☐ (c) Fatty acids
- ☐ (d) Prozymes
- ☐ (e) Vitamins

34 In a mammal, which organ has the function of storing food after it has been eaten, and then begins digesting some of this food?

- ☐ (a) Heart
- ☐ (b) Intestine
- ☐ (c) Kidney
- ☐ (d) Liver
- ☐ (e) Stomach

35 What are the functions of the stomach?

- ☐ (a) To digest only lipids (fats) and carbohydrates
- ☐ (b) To absorb the products of food digestion into the bloodstream
- ☐ (c) To break down food mechanically and begin the chemical digestion of proteins
- ☐ (d) To filter digestible from indigestible foods before they reach the intestines
- ☐ (e) To digest water and mineral salts

36 Your stomach produces hydrochloric acid. Which of the following is a function of this acid?

- ☐ (a) To help build the products of digestion into useful substances
- ☐ (b) To aid the movement of food through the gut
- ☐ (c) To build up the lining of your stomach
- ☐ (d) To kill bacteria taken in with food
- ☐ (e) To enable the enzymes of the small intestine to work

37 In a mammal, which organ has the function of digesting food and absorbing the useful products of this digestion into the bloodstream?

- ☐ (a) Heart
- ☐ (b) Intestine
- ☐ (c) Kidney
- ☐ (d) Liver
- ☐ (e) Stomach

38 What is the name of the enzyme responsible for the digestion of starch?

- ☐ (a) Amylase
- ☐ (b) Glucose
- ☐ (c) Maltase
- ☐ (d) Peptidase
- ☐ (e) Protease

39 What is the name of the molecule that results from the digestion of starch?

- ☐ (a) Fructose
- ☐ (b) Glucose
- ☐ (c) Glycogen
- ☐ (d) Lactose
- ☐ (e) Sucrose

40 What is the name of the molecule broken down by the enzyme amylase?

- ☐ (a) Actin
- ☐ (b) Glucose
- ☐ (c) Maltose
- ☐ (d) Protein
- ☐ (e) Starch

41 What is the function of carbohydrases within the mammalian digestive system?

- ☐ (a) To digest complex carbohydrates
- ☐ (b) To digest amino acids
- ☐ (c) To synthesise glucose
- ☐ (d) To synthesise all carbohydrates
- ☐ (e) To synthesise nucleic acids

42 Which of the following best describes proteases?

- ☐ (a) Enzymes that synthesise fats
- ☐ (b) Enzymes that digest proteins
- ☐ (c) Enzymes that synthesise proteins
- ☐ (d) Enzymes that synthesise sugars
- ☐ (e) Enzymes that digest sugars

43 Which of the following best describes the role of lipases in the human body?

- ☐ (a) To construct fatty acid molecules
- ☐ (b) To construct fat molecules
- ☐ (c) To digest fatty acid molecules
- ☐ (d) To digest fat molecules
- ☐ (e) To digest alcohol molecules

44 Which of the following nutrients is broken down to amino acids in the process of digestion?

☐ (a) Carbohydrates
☐ (b) Fats
☐ (c) Lipids
☐ (d) Minerals
☐ (e) Proteins

45 In digestion, what is the result when proteins are broken down?

☐ (a) Amino acids
☐ (b) Fatty acids
☐ (c) Glucose
☐ (d) Starch
☐ (e) Sugars

46 Which of the following foods is broken down to glucose in digestion?

☐ (a) Amylase
☐ (b) Fat
☐ (c) Lipids
☐ (d) Protein
☐ (e) Starch

47 Which group of enzymes is produced in your salivary glands, pancreas and small intestine?

☐ (a) Biles
☐ (b) Carbohydrases
☐ (c) Lipases
☐ (d) Pepsins
☐ (e) Proteases

48 Which types of digestive enzymes are produced by the pancreas?

☐ (a) Carbohdrases, proteases and lipases
☐ (b) Carbohydrases and lipases only
☐ (c) Carbohydrases and proteases only
☐ (d) Proteases and lipases only
☐ (e) Proteases only

49 The products of digestion in humans are usually water soluble. Why is this important?

☐ (a) Because it makes them easy to mix in the stomach
☐ (b) Because it makes them easier to separate from the unwanted products
☐ (c) Because it makes them easier to pass into the large intestine
☐ (d) Because it means that they can be transported in the blood
☐ (e) Because it means that they can be transported in the lymph system

50 What happens to the useful products of digestion once digestion is over?

☐ (a) They pass into the colon
☐ (b) They pass directly into the kidneys
☐ (c) They pass into the bloodstream
☐ (d) They pass into the rectum
☐ (e) They pass directly to the heart

51 Into which structure are the products of carbohydrate digestion absorbed during the human digestive process?

☐ (a) Artery inside a villus
☐ (b) Capillary inside a villus
☐ (c) Lacteal vessel inside a villus
☐ (d) Neurone inside a villus
☐ (e) Vein inside a villus

52 Into which structure, located within the villi, are the products of protein digestion absorbed?

☐ (a) Arteries
☐ (b) Capillaries
☐ (c) Lacteals
☐ (d) Lymph vessels
☐ (e) Veins

Higher Level only

53 In the human digestive system, which type of food molecules have their digestion speeded up by bile salts?

☐ (a) Amino acids
☐ (b) Carbohydrates
☐ (c) Fats
☐ (d) Proteins
☐ (e) Vitamins

54 Which of the following substances will emulsify fats?

☐ (a) Amylase
☐ (b) Bile
☐ (c) Carbohydrase
☐ (d) Lipase
☐ (e) Protease

55 Which of the following is responsible for storing bile salts that emulsify, or break down, lipids?

☐ (a) Gall bladder
☐ (b) Ileum
☐ (c) Kidney
☐ (d) Pancreas
☐ (e) Salivary glands

Human circulation *(Double Award only)*

The heart pumps about 9,000 litres of blood around the body each day! This blood is pumped through arteries into arterioles then capillaries and back through venules and veins to the heart. In all there are about 100,000 kilometres of these blood vessels in the adult human. Most of these blood vessels are tiny capillaries that mingle closely with the cells that they supply.

 KEY FACTS

• **Heart** This consists of two sides that are similar. Each side has an atrium, which receives blood and pumps it into a ventricle, which then pumps the blood out of the heart. Valves in the heart and in the veins make sure blood flows in one direction only.

• **Main circulatory system** The heart pumps blood around the body via the arteries, then the capillaries, where the exchange of substances between the blood and tissues occur, and finally the veins, which return the blood to the heart.

• **Secondary circulatory system** There is a second system of arteries, capillaries and veins, which supply

the lungs with blood. So, the blood goes through the heart twice on each journey around the body.

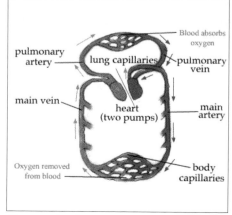

Human circulatory system

QUESTIONS

56 The following diagram shows the major internal organs in the body cavity of a mammal. Which letter correctly labels the heart?

- ☐ (a) V
- ☐ (b) W
- ☐ (c) X
- ☐ (d) Y
- ☐ (e) Z

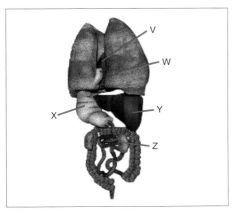

Q56

57 What is the the function of the heart?

- ☐ (a) To absorb oxygen from the atmosphere
- ☐ (b) To filter waste products from the blood
- ☐ (c) To produce new red blood cells
- ☐ (d) To produce new white blood cells
- ☐ (e) To pump blood around the body

58 Which structure is labelled U in the diagram of a mammalian heart?

- ☐ (a) Aorta
- ☐ (b) Left atrium
- ☐ (c) Right atrium
- ☐ (d) Left ventricle
- ☐ (e) Right ventricle

59 Which structure is labelled V in the diagram of a mammalian heart?

- ☐ (a) Left atrium
- ☐ (b) Right atrium
- ☐ (c) Left ventricle
- ☐ (d) Right ventricle
- ☐ (e) Heart valve

60 Which structure is labelled W in the diagram of a mammalian heart?

- ☐ (a) Aorta
- ☐ (b) Left atrium
- ☐ (c) Right atrium
- ☐ (d) Left ventricle
- ☐ (e) Right ventricle

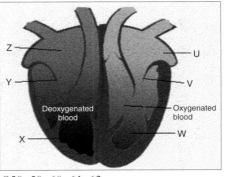

Q58, 59, 60, 61, 62

61 Which structure is labelled X in the diagram above?

- ☐ (a) Left atrium
- ☐ (b) Right atrium
- ☐ (c) Left ventricle
- ☐ (d) Right ventricle
- ☐ (e) Vena cava

62 Which structure is labelled Z in the diagram above?

- ☐ (a) Left atrium
- ☐ (b) Right atrium
- ☐ (c) Left ventricle
- ☐ (d) Right ventricle
- ☐ (e) Heart valve

63 True ☐ or false ☐ ?
The chamber with the thickest walls in the heart is the right ventricle.

64 True ☐ or false ☐ ?
Arteries are different from veins in that they carry oxygenated blood while veins carry de-oxygenated blood.

65 The following diagram shows the circulatory system. What is the name of the blood vessel labelled W?

- ☐ (a) Aorta
- ☐ (b) Hepatic portal vein
- ☐ (c) Pulmonary artery
- ☐ (d) Pulmonary vein
- ☐ (e) Vena cava

66 What is the name of the blood vessel labelled Y in the following diagram?

- ☐ (a) Aorta
- ☐ (b) Hepatic portal vein
- ☐ (c) Pulmonary artery
- ☐ (d) Pulmonary vein
- ☐ (e) Vena cava

67 What is the name of the blood vessel labelled T in the following diagram?

- ☐ (a) Aorta
- ☐ (b) Hepatic portal vein
- ☐ (c) Pulmonary artery
- ☐ (d) Pulmonary vein
- ☐ (e) Vena cava

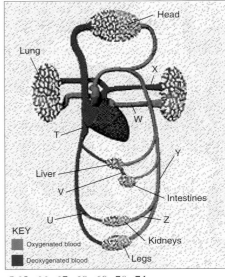

Q65, 66, 67, 68, 69, 70, 71

68 What is the name of the blood vessel labelled X in the diagram above?

- ☐ (a) Aorta
- ☐ (b) Hepatic portal vein
- ☐ (c) Pulmonary artery
- ☐ (d) Pulmonary vein
- ☐ (e) Vena cava

69 What is the name of the blood vessel labelled Z in the diagram above?

- ☐ (a) Aorta
- ☐ (b) Intestinal artery
- ☐ (c) Pulmonary artery
- ☐ (d) Renal artery
- ☐ (e) Renal vein

70 What is the name of the blood vessel labelled U in the diagram above?

- ☐ (a) Renal vein
- ☐ (b) Hepatic vein
- ☐ (c) Hepatic portal vein
- ☐ (d) Renal artery
- ☐ (e) Hepatic artery

71 Which letter correctly labels the hepatic portal vein in the diagram above?

- ☐ (a) V
- ☐ (b) W
- ☐ (c) X
- ☐ (d) Y
- ☐ (e) Z

72 What causes the rhythm of your pulse?

☐ (a) The movements of your heart pumping blood into capillaries
☐ (b) The movements of your heart pumping blood into veins
☐ (c) The movements of your heart pumping blood into arteries
☐ (d) The movements of your lungs pumping blood into veins
☐ (e) The movements of your lungs pumping blood into arteries

73 Why do arteries have thicker walls than veins?

☐ (a) To produce new red blood cells in response to losses and cell ageing
☐ (b) To cope with the extra pressure of blood coming direct from the heart
☐ (c) To help the heart pump the blood around the body at high pressure
☐ (d) To prevent bacteria moving through the artery walls and into the blood
☐ (e) For protection, because they are close to the surface of the body

74 Which of the following explains why veins have valves and arteries do not?

☐ (a) To cope with lower blood pressure
☐ (b) To cope with higher blood pressure
☐ (c) To prevent bacteria entering the heart
☐ (d) To prevent lipids reaching the heart
☐ (e) To prevent shocks reaching the heart

75 Which of the following is a correct difference between arteries and veins?

☐ (a) Arteries possess valves attached to their walls and veins do not
☐ (b) Arteries have thinner and less muscular walls than veins
☐ (c) Arteries carry oxygenated blood and veins carry deoxygenated blood
☐ (d) Arteries carry blood at low pressure and veins at high pressure
☐ (e) Arteries carry blood away from the heart but veins take blood back to the heart

76 In which of the following ways do arteries and veins differ?

☐ (a) Arteries are equipped with valves and veins have no valves
☐ (b) Arteries have thin, flexible walls and veins have thicker, muscular walls
☐ (c) Arteries carry blood at a higher pressure and veins at a lower pressure
☐ (d) Arteries carry deoxgenated blood and veins carry oxygenated blood
☐ (e) Arteries carry blood towards the heart and veins carry blood away from the heart

77 Why does your pulse rate increase during hard exercise?

☐ (a) The heart is beating faster to rid the muscles of more waste oxygen made in exercise
☐ (b) The heart is beating faster to rid the muscles of more waste urea made in exercise
☐ (c) The heart is beating faster to rid the muscles of more waste glucose made in exercise
☐ (d) The heart is beating faster to supply the muscles with more oxygen
☐ (e) The heart is beating faster to supply the muscles with more carbon dioxide

78 Why should you not have too much fat in your diet?

☐ (a) It lowers your immunity to disease
☐ (b) It causes blocking of arteries
☐ (c) It causes you to become sterile
☐ (d) It causes arthritis of the joints
☐ (e) It causes the disease haemophilia

79 Arteries divide up into a smaller type of vessel which, in turn, divides into capillaries. What is the name of these smaller vessels that feed the capillaries?

☐ (a) Arteria
☐ (b) Arterioles
☐ (c) Atria
☐ (d) Veins
☐ (e) Venules

80 In the human circulatory system, a red blood cell has to go through the heart twice before it can return to its starting position. What is this type of circulatory system known as?

☐ (a) Ventricular circulatory system
☐ (b) Darwinian circulatory system
☐ (c) Atrial circulatory system
☐ (d) Double circulatory system
☐ (e) Pulmonary circulatory system

Composition and function of blood *(Single and Double Awards)*

Blood keeps the cells in a more or less constant environment. It supplies nutrients and removes waste, provides a central heating system, controls the activities of cells by circulating hormones, and protects against infection. Red and white blood cells floating in liquid plasma make up the four or five litres of blood in our bodies.

 KEY FACTS

• **Platelets** These are small fragments of bone marrow cells with no nucleus; they help the blood to clot.

• **Red blood cells** These are biconcave in shape and filled with haemoglobin, which carries oxygen from the lungs to the organs.

• **White blood cells** These fight infection by releasing antitoxins, producing antibodies, or ingesting microbes.

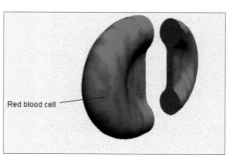
Red blood cell

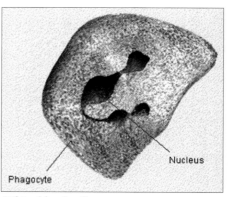
White blood cell

QUESTIONS

81 Which of the following is the most accurate description of the structure of our blood?

☐ (a) Red cells and white cells
☐ (b) Red cells, white cells and blue cells
☐ (c) Red, white and blue cells, and plasma
☐ (d) Red cells and plasma
☐ (e) Red cells, white cells and plasma

82 True ☐ or false ☐ ?
Blood consists of red blood cells, white blood cells, platelets and plasma.

83 True ☐ or false ☐ ?
Blood plasma contains a number of dissolved substances that it transports round the body. These include nutrients, carbon dioxide, urea and hormones.

84 Natasha Young was given a slide to inspect under the microscope. Once she focused the microscope she saw the following image. What are the structures labelled Y in the following diagram?

☐ (a) Blue blood cells
☐ (b) Button cells
☐ (c) Red blood cells
☐ (d) Scarlet blood cells
☐ (e) White blood cells

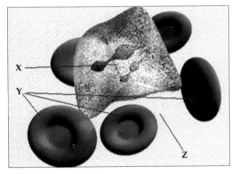

Q84, 85

85 Frederick Lapse was given a slide to inspect under the microscope. Once the microscope was in focus he saw the image above. What is the structure labelled X in the diagram above?

☐ (a) Haemocyte
☐ (b) Haemoglobin
☐ (c) Red blood cell
☐ (d) White blood cell
☐ (e) Yellow blood cell

86 What shape is a red blood cell?

☐ (a) Biconcave
☐ (b) Biconvex
☐ (c) Concave
☐ (d) Convex
☐ (e) Spherical

87 Amanda Day was given a slide with blood on it to look at under the microscope. Once she got the microscope in focus she saw the following image. What is labelled Z in the following diagram?

☐ (a) Glucose
☐ (b) Haemoglobin
☐ (c) Plasma
☐ (d) Water
☐ (e) White blood cell

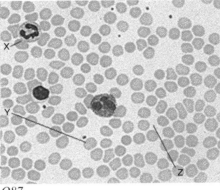

Q87

88 Which of the following best describes blood platelets?

☐ (a) Small cells that carry carbon dioxide
☐ (b) Small fragments of cells with no nuclei
☐ (c) Similar to red blood cells, but with nuclei
☐ (d) Large cells that can engulf bacteria
☐ (e) Large cells that prevent blood leaving arteries and veins

89 Which of the following is not found in mammalian blood?

☐ (a) Chloroplasts
☐ (b) Plasma proteins
☐ (c) Red blood cells
☐ (d) Sodium ions
☐ (e) White blood cells

90 Which of the following would not be found in a sample of human blood?

☐ (a) Hormones
☐ (b) Plasma proteins

☐ (c) Blue blood cell
☐ (d) White blood cell
☐ (e) Red blood cell

91 What is the function of haemoglobin?

☐ (a) To carry carbon dioxide to the tissues
☐ (b) To remove disease organisms from the body
☐ (c) To remove clots from the blood
☐ (d) To carry oxygen around the body
☐ (e) To carry glucose around the body

92 Within minutes of a minor accident, for example, cutting the skin on your finger, the blood flow begins to slow down and eventually stops. How does the body manage to stop the blood flow so quickly and neatly?

☐ (a) A blood clot forms inside each capillary so that the blood stops entering the injury
☐ (b) A layer of skin forms across the top of the cut, keeping the blood flow under the skin
☐ (c) The sides of the cut are pulled together by strands of muscle beneath the skin
☐ (d) Small segments of capillary are fitted into the damaged sectors, like new pipes
☐ (e) The heart reduces the blood pumping to the injury so that the blood flow decreases

93 What is the name of the insoluble protein that forms threads, which will trap red blood cells and lead to the formation of a clot over a wound?

☐ (a) Antibody
☐ (b) Antigen
☐ (c) Fibrin
☐ (d) Fibrinogen
☐ (e) Haemoglobin

94 Many bacteria cause disease by releasing damaging toxins inside our bodies. What does the human body do to counteract this?

☐ (a) Platelets attack the toxins
☐ (b) Red blood cells attach to the toxins neutralising them
☐ (c) Haemoglobin neutralises the toxins
☐ (d) White blood cells release antitoxins
☐ (e) White blood cells release antigens

Human breathing *(Double Award only)*

The whole thorax is involved in breathing but the lungs and the heart are its major organs. The ribcage surrounding the lungs, and the diaphragm below it, are responsible for inflating and deflating the lungs. The lungs provide an enormous surface area for oxygen and carbon dioxide to diffuse into and out of the lungs. The lungs can hold about 6.5 litres of air. The principle behind breathing is that the volume of the lungs is increased and the pressure within them reduced so that air can rush in. The reverse happens when breathing out.

 KEY FACTS

• **Trachea (windpipe)** This connects the mouth and the lungs, then splits into two bronchi, one for each lung. Rings of cartilage keep the trachea open at all times and hair-like cilia and mucus trap any unwanted particles in the air passing through.

• **Bronchi** These split into many branches called bronchioles, which end in tiny air sacs called alveoli.

• **Alveoli** These are surrounded by capillaries and are where the gas exchange between oxygen entering the blood and carbon dioxide leaving the blood takes place.

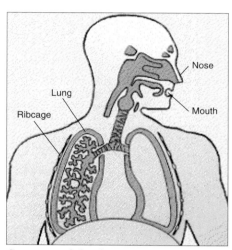
Structure of the thorax

• **Ribs** These encase the lungs in the chest, providing protection, and are connected to each other by intercostal rib muscles, which can change the shape and the volume of the ribcage.

• **Diaphragm** This is a large muscular sheet that seals off the bottom of the thorax.

• **Inhaling** When breathing in, the diaphragm contracts, changing its shape from a dome to a flatter sheet. The intercostal rib muscles contract, pulling the ribcage up and out. These actions increase the volume of the chest, which reduces the pressure inside the lungs so that air is pushed into the lungs.

• **Exhaling** When breathing out, the reverse happens. The diaphragm relaxes becoming dome-shaped again. The rib muscles relax, letting the ribcage fall back, which reduces the volume of the chest. The pressure inside the lungs increases, and air is forced out of the lungs.

QUESTIONS

95 The following diagram shows the internal organs of a mammal. Which letter correctly labels a lung?

☐ (a) V
☐ (b) W
☐ (c) X
☐ (d) Y
☐ (e) Z

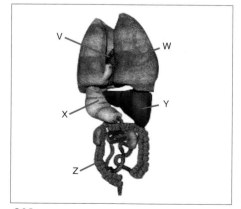
Q95

96 What are the the functions of the lungs?

☐ (a) To absorb carbon dioxide and expel oxygen
☐ (b) To absorb oxygen and get rid of carbon dioxide
☐ (c) To absorb water and expel oxygen
☐ (d) To circulate oxygen around the body
☐ (e) To filter waste products out of the blood

97 In a mammal, which organ has the function of extracting oxygen from the air into the blood?

☐ (a) Heart
☐ (b) Intestine
☐ (c) Liver
☐ (d) Lung
☐ (e) Stomach

98 In the diagram showing the breathing system of a human, what is the name of the structure labelled V?

☐ (a) Alveoli
☐ (b) Bronchiole
☐ (c) Bronchus
☐ (d) Intercostal (rib) muscle
☐ (e) Trachea

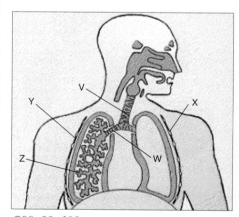
Q98, 99, 100

99 In the diagram showing the breathing system of a human, what is the name of the structure labelled W?

☐ (a) Alveoli
☐ (b) Bronchiole
☐ (c) Bronchus
☐ (d) Intercostal (rib) muscle
☐ (e) Trachea

100 In the diagram showing the breathing system of a human, what is the name of the structure labelled Z?

- ☐ (a) Alveolus
- ☐ (b) Bronchiole
- ☐ (c) Bronchus
- ☐ (d) Bronco
- ☐ (e) Trachea

101 In the diagram showing the breathing system of a human, what is the name of the structure labelled X?

- ☐ (a) Diaphragm
- ☐ (b) Intercostal (rib) muscle
- ☐ (c) Intermediate muscle
- ☐ (d) Lung
- ☐ (e) Rib

102 In the diagram showing the breathing system of a human, what is the name of the structure labelled Y?

- ☐ (a) Diaphragm
- ☐ (b) Intercostal (rib) muscle
- ☐ (c) Intermediate muscle
- ☐ (d) Lung
- ☐ (e) Rib

103 What is the name of the structure labelled Z in the following diagram?

- ☐ (a) Diaphragm
- ☐ (b) Intercostal (rib) muscle
- ☐ (c) Intermediate muscle
- ☐ (d) Lung
- ☐ (e) Rib

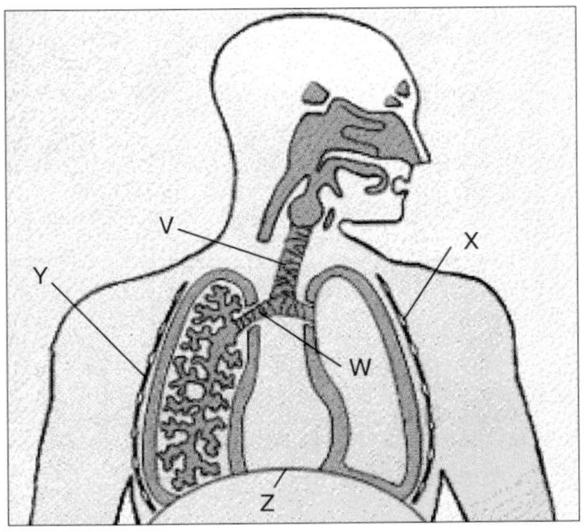

Q101, 102, 103

104 True ☐ or false ☐ ?
During inhalation, the external intercostal muscles relax and the diaphragm contracts.

105 True ☐ or false ☐ ?
The lungs are the surface at which the body gains oxygen and gets rid of wastes, such as carbon dioxide and urea.

106 What is the name of the tube that carries air from the mouth or nose to the bronchi?

- ☐ (a) Alveolus
- ☐ (b) Bronchus
- ☐ (c) Hornpipe
- ☐ (d) Larynx
- ☐ (e) Trachea

107 The trachea divides as it approaches the lungs so that both lungs are supplied with air. Which of the following is the name given to the tubes that supply each lung?

- ☐ (a) Alveoli
- ☐ (b) Bronchi
- ☐ (c) Bronchioles
- ☐ (d) Bronchitis
- ☐ (e) Windpipe

108 What are the names of the two sets of structures that change the volume of the chest in breathing?

- ☐ (a) Alveoli and intercostal muscles
- ☐ (b) Diaphragm and extracostal muscles
- ☐ (c) Diaphragm and intercostal muscles
- ☐ (d) Ribs and intercostal muscles
- ☐ (e) Ribs and extracostal muscles

Higher Level only

109 Which of the following most accurately describes the mechanism that increases the volume of the chest in human inhalation?

- ☐ (a) Intercostal muscles contract and diaphragm muscles contract
- ☐ (b) Intercostal muscles contract and diaphragm muscles relax
- ☐ (c) Intercostal muscles relax and diaphragm muscles contract
- ☐ (d) Intermediate muscles relax and diaphragm muscles relax
- ☐ (e) Intercostal muscles relax and diaphragm muscles relax

110 Which of the following best describes the reason why air leaves the lungs during human exhalations?

- ☐ (a) Elastic lung tissue and weight of raised chest push air out of lungs
- ☐ (b) Intercostal muscles contract and diaphragm muscles contract

- ☐ (c) Intercostal muscles contract and diaphragm muscles relax
- ☐ (d) Intercostal muscles relax and diaphragm muscles relax
- ☐ (e) Weight of lung tissue and elastic ribs push air out of lungs

111 What happens to the volumes of the chest and the lungs when both the intercostal muscles and the diaphragm muscles contract?

- ☐ (a) Chest volume remains constant and lung volume decreases
- ☐ (b) Chest volume remains constant and lung volume increases
- ☐ (c) Lung volume remains constant and chest volume decreases
- ☐ (d) Chest volume increases and lung volume also increases
- ☐ (e) Chest volume decreases and lung volume decreases

112 What happens to the air pressure within the lungs during the course of one cycle of breathing?

- ☐ (a) Pressure increases as the muscles relax and decreases as the muscles contract
- ☐ (b) Pressure decreases as the muscles relax and increases as the muscles contract
- ☐ (c) Pressure increases as the muscles relax and also increases as the muscles contract
- ☐ (d) Pressure decreases as the muscles relax and also decreases as the muscles contract
- ☐ (e) Pressure in the lungs has no relationship to the contractions of these two muscle groups

Foundation and Higher Levels

113 Which of the following diffuses through capillary walls from the blood into the tissues?

- ☐ (a) Carbon dioxide
- ☐ (b) Nitrogen
- ☐ (c) Oxygen
- ☐ (d) Red blood cells
- ☐ (e) Urea

114 Across the membranes of which structures does carbon dioxide diffuse when it is excreted from the bloodstream to the atmosphere?

- ☐ (a) Alveoli
- ☐ (b) Bronchi
- ☐ (c) Bronchioles
- ☐ (d) Diaphragm
- ☐ (e) Intercostal muscles

115 By which process does oxygen leave the alveoli and enter the red blood cells?

- ☐ (a) Active transport
- ☐ (b) Breathing
- ☐ (c) Diffusion
- ☐ (d) Osmosis
- ☐ (e) Respiration

116 The lungs are adapted to take oxygen from the air and allow it to diffuse into the blood as quickly as possible. Which of the following features of the lungs does not help in this process?

- ☐ (a) Large surface area
- ☐ (b) Moist surface
- ☐ (c) Mucus-secreting cells
- ☐ (d) Rich blood supply
- ☐ (e) Thin-walled air sacs

117 After oxygen moves from the alveoli into the bloodstream, how is it carried in the blood around the body?

- ☐ (a) Attached to antibody molecules in solution within the blood plasma
- ☐ (b) Attached to proteins in the cell membrane of the red blood cells
- ☐ (c) Attached to proteins in the chromosomes of the white blood cells
- ☐ (d) Attached to the haemoglobin protein carried within the red blood cells

- ☐ (e) Attached to the haemoglobin carried within the blood mitochondria

118 Where exactly is carbon dioxide carried when being transported from respiring organs to the lungs by the bloodstream?

- ☐ (a) In the lymphocyte cells and red blood cells
- ☐ (b) In the phagocyte cells and red blood cells
- ☐ (c) In the phagocyte cells and lymphocyte cells
- ☐ (d) In the red blood cells and the blood plasma
- ☐ (e) In the blood plasma only

119 Which of the following First Aid measures could not be used to check if a person is breathing?

- ☐ (a) Use your middle finger to feel the pulse on the inside of their wrist or in their neck
- ☐ (b) Place a mirror close to their mouth and nose, and see if it mists up with condensation
- ☐ (c) Place your cheek against their mouth, and see if you can feel them breathing out
- ☐ (d) Place your ear against their mouth, and see if you can hear them breathing out
- ☐ (e) Place your hand on their chest, and see if you can feel any movement

120 In inhaled air there is 21% oxygen. What percentage of oxygen would you expect there to be in exhaled air, if the person breathing was not undergoing any strenuous activity?

- ☐ (a) 9
- ☐ (b) 12
- ☐ (c) 16
- ☐ (d) 21
- ☐ (e) 24

121 In inhaled air there is 0.03% carbon dioxide. What percentage of carbon dioxide would you expect there to be in exhaled air, if the person breathing was not undergoing any strenuous activity?

- ☐ (a) 0.001
- ☐ (b) 0.003
- ☐ (c) 1
- ☐ (d) 4
- ☐ (e) 7

122 In inhaled air there is 78% nitrogen. What percentage of nitrogen would you expect there to be in exhaled air, if the person breathing was not undergoing any strenuous activity?

- ☐ (a) 68
- ☐ (b) 76
- ☐ (c) 78
- ☐ (d) 80
- ☐ (e) 88

Human respiration *(Double Award only)*

Energy for most life processes comes from food that is eaten (or, in plants, made by photosynthesis). Respiration releases energy from food. More energy is released if respiration can use oxygen. This is aerobic respiration. When running fast, the supply of oxygen may not be sufficient for aerobic respiration to provide the energy required. Some organisms live where there is no oxygen available. In both of these circumstances, respiration can release small amounts of energy from food without the need for oxygen.

Anaerobic respiration

 ## KEY FACTS

- **Aerobic respiration** This occurs when there is enough oxygen present. Aerobic respiration uses up the oxygen and also uses up sugar, such as glucose. Energy is released, which can be used in many living processes. Carbon dioxide and water are waste products of the reaction.

- **Anaerobic respiration** This occurs when there is not enough oxygen present for aerobic respiration, for example, during vigorous exercise. Energy is still released but not as much as in aerobic respiration. This kind of respiration still requires a sugar, such as glucose, but produces a different waste product called lactic acid.

- **Lactic acid** This is a mild poison that must be removed from the body. Aching leg muscles after a sprint are due to the presence of lactic acid. Oxygen is required to break the lactic acid down into carbon dioxide and water. The oxygen needed is called the 'oxygen debt'. This is why you breathe rapidly after exercise.

QUESTIONS

123 Which of the following is necessary for aerobic respiration in animals?

- ☐ (a) Carbon dioxide
- ☐ (b) Carbon monoxide
- ☐ (c) Nitrogen
- ☐ (d) Oxygen
- ☐ (e) Water

124 Which of the following is necessary for aerobic respiration in plants?

- ☐ (a) Carbon dioxide
- ☐ (b) Carbon monoxide
- ☐ (c) Nitrogen
- ☐ (d) Oxygen
- ☐ (e) Water

125 Oxygen is needed in which of the following processes?

- ☐ (a) Diffusion
- ☐ (b) Osmosis
- ☐ (c) Photosynthesis
- ☐ (d) Respiration
- ☐ (e) Transpiration

126 Which of the following is a waste product of aerobic respiration?

- ☐ (a) Carbon
- ☐ (b) Carbon dioxide
- ☐ (c) Carbon monoxide
- ☐ (d) Nitrogen
- ☐ (e) Oxygen

127 Which of the following is a useful product of aerobic respiration?

- ☐ (a) Energy in a usable form
- ☐ (b) Oxygen as a gas
- ☐ (c) Glucose as a food
- ☐ (d) Hydrogen as a gas
- ☐ (e) Carbon monoxide as a gas

128 How exactly is oxygen transported around the body?

- ☐ (a) Attached as oxygen ions to the blood plasma
- ☐ (b) Attached to haemoglobin in the red cells
- ☐ (c) Attached to haemoglobin in the white cells
- ☐ (d) Attached to haemoglobin in the blood plasma
- ☐ (e) Attached to myoglobin in the muscle cells

129 Which of the following best describes the gas exchange(s) you would expect to find between the blood in a capillary and a muscle cell?

- ☐ (a) Oxygen diffuses from the cells of the muscle into the blood plasma
- ☐ (b) Oxygen diffuses from muscle cells to blood, and the reverse for carbon dioxide
- ☐ (c) Carbon dioxide diffuses from the muscle cell to the blood plasma
- ☐ (d) Carbon dioxide diffuses from muscle cell to blood, and the reverse for oxygen
- ☐ (e) Carbon dioxide diffuses to the muscle cell from the blood plasma

130 Which of the following is necessary if a cell is to respire aerobically?

- ☐ (a) Blood
- ☐ (b) Carbon dioxide
- ☐ (c) Hydrogen
- ☐ (d) Nitrogen
- ☐ (e) Oxygen

131 Which of the following substances is the usual fuel for the process of respiration?

- ☐ (a) Haemoglobin
- ☐ (b) Glucose
- ☐ (c) Glycogen
- ☐ (d) Starch
- ☐ (e) Sucrose

132 What is the cellular process that provides all the energy required for a mammal to maintain a constant internal temperature?

- ☐ (a) Respiration
- ☐ (b) Shivering
- ☐ (c) Sweating
- ☐ (d) Vasoconstriction
- ☐ (e) Vasodilation

133 The heart rate increases during exercise because the muscles need more energy than when the body is inactive. What is the name of the process that provides this energy?

- ☐ (a) Breathing
- ☐ (b) Expiration
- ☐ (c) Inspiration
- ☐ (d) Pulsation
- ☐ (e) Respiration

134 Which of the following terms is used to describe respiration in the absence of oxygen?

- ☐ (a) Aerobic
- ☐ (b) Anaerobic
- ☐ (c) Debit
- ☐ (d) Lactic
- ☐ (e) Oxyless

Higher Level only

135 Which of the following is the waste product produced when your muscles respire anaerobically?

- ☐ (a) Carbon dioxide
- ☐ (b) Carbon monoxide
- ☐ (c) Ethanoic acid
- ☐ (d) Ethanol
- ☐ (e) Lactic acid

136 Which of the following terms is used for the time it takes a pulse rate to return to its resting level after a period of exercise?

- ☐ (a) Dropping zone
- ☐ (b) Exercise period
- ☐ (c) Recovery period
- ☐ (d) Recuperation zone
- ☐ (e) Resting period

137 Phil, Angus and Trevor all have a resting pulse rate of 67 beats per minute. They all undergo an identical exercise after which their pulses are again taken and the results are as follows: Phil = 98, Angus = 95, and Trevor = 100. They also see how long it takes for their pulses to return to normal and the results are as follows: Phil = 180 seconds, Angus = 210 seconds, and Trevor = 197 seconds. Who is the fittest and who is the least fit?

- ☐ (a) Fittest is Phil and the least fit is Angus
- ☐ (b) Fittest is Angus and the least fit is Trevor
- ☐ (c) Fittest is Phil and the least fit is Trevor
- ☐ (d) Fittest is Angus and the least fit is Phil
- ☐ (e) Fittest is Trevor and the least fit is Phil

138 In the absence of oxygen, yeast converts sugar into alcohol and carbon dioxide. What is this process called?

- ☐ (a) Aerobic respiration
- ☐ (b) Brewing
- ☐ (c) Distillation
- ☐ (d) Fermentation
- ☐ (e) Wine making

139 Fermentation is a type of anaerobic respiration. In this process alcohol is one product. What is the other product?

- ☐ (a) Carbon dioxide
- ☐ (b) Oxygen
- ☐ (c) Proteins
- ☐ (d) Sugars
- ☐ (e) Water

140 Which of the following does not use energy from respiration?

- ☐ (a) Active transport of materials across cell membranes
- ☐ (b) Contraction of muscles
- ☐ (c) Diffusion of dissolved salts
- ☐ (d) Maintenance of body temperature
- ☐ (e) Manufacture of molecules

141 During long periods of vigorous activity, muscles become tired. If insufficient oxygen is reaching the muscles, they cannot respire aerobically. In this situation anaerobic respiration takes over. During anaerobic respiration, what is produced and does it produce more or less energy than aerobic respiration?

- ☐ (a) Oxygen is produced and more energy
- ☐ (b) Oxygen is produced and less energy
- ☐ (c) Lactic acid is produced and more energy
- ☐ (d) Lactic acid is produced and less energy
- ☐ (e) Starch is produced and more energy

142 During anaerobic respiration, the incomplete breakdown of glucose produces lactic acid. As this breakdown is incomplete, much less energy is produced than during aerobic respiration. The lactic acid that builds up is toxic so this must be broken down. What is the oxygen required to get rid of this lactic acid called?

- ☐ (a) Haemoglobin cover
- ☐ (b) Haem debt
- ☐ (c) Oxygen debt
- ☐ (d) Oxygen owed
- ☐ (e) Recovery supply

Human nervous system *(Single and Double Awards)*

Animals need a rapid response system to survive. The senses detect changes in the environment of an animal and convert these physical changes into nerve impulses. The nervous system transmits these impulses and co-ordinates a response very rapidly. The brain is the co-ordinating centre with more than 20 billion nerve cells at birth. We lose thousands every day, which are not replaced. However, we don't seem to notice this until we reach very old age. The nerve cell, or neurone, can pass on impulses at 50 metres per second.

The simplest of co-ordinated actions by the body is the reflex arc. This can involve just two neurones as in the knee jerk. Usually it involves three neurones, one carrying the impulse from the sense organ to the central nervous system, a second in the central nervous system passing the impulse to the third, which takes the impulse to the muscle, which will carry out the response. As the conscious part of the brain is not used, the response is very rapid and the person is not immediately aware of what is happening. You might have experienced this when picking up a hot object: you probably dropped it before you were even aware that it was hot.

 KEY FACTS

• **Central nervous system (CNS)** This consists of the brain and the spinal cord. It is connected to the rest of the body by a system of nerves.

• **Sense organs** Certain areas of the body contain specialised cells for receiving stimuli: the eyes contain light sensitive cells, the ears contain sound and balance sensitive cells, the tongue contains taste receptor cells, the nose contains smell sensitive cells, and the skin contains many receptor cells including those which detect touch.

• **Stimulus to response** Receptors are able to detect stimuli and messages get sent to the CNS as nerve impulses along nerve cells, or neurones. The CNS then co-ordinates a response to these stimuli. Nerve impulses are sent from the CNS along neurones to an effector, which then carries out the response. The way a body responds to a stimulus from a sense organ can be summarised as follows:
stimulus → receptor → co-ordinator → effector → response

• **Reflex arc** This involves a nerve impulse, which is an electrical signal, carried via neurones and across synapses. A reflex arc involves as few neurones as possible, so making us able to respond rapidly to a stimulus. Examples of reflex arcs are the knee-jerk reaction and a hand being pulled away from a hot object.

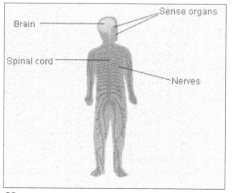

Human nervous system

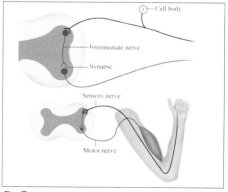

Reflex arc

• **Sensory neurone** The stimulus will start a nerve impulse that is carried to the CNS via a sensory neurone.

• **Relay neurone** In the CNS, the nerve impulse must be sent to a relay neurone over a tiny gap, called a synapse, between the two cells. When the nerve impulse reaches the synapse, it causes a chemical called a neurotransmitter to be released. This chemical crosses the synapse and causes a new nerve impulse in the relay neurone.

• **Motor neurone** This next neurone is long and thin. Again the nerve impulse must cross a synapse between the two cells using a neurotransmitter. The nerve impulse now leaves the CNS via the motor neurone and is carried to an effector, such as a muscle, which carries out a response.

QUESTIONS

143 True ☐ or false ☐ ?
Humans have five main senses: hearing, sight, smell, taste and touch.

144 True ☐ or false ☐ ?
The sense organs: the eye, the ear, the nose, the tongue and the skin, are all part of the central nervous system.

145 True ☐ or false ☐ ?
The eye is part of the central nervous system.

146 Which of the following correctly lists the five human senses?

☐ (a) Happiness, sadness, anger, pity and grief
☐ (b) Happiness, sadness, anger, pain and joy
☐ (c) Sound, hearing, greed, touch and smell
☐ (d) Sight, hearing, taste, touch and smell
☐ (e) Sight, sound, smell, touch and taste

147 Which of the following is not an example of a human sense?

☐ (a) Hearing
☐ (b) Indigestion
☐ (c) Sight
☐ (d) Taste
☐ (e) Touch

148 To which of the following stimuli is the skin not sensitive?

☐ (a) Humidity
☐ (b) Pain
☐ (c) Pressure
☐ (d) Temperature
☐ (e) Touch

149 To which of the following types of stimuli is the skin not sensitive?

☐ (a) Acidity
☐ (b) Pain
☐ (c) Pressure
☐ (d) Temperature
☐ (e) Touch

150 The skin has no sensory receptors for which of the following?

☐ (a) Light
☐ (b) Pain
☐ (c) Pressure
☐ (d) Temperature
☐ (e) Touch

151 In the following diagram, which letter correctly labels the brain?

☐ (a) V
☐ (b) W
☐ (c) X
☐ (d) Y
☐ (e) Z

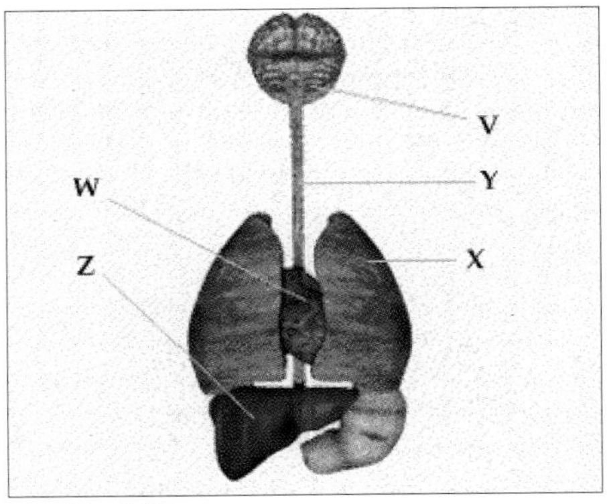

Q151, 152

152 In the diagram above, which letter labels the spinal cord?

☐ (a) V
☐ (b) W
☐ (c) X
☐ (d) Y
☐ (e) Z

153 Which of the following best describes the function of the brain?

☐ (a) To warm the blood pumped around the body by the heart
☐ (b) To form images from the eyes, so that you can see
☐ (c) To control movements of the arms and legs
☐ (d) To control most of your behaviour, both unconscious and conscious
☐ (e) To control only your unconscious actions, such as the beating of your heart

154 Which of the following best describes the human nervous system?

☐ (a) All body organs, the nerves, the spinal cord and the brain
☐ (b) Digestive organs, the sensory receptors and the brain
☐ (c) Motor and sensory nerves, the spinal cord and the brain
☐ (d) Spinal cord, the endocrine glands and the brain
☐ (e) Sense organs, all nerves, the spinal cord and the brain

155 Which of the following is not a part of the human nervous system?

☐ (a) Brain
☐ (b) Nerves
☐ (c) Sense organs
☐ (d) Skull
☐ (e) Spinal cord

156 Which of the following is not a part of the human nervous system?

☐ (a) Backbone
☐ (b) Brain
☐ (c) Nerves
☐ (d) Neurones
☐ (e) Spinal cord

157 In which part of your body might you find receptors highly sensitive to vibrations?

☐ (a) Ears
☐ (b) Eyes
☐ (c) Nose
☐ (d) Stomach
☐ (e) Tongue

158 Sense organs have cells in them called receptors. Receptors can change a stimulus into a nerve impulse. Which of the following is not a characteristic of a nerve impulse?

☐ (a) It is rapid
☐ (b) It can be carried in the blood
☐ (c) It is carried in a neurone
☐ (d) It is like an electrical impulse
☐ (e) It can start a muscle contraction

Higher Level only

159 True ☐ or false ☐ ?
A reflex action is an immediate response to a stimulus. It involves only the brain.

160 William Edwards touched a plate he thought was cold whereas, in fact, it was very hot. Almost as soon as his finger touched the plate, he pulled his hand away. What type of response is this?

☐ (a) A cortex
☐ (b) An influction
☐ (c) An instruction
☐ (d) A reflection
☐ (e) A reflex

161 The following diagram shows the reflex arc that causes the withdrawal of your hand from a hot object. Where would the stimulus of the hot object be detected?

☐ (a) V
☐ (b) W
☐ (c) X

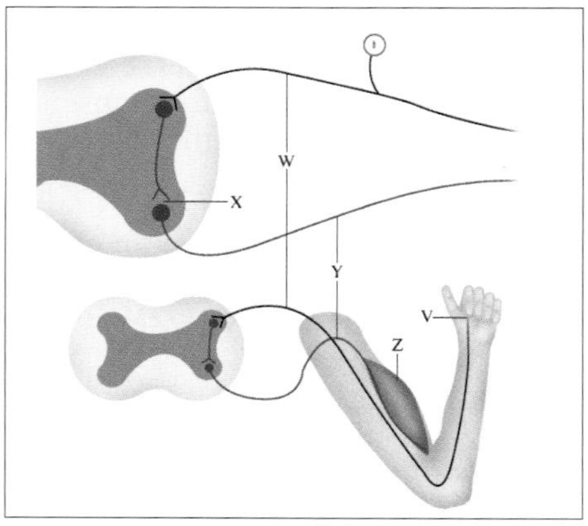

Q161, 162, 163, 164, 165

☐ (d) Y
☐ (e) Z

162 Which structure is labelled W in the diagram above?

☐ (a) Cell body
☐ (b) Motor nerve fibre
☐ (c) Sensory nerve fibre
☐ (d) Sensory receptor
☐ (e) Synapse

163 Which structure is labelled X in the diagram above?

☐ (a) Cell body
☐ (b) Motor nerve fibre
☐ (c) Sensory nerve fibre
☐ (d) Sensory receptor
☐ (e) Synapse

164 Which structure is labelled Y in the diagram above?

☐ (a) Effector muscle
☐ (b) Intermediate nerve fibre

☐ (c) Motor nerve fibre
☐ (d) Sensory nerve fibre
☐ (e) Synapse

165 Which structure is labelled Z in the diagram of a reflex arc?

☐ (a) Affector (sensory) nerve fibre
☐ (b) Afferent (sensory) cell body
☐ (c) Effector (biceps muscle)
☐ (d) Effector (motor) nerve fibre
☐ (e) Sensory receptor in the hand

166 Which of the following is an adaptation of a motor neurone to its function?

☐ (a) It can move around the body
☐ (b) It has more than one nucleus
☐ (c) It is biconcave
☐ (d) It is very long and thin
☐ (e) It has no nucleus

167 In a reflex arc, which type of nerve fibre stimulates the effector muscle to contract?

☐ (a) Grey fibre
☐ (b) Intermediate fibre
☐ (c) Motor fibre
☐ (d) Sensory fibre
☐ (e) White fibre

168 What is the name given to a junction between two nerves?

☐ (a) Circuit
☐ (b) Conjunctiva
☐ (c) Ozone
☐ (d) Synapse
☐ (e) T junction

Human eye *(Single and Double Awards)*

The eye is a sense organ that changes light wave energy into nerve impulses in the optic nerve. These impulses are then used by the brain to produce a 'picture' of what the person has seen. The eye is an extremely sensitive organ in mammals. It can focus on objects at different distances using a lens that changes shape. It can control the amount of light entering the eye by opening or closing the pupil. It consists of a series of structures that all play a role in how the eye functions in response to light.

 KEY FACTS

• **Retina** This is at the back of the eye and contains the light sensitive cells, rods and cones, which convert the light signals into nerve impulses.

• **Optic nerve** This contains all the neurones going from the eye to the brain.

• **Cornea** This is the transparent part of the tough outer coating of the eye and bends the light as it enters the eye.

• **Iris** This is the coloured part of the eye surrounding the pupil. It contains muscles, which can open and close the pupil so that only the right amount of light enters the eye.

• **Lens** This focuses light onto the retina. Its shape can be changed by contracting or relaxing muscles in the ciliary body. These muscles are circular and are attached to the lens by the suspensory ligaments. Contracting the muscles allows the eye to focus on objects close to the eye.

QUESTIONS

169 The following diagram shows a cross-section through the human eye. Which letter correctly labels the cornea?

- ☐ (a) V
- ☐ (b) W
- ☐ (c) X
- ☐ (d) Y
- ☐ (e) Z

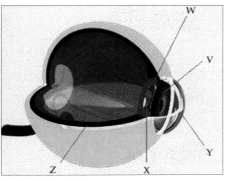

Q169, 170, 171

170 The diagram above shows a cross-section through the human eye. Which letter correctly labels the lens?

- ☐ (a) V
- ☐ (b) W
- ☐ (c) X
- ☐ (d) Y
- ☐ (e) Z

171 The diagram above shows a cross-section through the human eye. Which letter correctly labels the iris?

- ☐ (a) V
- ☐ (b) W
- ☐ (c) X
- ☐ (d) Y
- ☐ (e) Z

172 The following diagram shows a cross-section through the human eye. Which letter correctly labels the retina?

- ☐ (a) V
- ☐ (b) W
- ☐ (c) X
- ☐ (d) Y
- ☐ (e) Z

173 The following diagram shows a cross-section through the human eye. Which letter correctly labels the optic nerve?

- ☐ (a) V
- ☐ (b) W
- ☐ (c) X
- ☐ (d) Y
- ☐ (e) Z

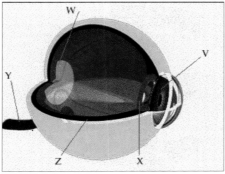

Q172, 173

174 In the mammalian eye, what is the function of the cornea?

- ☐ (a) To bend light entering the eye
- ☐ (b) To house the light sensitive cells
- ☐ (c) To protect the eye from damage
- ☐ (d) To prevent reflections within the eye
- ☐ (e) To hold the lens securely in place

175 In the mammalian eye, what is the function of the lens?

- ☐ (a) To control the amount of light that enters the eye
- ☐ (b) To help focus the light onto the retina
- ☐ (c) To help protect the eye from physical damage
- ☐ (d) To change the light image into nerve impulses
- ☐ (e) To prevent stray light reflections within the eye

176 Which part of the eye is most effective at bending the light that enters the eye?

- ☐ (a) Choroid
- ☐ (b) Cornea
- ☐ (c) Lens
- ☐ (d) Retina
- ☐ (e) Vitreous humour

177 Which part of the eye allows it to focus both on objects that are very close and objects that are very far away?

- ☐ (a) Choroid
- ☐ (b) Iris
- ☐ (c) Lens
- ☐ (d) Optic nerve
- ☐ (e) Retina

178 Which part of the eye is responsible for changing the light image into nerve impulses that can be interpreted by the brain?

- ☐ (a) Cornea
- ☐ (b) Iris
- ☐ (c) Lens
- ☐ (d) Optic nerve
- ☐ (e) Retina

179 In the mammalian eye, what is the function of the retina?

- ☐ (a) To control the amount of light that enters the eye
- ☐ (b) To ensure the correct amount of light enters the eye
- ☐ (c) To transport nerve impulses from the eye to the brain
- ☐ (d) To change the light image into nerve impulses
- ☐ (e) To prevent light leaking into the brain behind

180 In the mammalian eye, what is the function of the optic nerve?

- ☐ (a) To change the light image into nerve impulses
- ☐ (b) To control the amount of light that enters the eye
- ☐ (c) To ensure no light is reflected within the eye
- ☐ (d) To house and protect the light sensitive cells
- ☐ (e) To transmit nerve impulses from the eye to the brain

181 Which part of the eye is responsible for controlling the amount of light that falls on the retina?

- ☐ (a) Cornea
- ☐ (b) Iris
- ☐ (c) Lens
- ☐ (d) Retina
- ☐ (e) Sclera

182 Which of the following best describes the function of the iris in the mammalian eye?

- ☐ (a) To change images into nerve impulses
- ☐ (b) To control the amount of light entering the eye
- ☐ (c) To focus light sharply on to the cornea
- ☐ (d) To focus light sharply on to the retina
- ☐ (e) To focus light sharply on to the lens

183 What happens to the radial and circular muscles in the iris when a bright light is shone on the eye?

- ☐ (a) The circular muscles contract and the radial muscles relax
- ☐ (b) The circular muscles relax and the radial muscles relax
- ☐ (c) The circular muscles contract and the radial muscles contract
- ☐ (d) The circular muscles relax and the radial muscles contract
- ☐ (e) There's no change to either muscle group

184 What happens to the radial muscles in the iris when a person walks into a darkened room?

- ☐ (a) The radial muscles become contracted
- ☐ (b) The radial muscles become relaxed
- ☐ (c) The radial muscles become thinner
- ☐ (d) The radial muscles become slower
- ☐ (e) The radial muscles become faster

185 Toby Thorpe has been caught sleeping in a biology lesson, but before his teacher wakes him up, she tells the class to gather round and look at Toby's eyes as soon as he opens them. What would you expect the students to see?

- ☐ (a) Toby's lenses increasing in size
- ☐ (b) Toby's lenses decreasing in size
- ☐ (c) Toby's pupils increasing in size
- ☐ (d) Toby's pupils decreasing in size
- ☐ (e) Toby's irises decreasing in size

186 Which of the following terms best describes the type of response shown by the reaction of the iris to a change in light intensity?

- ☐ (a) Deflux
- ☐ (b) Influx
- ☐ (c) Instinct
- ☐ (d) Reflex
- ☐ (e) Reflux

Higher Level only

187 What is the function of the sensory cells called rods?

- ☐ (a) To detect light colour
- ☐ (b) To detect light intensity
- ☐ (c) To detect gravity
- ☐ (d) To detect sound
- ☐ (e) To detect pressure

188 What is the function of the sensory cells called cones?

- ☐ (a) To detect colour of light
- ☐ (b) To detect intensity of light
- ☐ (c) To detect airborne scents
- ☐ (d) To detect pain on the skin surface
- ☐ (e) To detect changes in temperature

189 Which of the following controls the shape of the lens in your eye?

- ☐ (a) Ciliary muscles
- ☐ (b) Cornea
- ☐ (c) Iris
- ☐ (d) Pupil
- ☐ (e) Suspensory ligaments

190 Ciliary muscles change the shape of the lens so our eyes can accommodate and focus on objects at varying distances away from them. What is the name given to the ligaments that attach the ciliary muscle to the lens?

- ☐ (a) Ciliary
- ☐ (b) Cornea
- ☐ (c) Hare
- ☐ (d) Retinal
- ☐ (e) Suspensory

Human hormones *(Single and Double Awards)*

Rapid responses to a stimulus are co-ordinated by the nervous system. Slow, long term responses are usually co-ordinated by hormones that communicate through the blood circulatory system. The two systems are linked in the brain. Think what happens to you when you pick up the courage to go on a big dipper! There is a sudden rapid response of total fright followed by longer term fear until you get off the ride. Insulin is a natural hormone that ensures body cells have a constant supply of energy-giving sugars. Medical uses of hormones include the prevention of pregnancy (contraception), the promotion of fertility, and the treatment of diabetes.

KEY FACTS

- **Hormones** These are chemicals in the body that affect the way certain target organs work. They are often referred to as 'chemical messengers'. Hormones are produced by glands and are secreted into the bloodstream, which carries them to their target organs.

- **Sex hormones** These control the start of puberty, when gametes (sex cells) begin to be produced. At this time, secondary sexual characteristics, such as the voice breaking in boys or breast development in girls, also become apparent due to the sex hormones. In men, the main hormone is testosterone, which is produced by the testes. In women, the main hormones are oestrogen and progesterone, which are produced in the ovaries. Female sex hormones control the development and release of eggs from the ovaries, and the menstrual cycle.

- **Oral contraception** This is otherwise known as the Pill. It is a small dose of female sex hormones that prevent the ovaries releasing any eggs. Using this, a woman can avoid becoming pregnant because there are no eggs to be fertilised.

- **Fertility drugs** These are small doses of different female sex hormones that stimulate the release of eggs from the ovaries, increasing the chances of fertilisation.

(Double Award only)

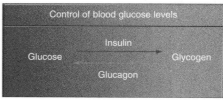

Control of blood sugar levels

- **Insulin** This is a hormone produced by the pancreas that targets the liver. In the liver, it causes the cells to convert excess glucose in the blood into glycogen, which is then stored in the liver. In this way blood sugar levels are controlled.

• **Diabetes** This is a disease in which a person cannot control his or her blood sugar levels because the pancreas does not produce enough insulin. To treat the disease, the patient is injected with insulin. Diabetics also need to control their diet carefully.

QUESTIONS

191 Which of the following best defines a hormone?

☐ (a) A chemical released into the blood that will affect the activity of a target organ or organs
☐ (b) A chemical released into the blood that will affect sexual development of the person
☐ (c) A chemical released by the brain that will affect behaviour and mood
☐ (d) A chemical released into the nervous system that affects target organs
☐ (e) A chemical released into the intestine that affects the metabolism of all body cells

192 True ☐ or false ☐ ?
Hormones travel round the body via the nervous system.

193 What is defined as 'a chemical released from a gland that travels in the blood and will affect the activity of a target organ, or organs'?

☐ (a) Antibody
☐ (b) Antigen
☐ (c) Enzyme
☐ (d) Hormone
☐ (e) Nervous impulse

194 Which of the following identifies two differences between a message sent by a hormone and one sent by a nerve?

☐ (a) The hormonal message will be quicker and more powerful
☐ (b) The hormonal message will be slower and more powerful
☐ (c) The hormonal message will be slower and will last longer
☐ (d) The hormonal message will be faster and more specific in its targets
☐ (e) The nervous message will be faster and less specific in its targets

195 Where is the hormone testosterone produced?

☐ (a) Adrenal gland
☐ (b) Pancreas
☐ (c) Pineal gland
☐ (d) Pituitary gland
☐ (e) Testes

196 Which hormone causes the voice of a male to deepen at puberty?

☐ (a) Adrenalin
☐ (b) Oestrogen
☐ (c) Progesterone
☐ (d) Testosterone
☐ (e) Toblerone

197 Which of the following changes is not caused by testosterone?

☐ (a) A decrease in body hair
☐ (b) An enlargement of the sexual organs
☐ (c) An increased sex drive
☐ (d) A muscle enlargement
☐ (e) The voice becomes lower

198 Which organ produces the hormones oestrogen and progesterone?

☐ (a) Liver
☐ (b) Ovary
☐ (c) Pancreas
☐ (d) Pituitary gland
☐ (e) Thyroid gland

Higher Level only

199 Which of the following is a function of oestrogen?

☐ (a) To prepare the vaginal lining for the newly-fertilised ovum
☐ (b) To attract the sperm towards the ovum in the Fallopian tubes
☐ (c) To trigger the shedding of the uterus lining in menstruation
☐ (d) To trigger the development of a thicker uterus lining
☐ (e) To trigger the development of the ovum in the ovaries

200 Which of the following are found in a typical oral contraceptive pill?

☐ (a) Adrenalin and progesterone
☐ (b) Oestrogen and progesterone
☐ (c) Oestrogen and testosterone
☐ (d) Progesterone and testosterone
☐ (e) Testosterone and adrenalin

201 Which reproductive event is the oral contraceptive pill supposed to prevent?

☐ (a) Fertilisation
☐ (b) Menstruation
☐ (c) Meiosis
☐ (d) Mitosis
☐ (e) Ovulation

202 Which of the following hormones might be given to an infertile man in an attempt to increase his chances of fathering a child?

☐ (a) Adrenalin
☐ (b) Insulin
☐ (c) Oestrogen
☐ (d) Testosterone
☐ (e) Thyroxine

203 Which of the following hormones may be used in the hormone replacement therapy (HRT) undergone by a woman in menopause?

☐ (a) ADH
☐ (b) Adrenalin
☐ (c) Insulin
☐ (d) Progesterone
☐ (e) Thyroxine

204 The human menstrual cycle is usually regarded as 'starting' with the start of bleeding on day one of the 28-day cycle. As the cycle progresses through days 1 – 5, which of the following happens?

☐ (a) Fertilised egg waits in oviduct
☐ (b) Ovaries transport eggs to the cervix
☐ (c) Uterus lining is broken down
☐ (d) Uterus lining is thickened
☐ (e) Uterus produces oestrogen

205 Which of the following is caused by the follicle stimulating hormone (FSH) during the menstrual cycle?

☐ (a) The inhibition of oestrogen production
☐ (b) The inhibition of LH production
☐ (c) The maturing of an egg
☐ (d) Menstruation
☐ (e) Ovulation

206 During the menstrual cycle, which of the following hormones stimulates the ovaries to produce oestrogens?

- ☐ (a) Adrenaline
- ☐ (b) FSH
- ☐ (c) HCG
- ☐ (d) Progesterone
- ☐ (e) Testosterone

207 The following diagram shows the position of the endocrine glands in a woman. Which letter correctly identifies the pituitary gland?

- ☐ (a) V
- ☐ (b) W
- ☐ (c) X
- ☐ (d) Y
- ☐ (e) Z

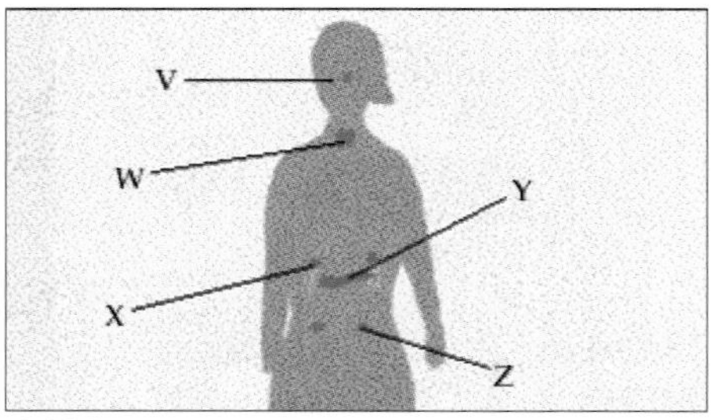

Q207

208 Which of the following hormones stimulates the pituitary gland in a woman to produce luteinizing hormone (LH)?

- ☐ (a) Adrenaline
- ☐ (b) FSH
- ☐ (c) Oestrogens
- ☐ (d) PH
- ☐ (e) Progesterone

209 Which of the following hormones stimulates the release of the egg on about day 14 of the menstrual cycle (the middle of the cycle)?

- ☐ (a) FSH
- ☐ (b) Glucagon
- ☐ (c) LH
- ☐ (d) Oestrogens
- ☐ (e) Progesterone

210 Which of the following hormones is used as a fertility drug for women whose hormone levels are too low to stimulate the eggs to mature.

- ☐ (a) FSH
- ☐ (b) LH
- ☐ (c) Oestrogen
- ☐ (d) Progesterone
- ☐ (e) Testosterone

211 The following diagram shows the position of the endocrine glands in a man. Which letter correctly identifies the adrenal gland?

- ☐ (a) V
- ☐ (b) W
- ☐ (c) X
- ☐ (d) Y
- ☐ (e) Z

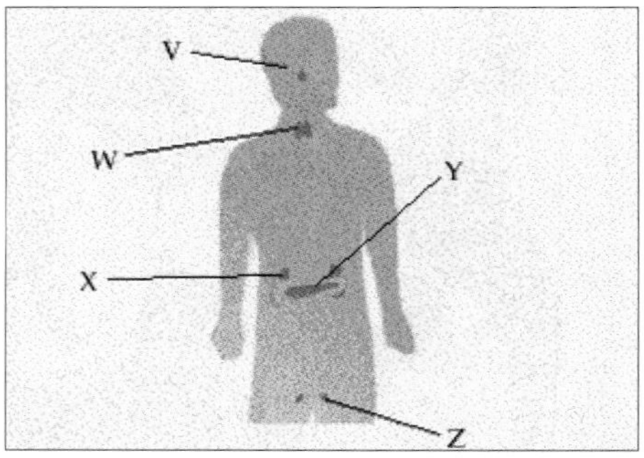

Q211

212 Which organ releases the hormone adrenalin?

- ☐ (a) Adrenal gland
- ☐ (b) Ovary
- ☐ (c) Pancreas
- ☐ (d) Pituitary gland
- ☐ (e) Thyroid gland

213 Which of the following hormones is most likely to be produced by a woman in response to a stressful situation?

- ☐ (a) Adrenalin
- ☐ (b) Insulin
- ☐ (c) Oestrogen
- ☐ (d) Somatotrophin
- ☐ (e) Thyroxine

214 Which of the following responses is not caused by the release of adrenalin?

- ☐ (a) Deeper breathing
- ☐ (b) Decreased body temperature
- ☐ (c) Faster pulse rate
- ☐ (d) Glycogen converted to glucose
- ☐ (e) Tensing of the body muscles

(Double Award only)

215 When the blood glucose rises above its normal level, what chemical is released by the pancreas to correct it?

- ☐ (a) Adrenalin
- ☐ (b) Glycogen
- ☐ (c) Glucagon

- ☐ (d) Insulin
- ☐ (e) Oestrogen

216 During which circumstances is insulin released into the blood?

- ☐ (a) When glucose levels in the blood are too high
- ☐ (b) When glucose levels in the blood are too low
- ☐ (c) When water levels in the blood are too high
- ☐ (d) When water levels in the blood are too low
- ☐ (e) When the body receives a sudden shock

217 Under which circumstances is glucagon released into the blood?

- ☐ (a) When glucose levels in the blood are too high
- ☐ (b) When glucose levels in the blood are too low
- ☐ (c) When water levels in the blood are too high
- ☐ (d) When water levels in the blood are too low
- ☐ (e) When the body receives a sudden shock

218 Which organ in the body senses any change in blood glucose level?

- ☐ (a) Brain
- ☐ (b) Kidney
- ☐ (c) Intestines
- ☐ (d) Liver
- ☐ (e) Pancreas

219 What is the function of insulin?

- ☐ (a) To convert glucose to glycogen
- ☐ (b) To convert glucose to glucagon
- ☐ (c) To convert glycogen to glucagon
- ☐ (d) To convert glycogen to glucose
- ☐ (e) To convert glucagon to glucose

220 What is the function of the hormone glucagon?

- ☐ (a) To convert adrenalin to insulin
- ☐ (b) To convert adrenalin to glycogen
- ☐ (c) To convert insulin to adrenalin
- ☐ (d) To convert glycogen to glucose
- ☐ (e) To convert glucose to glycogen

Importance of homeostasis *(Single and Double Awards)*

Your body is the site of an amazing range of really complex chemical reactions. As with any chemical reaction, there are certain conditions in which they can work best. Homeostasis keeps the body in more or less the best conditions for all these chemical reactions to work.

Carbon dioxide could make the blood more acidic than it should be for all chemical reactions to proceed quickly. It is important to get this out of the body as soon as possible.

You will know from your chemistry studies that the rate of a chemical reaction increases as the temperature increases. Enzymes work faster when the temperature is higher, but they are destroyed if the temperature is too high. Therefore, it is important to keep the body at the correct temperature.

 KEY FACTS

• **Homeostasis** This word means 'staying the same', and in the body this means maintaining a constant internal environment. It is important that the human body maintains a constant internal environment so that all the chemical reactions, which occur to keep a person healthy and alive, happen in the right conditions. If the conditions change too much, the reactions may not occur at the right speed and then the wrong amounts of substances may be present.

• **Constant conditions** The conditions that the body tries to keep constant include levels of waste products, water levels, and body temperature. For example, if the body became too hot, some enzymes might stop working, essential chemical

processes would not take place and the person would die.

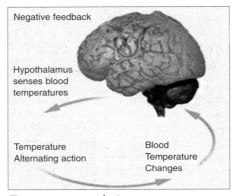

Temperature regulation

• **Temperature regulation in the liver** The chemical reactions in the liver produce much of the body's heat. If the temperature is too high, reactions are speeded up. If the temperature is too low, reactions are slowed down. The brain can detect

whether the body temperature is too high or too low.

• **High body temperature** If the body temperature is too high, nerve impulses are sent to the blood vessels in the skin, which then dilate (expand), and blood flow increases in the skin allowing heat to be lost from the blood to the surroundings. Sweat glands release sweat, which evaporates, cooling the body down.

• **Low body temperature** If the body temperature is too low, the blood vessels in the skin constrict (get thinner), reducing blood flow and reducing heat loss from the body. The sweat glands stop releasing sweat. Sometimes the muscles contract, or shiver, releasing some energy as heat.

(Double Award only)

• **Excretion in the lungs** The lungs provide a large surface area at which carbon dioxide is diffused out of the bloodstream and then exhaled out of the body. Carbon dioxide is a waste product of respiration. It is produced by all the cells in the body and diffused into the bloodstream. If carbon dioxide is allowed to build up in the blood, it lowers the pH of the blood and the conditions are then not suitable for normal chemical reactions.

QUESTIONS

221 True ☐ or false ☐ ?
Homeostasis is about keeping conditions inside the body constant.

222 True ☐ or false ☐ ?
Sweating has an important function in maintaining a constant body temperature.

223 Which of the following statements are true? X: We lose water by breathing. Y: Our body temperature should be approximately 47°C. Z: Our blood sugar level should remain constant despite the effects of feeding.

☐ (a) X and Y
☐ (b) X and Z

☐ (c) Y and Z
☐ (d) X only
☐ (e) X, Y and Z

224 The developing human baby, or fetus, needs a steady stable environment in which to grow. This is provided by the mother. Which structure helps to ensure that the fetus gets the nourishment it needs?

☐ (a) Heart
☐ (b) Liver
☐ (c) Lungs
☐ (d) Pancreas
☐ (e) Placenta

225 The lungs help in the processes of homeostasis. Which of the following substances is kept at a very low level in the body by the lungs?

☐ (a) Carbon dioxide
☐ (b) Salts
☐ (c) Sugar
☐ (d) Urea
☐ (e) Water

226 Which of the following substances diffuses through capillary walls, out of the tissues and into the blood?

☐ (a) Amino acids
☐ (b) Carbon dioxide
☐ (c) Glucose
☐ (d) Nitrogen
☐ (e) Oxygen

227 What part(s) of the blood is/are involved in the transport of carbon dioxide?

- ☐ (a) Carboxy-haemoglobin
- ☐ (b) Haemoglobin and plasma
- ☐ (c) Haemoglobin
- ☐ (d) Oxyhaemoglobin
- ☐ (e) Plasma

228 Which of the following best describes the gas exchange processes that occur between the alveoli and blood?

- ☐ (a) Both oxygen and carbon dioxide diffuse from the lung alveoli into the bloodstream
- ☐ (b) Both oxygen and carbon dioxide diffuse from the bloodstream into the lung alveoli
- ☐ (c) Oxygen diffuses from the blood to the alveoli, whilst carbon dioxide does the reverse
- ☐ (d) Carbon dioxide diffuses from the blood to the alveoli, whilst oxygen does the reverse
- ☐ (e) Carbon dioxide alone diffuses from the lung alveoli into the bloodstream

229 The following diagram shows the major internal organs of a typical mammal. Which letter correctly labels a kidney?

- ☐ (a) V
- ☐ (b) W
- ☐ (c) X
- ☐ (d) Y
- ☐ (e) Z

Q229

230 Which of the following best describes the function of the human kidneys?

- ☐ (a) To filter the air we inhale and allow it to be exposed to white

blood cells
- ☐ (b) To filter waste products out of the blood and to produce urine that is stored in the bladder
- ☐ (c) To filter waste products out of the blood and to produce faeces that are stored in the colon
- ☐ (d) To finish off the process of digestion by filtering the faeces before egestion
- ☐ (e) To finish the production of red blood cells by adding urea to their haemoglobin

231 In a mammal, which organ has the function of removing the waste products from the blood for excretion through the bladder?

- ☐ (a) Intestine
- ☐ (b) Kidney
- ☐ (c) Liver
- ☐ (d) Lung
- ☐ (e) Stomach

232 Which of the following reasons explains why water is so important to mammals?

- ☐ (a) It is used in the chemical reactions of the body
- ☐ (b) It acts as a medium for the chemical reactions of the body
- ☐ (c) It is vital in transporting many chemicals, such as glucose
- ☐ (d) It is used in the removal of waste
- ☐ (e) All are valid reasons

233 In which two ways do we obtain the water essential to our survival?

- ☐ (a) Assimilation and egestion
- ☐ (b) Ingestion and digestion
- ☐ (c) Ingestion and egestion
- ☐ (d) Ingestion and respiration
- ☐ (e) Respiration and digestion

234 Which of the following best describes how water can be lost from our bodies?

- ☐ (a) In exhaled air
- ☐ (b) In sweat
- ☐ (c) In urine
- ☐ (d) In urine and sweat
- ☐ (e) In urine, sweat and exhaled air

235 What is the usual body temperature of a healthy human?

- ☐ (a) 29°C
- ☐ (b) 31°C
- ☐ (c) 33°C
- ☐ (d) 35°C
- ☐ (e) 37°C

236 In which three ways do our bodies lose water during a typical summer day?

- ☐ (a) Excretion, assimilation, inspiration
- ☐ (b) Perspiration, exhalation, excretion
- ☐ (c) Perspiration, assimilation, agglutination
- ☐ (d) Perspiration, digestion, excretion
- ☐ (e) Perspiration, assimilation, digestion

237 Which change generally produces the response of sweating?

- ☐ (a) A decrease in environmental temperature
- ☐ (b) A decrease in core body temperature
- ☐ (c) A rise in environmental temperature
- ☐ (d) A rise in core body temperature
- ☐ (e) Any change in core temperature

238 Which of the following changes would decrease the rate of water loss from the body of a swimsuited bather on a beach in summer?

- ☐ (a) An energetic game of volleyball
- ☐ (b) An increase in air temperature
- ☐ (c) The application of suntan lotion
- ☐ (d) A meal of fish and chips with extra salt
- ☐ (e) A long drink of cool lemonade

239 Where is sweat produced?

- ☐ (a) The sweat arteries in the skin
- ☐ (b) The sweat follicles in the skin
- ☐ (c) The sweat glands in the skin
- ☐ (d) The sweat pores in the skin
- ☐ (e) The sweat veins in the skin

240 How exactly does sweat cool the body?

- ☐ (a) When sweat is produced, it is a cool liquid that then cools the skin directly
- ☐ (b) Sweat glues skin hairs together and so lowers the insulation by the hairs
- ☐ (c) Sweat constricts the skin capillaries so that more body heat is lost
- ☐ (d) Sweat becomes warm with body heat and takes this heat away in drips

☐ (e) As the sweat evaporates, it takes body heat away with it

241 Which of the following fluids can help cool the body by its evaporation?

☐ (a) Blood
☐ (b) Plasma
☐ (c) Sweat
☐ (d) Urea
☐ (e) Urine

242 The following diagram shows a cross-section of human skin. If the body needs cooling down, sweat will be produced by sweat glands located in the skin. Which letter labels a sweat gland?

☐ (a) V
☐ (b) W
☐ (c) X
☐ (d) Y
☐ (e) Z

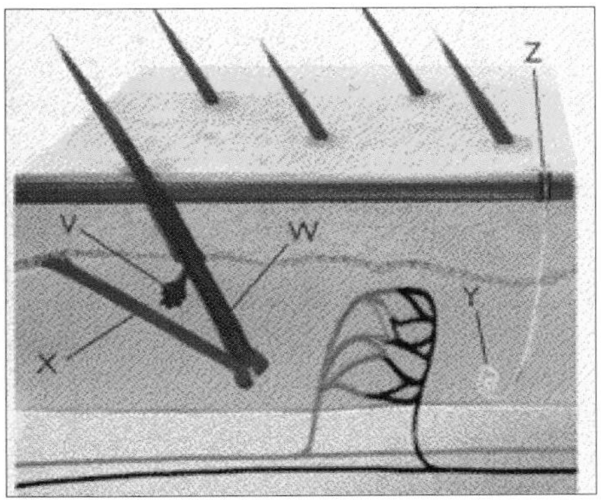

Q242

243 If your body is too hot it produces sweat to cool itself down. What is the name of the physical process that takes heat away from the body?

☐ (a) Conduction
☐ (b) Convection
☐ (c) Distillation
☐ (d) Evaporation
☐ (e) Radiation

244 What happens to the hair of most mammals if their body temperature rises?

☐ (a) The hair lies flat against the skin
☐ (b) The hair becomes very erect
☐ (c) The skin falls out of the follicles
☐ (d) Oil is secreted on to the hair
☐ (e) No response is shown

245 If your core body temperature drops below normal, what muscular response might your body show?

☐ (a) Involuntary slow contractions
☐ (b) Involuntary rapid contractions
☐ (c) Muscular cramps
☐ (d) Total muscular relaxation
☐ (e) Voluntary contractions

246 Which of the following best defines shivering?

☐ (a) Rapid involuntary muscle contractions in response to a drop in body temperature
☐ (b) Rapid involuntary muscle contractions in response to a rise in body temperature
☐ (c) Rapid voluntary muscle contractions in response to a rise in body temperature
☐ (d) Slow involuntary muscle contractions in response to a drop in body temperature
☐ (e) Slow involuntary muscle contractions in response to a rise in body temperature

247 To which of the following stimuli is shivering a reflex response?

☐ (a) Decrease in external temperature
☐ (b) Decrease in internal temperature
☐ (c) Increase in external temperature

☐ (d) Increase in internal temperature
☐ (e) Any change in internal temperature

248 Which of the following behaviours would not help maintain a constant and stable body temperature?

☐ (a) Altering the type of clothes you wear
☐ (b) Curling your body up into a tight ball
☐ (c) Jumping up and down on the spot
☐ (d) Moving between sunny and shady spots
☐ (e) Using under-arm deodorant

Higher Level only

249 What is meant by the term 'vasodilation'?

☐ (a) The erection of hairs on the skin
☐ (b) The lowering of hairs on the skin
☐ (c) The narrowing of skin capillaries
☐ (d) The secretion of sweat from the skin
☐ (e) The widening of skin capillaries

250 What is meant by the term 'vasoconstriction'?

☐ (a) The contraction of the hair erector muscles
☐ (b) The contraction of the sweat glands
☐ (c) The narrowing of skin capillaries
☐ (d) The relaxation of the hair erector muscles
☐ (e) The widening of capillaries in the skin

Excretion in the kidneys *(Single and Double Awards)*

The kidneys help to keep a constantly low level of urea in the blood. They do this by filtering the blood. Each of our kidneys contains 1 – 1.5 million tiny filters that have up to 200 litres of liquid passing through them each day. Not all of the water that passes through the kidney filters is excreted. Most of it is put back into the blood. How much is excreted depends on how much water we have been able to drink and how much we have lost, for example, in sweating.

 KEY FACTS

• **Liver** When breaking down excess amino acids, the liver produces the poisonous waste called urea, which then is released into the blood.

• **Kidney tubules** Blood enters the kidneys and is filtered under high pressure. Much of the contents of the plasma are passed into the kidney tubules. Substances required by the body are returned to the blood by being re-absorbed into capillaries that surround the tubule. Excess ions and excess water remain in the tubule along with the urea.

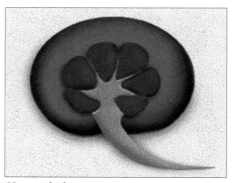

Human kidney

• **Bladder** The solution that passes to the bladder for storage before excretion is called urine.

• **Osmoregulation** The kidneys regulate the water content of the body. The body needs to maintain the correct water levels so that all the chemical reactions can happen at the right concentrations. When the kidneys filter the blood to remove urea, they also remove a large amount of water from the blood. How much water is reabsorbed back into the blood depends on how much water needs to be removed from the body.

• **ADH** The water content of the body is controlled by a hormone called ADH. This is produced by the pituitary gland when the water content of the blood is too low. ADH causes the kidneys to reabsorb more water, and the urine becomes concentrated. If the water content of the blood is too high, the pituitary gland releases less ADH, which causes the kidneys to reabsorb less water and this results in a more dilute urine.

 QUESTIONS

251 Which of the following names two human organs responsible for excreting waste products from the blood?

- ☐ (a) Heart and Liver
- ☐ (b) Kidneys and Heart
- ☐ (c) Kidneys and Liver
- ☐ (d) Kidneys and Lungs
- ☐ (e) Lungs and Liver

252 Which organ's function is often described as 'to filter the blood'?

- ☐ (a) Brain
- ☐ (b) Heart
- ☐ (c) Kidney
- ☐ (d) Lungs
- ☐ (e) Small intestine

253 Which of the following human organs produces urine?

- ☐ (a) Bladder
- ☐ (b) Intestine
- ☐ (c) Kidneys
- ☐ (d) Liver
- ☐ (e) Lungs

254 Which of the following correctly lists the major constituents of human urine?

- ☐ (a) Urea, glucose and water
- ☐ (b) Urea, waste salts and alcohol
- ☐ (c) Urea, waste salts and bile
- ☐ (d) Urea, waste salts and water
- ☐ (e) Urea, water and amino acids

255 Which of the following human organs is responsible for ensuring the body contains the correct amount of water?

- ☐ (a) Bladder
- ☐ (b) Heart
- ☐ (c) Kidneys
- ☐ (d) Liver
- ☐ (e) Lungs

256 Transplantation and/or using a kidney dialysis machine are two ways of treating kidney failure. Which of the following is an advantage of the kidney dialysis machine?

- ☐ (a) You can carry on a normal life
- ☐ (b) It can help in cases of sudden, rapid kidney failure
- ☐ (c) It is cheaper in the long run
- ☐ (d) It is easier to use

- ☐ (e) It can be carried around with you

Higher Level only

257 Which major organ is responsible for reducing the levels of poisonous urea in the blood plasma?

- ☐ (a) Brain
- ☐ (b) Heart
- ☐ (c) Kidneys
- ☐ (d) Liver
- ☐ (e) Lungs

258 Your bloodstream carries urea to your kidneys so that it can be excreted, but what was the original source of this urea?

- ☐ (a) Broken-down amino acids
- ☐ (b) Broken-down carbohydrates
- ☐ (c) Broken-down dietary fibre
- ☐ (d) Broken-down phospholipids
- ☐ (e) Broken-down vitamins

259 Where in the body is urea produced?

- ☐ (a) Brain
- ☐ (b) Heart
- ☐ (c) Kidneys

☐ (d) Liver
☐ (e) Lungs

260 In the following diagram of a kidney nephron, which letter labels the glomerulus?

☐ (a) V
☐ (b) W
☐ (c) X
☐ (d) Y
☐ (e) Z

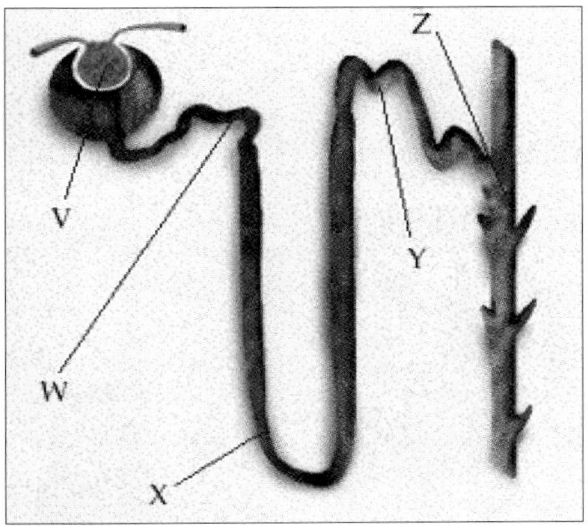

Q260

261 The following diagram shows a kidney nephron. Which letter correctly labels the Bowman's capsule?

☐ (a) V
☐ (b) W
☐ (c) X
☐ (d) Y
☐ (e) Z

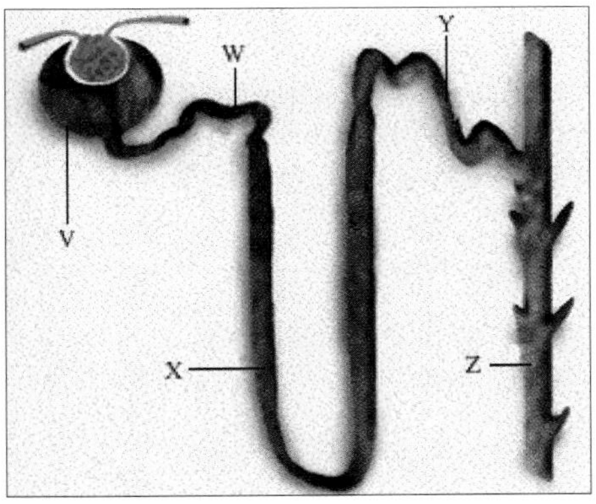

Q261, 262, 263, 264, 265

262 In the diagram above, which letter labels the collecting duct?

☐ (a) V
☐ (b) W
☐ (c) X
☐ (d) Y
☐ (e) Z

263 In the diagram of a kidney nephron, which letter labels the loop of Henle?

☐ (a) V
☐ (b) W
☐ (c) X
☐ (d) Y
☐ (e) Z

264 In the diagram of a kidney nephron, which letter labels the first convoluted tubule, sometimes called the proximal convolution?

☐ (a) V
☐ (b) W
☐ (c) X
☐ (d) Y
☐ (e) Z

265 In the diagram of a kidney nephron, which letter correctly labels the second convoluted (or distal) tubule?

☐ (a) V
☐ (b) W
☐ (c) X
☐ (d) Y
☐ (e) Z

266 Which part of the nephron is involved in the process known as ultrafiltration?

☐ (a) Bowman's capsule
☐ (b) Collecting duct
☐ (c) First convolution
☐ (d) Loop of Henle
☐ (e) Second convolution

267 In which part of the kidney nephron is the majority of tubule filtrate reabsorbed?

☐ (a) Bowman's capsule
☐ (b) Collecting duct
☐ (c) First convolution
☐ (d) Glomerulus
☐ (e) Second convolution

268 Which part of the nephron varies in size depending upon how much water the mammal needs to conserve?

☐ (a) Collecting duct
☐ (b) First convoluted tubule
☐ (c) Glomerulus
☐ (d) Loop of Henle
☐ (e) Second convoluted tubule

269 Which part of the nephron ensures, by regulating the amount of reabsorption, that the level of sodium chloride in the blood is maintained at the correct level?

☐ (a) Bowman's capsule
☐ (b) Collecting duct
☐ (c) First convolution
☐ (d) Glomerulus
☐ (e) Second convolution

270 Which part of the nephron exerts the final control over the concentration of the urine and adapts to changing levels of body water by altering the degree of reabsorption?

☐ (a) Bowman's capsule
☐ (b) Collecting duct
☐ (c) Glomerulus
☐ (d) Renal arteriole
☐ (e) Second convolution

271 Which substance, transported around the body in the blood and filtered out of the capillaries in the Bowman's capsule, is not reabsorbed back into the bloodstream from the kidney nephron?

☐ (a) Amino acids
☐ (b) Glucose
☐ (c) Urea
☐ (d) Vitamins
☐ (e) Water

272 Ultrafiltration in the kidney removes several substances from the blood and excretes them in the urine. What are the three major contents of human urine?

☐ (a) Amino acids, glucose and water
☐ (b) Amino acids, sodium chloride and water
☐ (c) Water, urea and amino acids
☐ (d) Water, urea and glucose
☐ (e) Water, urea and salts

273 If the water content in your blood was low, what hormone would be released from your pituitary gland?

☐ (a) ADH
☐ (b) Adrenaline
☐ (c) FSH
☐ (d) LH
☐ (e) Progesterone

41

274 It is a hot, breezy summer's day. Luke has just been for a run and he has not had a drink for a couple of hours. Which of the following statements is not true concerning the internal state of his body?

☐ (a) More water will be reabsorbed in the kidneys
☐ (b) The water content in his blood will be relatively low
☐ (c) The concentration of ADH in his blood will be relatively low
☐ (d) The urine in his bladder will be relatively concentrated
☐ (e) There is no major change in the amount of urea in his urine

275 It is a cold winter's day. Jonathan has just been watching television for three hours and during that time has drunk five cans of lemonade. Which of the following statements is not true concerning the internal state of his body?

☐ (a) More water will be reabsorbed in the kidneys
☐ (b) The water content in his blood will be relatively high
☐ (c) The concentration of ADH in his blood will be relatively low
☐ (d) The urine in his bladder will be relatively dilute
☐ (e) There is no major change in the amount of urea in his urine

Defence against disease *(Single and Double Awards)*

The human body has a range of defence mechanisms. The first line of defence is the skin. When there is a gap in the skin, the body brings other mechanisms into play. For example, when we eat food, the stomach produces a strong acid to kill the microbes. If a microbe penetrates these defences then the immune system kicks in and a complex range of cells and chemicals are used to attack the microbe. The immune system is also capable of learning from previous attacks so that you are less likely to suffer twice from the same infection.

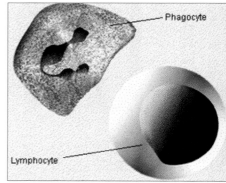

White blood cells

 KEY FACTS

• **Skin** This has an outer layer called the epidermis, which is made up of several layers of cells packed closely together. The cells near the outside are dead and overlap one another. They act as a barrier preventing unwanted micro-organisms from entering the body. If the skin is cut, the blood is able to clot, so preventing the entry of micro-organisms into the body.

• **White blood cells** If micro-organisms do manage to enter the body, white blood cells have several ways of defending the body from them. Some white blood cells produce antibodies, which are protein molecules that attach to the micro-organisms and kill them. Some white blood cells produce anti-toxins that neutralise toxins produced by microbes. Other white blood cells, called phagocytes, engulf micro-organisms and digest them.

• **Mucous membrane** This lines the respiratory tract and produces a sticky mucus, which traps microbes in the air. The mucus is then wafted up to the back of the throat by a muscular action where it is either swallowed and digested, or blown out through the nose.

• **Antigens and antibodies** These can be used to produce an artificial immunity against disease.

 QUESTIONS

276 Which of the following would not help you avoid infectious disease?

☐ (a) Brushing your teeth regularly
☐ (b) Eating food before the sell-by date on the packet
☐ (c) Ensuring meats are well-cooked before eating them
☐ (d) Keeping your body, especially hands, clean
☐ (e) Washing raw vegetables and fruit before eating them

277 True ☐ or false ☐ ?
The skin is one of the body's main defences against infection.

278 Which of the following body's defences plays no part in preventing viruses or bacteria getting into the body?

☐ (a) Acidic secretions from the stomach
☐ (b) Mucus from the nose
☐ (c) Tears from the eyes
☐ (d) Wax from the ears
☐ (e) White blood cells in your bloodstream

279 Which of the following is not directly used in the body's defence against infection?

☐ (a) Layers of dead, oily skin
☐ (b) Mucus from nose and throat
☐ (c) Stomach acid
☐ (d) Urine from the bladder
☐ (e) White blood cells

280 The following diagram shows a cross-section of human skin. Which letter correctly labels the oil gland?

☐ (a) V
☐ (b) W
☐ (c) X
☐ (d) Y
☐ (e) Z

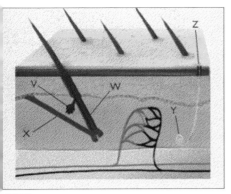

Q280

281 Which of the following helps to keep the lungs clean?

- ☐ (a) Adrenaline
- ☐ (b) Alveoli
- ☐ (c) Mucus-secreting cells
- ☐ (d) Platelets
- ☐ (e) Red blood cells

282 How does the shape of a white blood cell help it to defend your body against disease?

- ☐ (a) Its biconcave shape means it can carry oxygen efficiently to diseased parts of the body
- ☐ (b) Its large and changeable shape means it can capture, engulf and digest smaller organisms
- ☐ (c) Its length means messages can be sent more effectively to diseased parts of the body
- ☐ (d) Its small size helps it to form blood clots so helping to minimise any damage from invaders
- ☐ (e) Its streamlined shape means it can move faster to areas where disease needs to be fought

283 How do our white blood cells recognise invading disease organisms as being 'foreign'?

- ☐ (a) Recognise chemicals in the cell membranes
- ☐ (b) Recognise genes in the nucleus
- ☐ (c) Recognise different types of mitochondria
- ☐ (d) Recognise the overall body shape
- ☐ (e) Recognise the shape of the chromosomes

284 What is an antibody?

- ☐ (a) An inflammation reaction shown by the body when it becomes infected with a disease

- ☐ (b) A type of white blood cell that ingests and digests foreign particles in the body
- ☐ (c) A type of white blood cell that produces poisons to kill foreign organisms in the body
- ☐ (d) A protein molecule produced by white blood cells that helps to destroy foreign particles in the body
- ☐ (e) A DNA molecule produced by phagocytes that helps to kill foreign particles in the body

285 Which immune system molecules have the function of attaching themselves to foreign particles so that white blood cells can then engulf and digest these foreign particles?

- ☐ (a) Antibodies
- ☐ (b) Antigens
- ☐ (c) Anti-histamines
- ☐ (d) Anti-opposites
- ☐ (e) Anti-venoms

286 Some bacteria cause human disease by directly damaging the cells of their host. How else do bacteria manage to affect the body metabolism without directly attacking host cells?

- ☐ (a) By gradually destroying the immune system of their host
- ☐ (b) By gradually absorbing the blood plasma of their host
- ☐ (c) By producing poisons that interfere with the metabolism of the host
- ☐ (d) By preventing the red blood cells absorbing oxygen
- ☐ (e) By slowing down the nerve cells of their host

287 If a single bacterium capable of dividing every half hour enters your body, and no bacteria die, how many would you have in your body after 12 hours?

- ☐ (a) 64
- ☐ (b) 4,096
- ☐ (c) 262,144
- ☐ (d) 16,777,216
- ☐ (e) 33,554,432

Higher Level only

288 If a harmless form of a microbe that causes disease is injected into a person, the body forms a resistance to that disease. What is the name of this process?

- ☐ (a) Facilitation
- ☐ (b) Inoculation
- ☐ (c) Immuno-suppression
- ☐ (d) Vaccination
- ☐ (e) Vaso-dilation

289 Which of the following might be found in a vaccine?

- ☐ (a) Dead bacteria that are unable to infect and reproduce
- ☐ (b) Live bacteria that are healthy and able to infect and reproduce
- ☐ (c) Bacteria that are related to, and just as harmful as, the dangerous bacterium
- ☐ (d) Purified DNA that is isolated from cultures of the harmful bacterium
- ☐ (e) Red blood cells that have been in contact with the bacterium

290 The following graph shows a series of measurements of the concentration of measles' antibody in the body fluids of a boy. He had a vaccination against the disease early in his life, and then almost immediately caught the disease from a schoolfriend. Which of the following features of vaccination is shown clearly by this graph?

- ☐ (a) The primary response involved a more rapid increase in antibody levels
- ☐ (b) The secondary response involved a more rapid increase in antibody levels
- ☐ (c) The secondary response involved both the B-lymphocytes and T-lymphocytes
- ☐ (d) The secondary response produced lower antibody levels than the primary response
- ☐ (e) The primary increase in antibody levels lasted longer than the secondary response

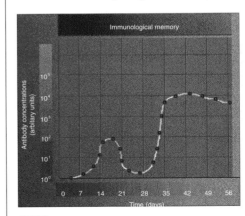

Q290

43

291 The following graph shows the antibody concentration of a person in response to a vaccination, and then to a 'booster' of the same vaccine. When did she have the booster?

☐ (a) 2 - 3 days
☐ (b) 6 - 7 days
☐ (c) 21 - 22 days
☐ (d) 28 - 29 days
☐ (e) 38 - 39 days

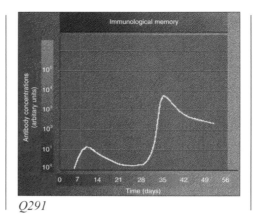

Q291

292 In 1794, a Gloucestershire doctor tried to make people immune to the serious disease of smallpox by infecting them with a dose of the relatively harmless cowpox. What was the name of this doctor?

☐ (a) Alexander Fleming
☐ (b) Christian Barnard
☐ (c) Edward Jenner
☐ (d) Florence Nightingale
☐ (e) Louis Pasteur

Use and abuse of drugs *(Single and Double Awards)*

Drugs alter the way our bodies work. The correct drug, used in the correct amounts at the correct time can make us feel better. The wrong drug, or a drug taken in the wrong amount, can cause us harm. We need to take advice about interfering with the chemistry of our body from people who are qualified to tell us.

Many drugs, used carefully, can benefit the body, for example, antibiotics and painkillers. Solvents, alcohol, tobacco and other drugs have an effect on body functions. Narcotic substances affect the nervous system. Depressants slow down people's reactions while stimulants speed up people's responses. Drugs change the chemical processes in people's bodies and this may affect their behaviour. People may become addicted to the drugs and suffer withdrawal symptoms without them.

 ## KEY FACTS

• **Solvents** These affect behaviour and may cause damage to the lungs, liver and brain.

• **Alcohol** This affects the nervous system by slowing down reactions, and may lead to lack of self-control, unconsciousness or even coma. It may cause damage to the liver (cirrhosis) and the brain.

• **Tobacco smoke** This contains nicotine, tar and carbon monoxide. Nicotine is addictive; tar causes lung cancer, bronchitis and emphysema; carbon monoxide slows the uptake of oxygen by the blood.

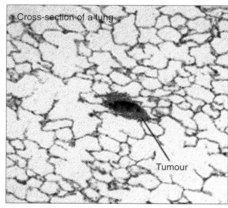

Cancer tumour in the lungs

 ## QUESTIONS

293 Which of the following terms best defines a 'substance produced by one organism that diffuses into its surroundings and is toxic to individuals of other species'?

☐ (a) Antibiotic
☐ (b) Antibody
☐ (c) Antiseptic
☐ (d) Disinfectant
☐ (e) Venom

294 Which of the following is an example of an antibiotic?

☐ (a) Aspirin
☐ (b) Cod Liver Oil
☐ (c) Nicotine
☐ (d) Paracetamol
☐ (e) Penicillin

295 What does an analgesic drug do?

☐ (a) Gives the taker a 'high'
☐ (b) Makes the taker's nerves very sensitive
☐ (c) Makes the taker fall asleep
☐ (d) Make the taker's heart beat at five to ten times its normal rate
☐ (e) Reduces pain

296 Which of the following drugs will speed up the actions of your nervous system?

☐ (a) Amphetamines
☐ (b) Barbiturates
☐ (c) Hallucinogens
☐ (d) Opiates
☐ (e) Tranquillisers

297 Narcotic substances that affect your mood can be classified as stimulants, depressants, painkillers or hallucinogens. Which body system do they all affect?

☐ (a) Breathing system
☐ (b) Excretory system
☐ (c) Nervous system
☐ (d) Reproduction system
☐ (e) Respiratory system

298 Which of the following substances is addictive to users?

☐ (a) Alcohol
☐ (b) Caffeine
☐ (c) Nicotine
☐ (d) Solvents
☐ (e) All of these options

299 Which of the following mood-influencing drugs is classified as a depressant?

- ☐ (a) Amphetamines
- ☐ (b) Caffeine
- ☐ (c) Cocaine
- ☐ (d) Glue solvents
- ☐ (e) Nicotine

300 True ☐ or false ☐ ?
Alcohol is a drug that is classified as a stimulant.

301 Which of the following mood-influencing drugs is classified as a stimulant?

- ☐ (a) Barbiturates
- ☐ (b) Caffeine
- ☐ (c) Glue solvents
- ☐ (d) Tranquillisers
- ☐ (e) Valium

302 Which of the following is a common reason why someone might try a mood-influencing drug?

- ☐ (a) Depression
- ☐ (b) Just to see what it's like
- ☐ (c) Peer group pressure
- ☐ (d) Stress
- ☐ (e) All of these options

303 Which of the following is a drug, made from poppies, that reduces pain by stopping nerve impulses in some parts of the brain?

- ☐ (a) Aspirin
- ☐ (b) Caffeine
- ☐ (c) Cannabis
- ☐ (d) Heroin
- ☐ (e) Nicotine

304 Which of the following diseases is not a risk to users of intravenous drugs?

- ☐ (a) AIDS
- ☐ (b) Hepatitis B
- ☐ (c) Herpes
- ☐ (d) Scurvy
- ☐ (e) Syphilis

305 Which of the following is socially acceptable, yet also a drug?

- ☐ (a) Exercise
- ☐ (b) Lager
- ☐ (c) Lemonade
- ☐ (d) Love
- ☐ (e) Sweets

306 Which of the following is not caused by a moderate intake of alcohol?

- ☐ (a) A decrease in emotional tension
- ☐ (b) An increase in metabolic rate
- ☐ (c) An increase in physical co-ordination
- ☐ (d) An increase in confidence
- ☐ (e) A sensation of warmth

307 What is the name of the liver condition caused by long-term alcohol abuse?

- ☐ (a) Catharsis
- ☐ (b) Cirrhosis
- ☐ (c) Cystitis
- ☐ (d) Cystic fibrosis
- ☐ (e) Diabetes

308 If a pint of bitter contains two units of alcohol, how many units of alcohol would be in a bottle of bitter containing four and a half pints?

- ☐ (a) 6 units
- ☐ (b) 7 units
- ☐ (c) 8 units
- ☐ (d) 9 units
- ☐ (e) 10 units

309 Which of the following diseases is associated with smoking?

- ☐ (a) Emphysema
- ☐ (b) Heart disease
- ☐ (c) Lung cancer
- ☐ (d) Throat cancer
- ☐ (e) All of these options

310 The following diagram shows a simple experiment set up to see what is in cigarette smoke. What is the liquid gathering at point X?

- ☐ (a) Carbon dioxide
- ☐ (b) Carbon monoxide
- ☐ (c) Nicotine solution
- ☐ (d) Tar mixture
- ☐ (e) Tobacco solution

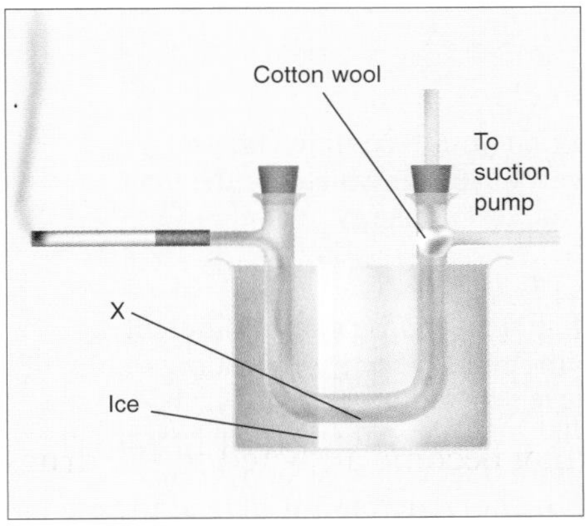

Q310

311 Which of these factors keep the lungs clean?

- ☐ (a) Antibiotics and detergents
- ☐ (b) Expulsion of air and antibiotics
- ☐ (c) Mucus and antibiotics
- ☐ (d) Mucus and cilia
- ☐ (e) Mucus and detergents

ANSWERS

Human diet

☐ **1** *(a)*
A balanced diet is one that includes protein, carbohydrate, fat, vitamins, minerals, vegetable fibre and water in the correct amounts. There is no need at all for any intake of alcohol in the human diet.

☐ **2** *(c)*
A balanced diet is one that includes protein, carbohydrate, fat, vitamins, minerals, vegetable fibre, and water in the correct amounts. Too much or too little of any one of the constituents of a balanced diet will lead to poor health.

☐ **3** *(b)*
Vegetable fibre consists mainly of indigestible cellulose from plant cell walls. This fibre adds bulk to the foodstuffs passing through the large intestine and helps them to retain water, causing the faeces to move more easily through the intestine, therefore avoiding constipation.

☐ **4** *(d)*
Carbohydrates, such as sugar and starch, and fats, such as butter and sunflower oil, are the main sources of energy in the human diet. Therefore, for a healthy diet, it is important to ensure the correct amounts of these two substances are included in meals, with more of the energy coming from carbohydrates, such as starches in rice and potatoes. Some energy can also be obtained from proteins, but normally most protein will be used in maintaining and repairing your tissues.

☐ **5** *False*
Starch is tested for with iodine solution, which is a light brown colour. The iodine then turns blue-black if starch is present.

A5

☐ **6** *(c)*
Fried potato contains fat and carbohydrate, which are the main sources of energy.

☐ **7** *(b)*
Different foods contain different amounts of energy depending on their levels of fat, protein and carbohydrate. Because fat contains more energy per gram than either carbohydrate or proteins, fatty foods will tend to have the highest energy content. Most cheeses contain a very high percentage of fat, and therefore lots of energy, whereas vegetables and turkey contain comparatively little fat.

☐ **8** *(b)*
All the constituents of a balanced diet must be eaten in the correct amounts. Any undereating or overeating does not only affect body weight, it can also often affect health. Fat contains by far the most energy per gram of weight, so overeating this component is particularly dangerous, and there is also some evidence that fats can lead to heart attacks and cancers. Eating too much starch is quite difficult since it satisfies your appetite so quickly.

☐ **9** *(d)*
We need proteins in our diet so that we can build our own proteins for growth. A lack of proteins in the diet causes a stunting of growth. Fibre in the diet helps the movement of food through the gut, and a deficiency of fibre in the diet can lead to constipation and an increased chance of bowel cancer. Lung cancer is nearly always caused by smoking.

A9

☐ **10** *(a)*
Fibre in the diet helps the movement of food through the gut, and so a deficiency in the diet can lead to constipation. Some of the more reactive constituents of fibre seem to do a more important job of lowering the incidence of bowel cancer, heart disease and some other serious conditions.

☐ **11** *(c)*
Carbohydrates and fats are the main sources of energy in our bodies, though we often have the balance wrong for a healthy diet, with too much fat and too little complex carbohydrate. Maintaining body temperature at 37°C requires a surprisingly large amount of energy, in fact most of the energy you use.

☐ **12** *(a)*
Fats, which are found in foods such as milk, cheese and butter, are needed to provide energy and for making cell membranes.

Human digestion

☐ **13** *(c)*
The gullet, or oesophagus, transports food from the mouth, where it is chewed, to the stomach, where chemical digestion by enzymes and acid begins. The gullet moves the food downwards by peristalsis – a rhythmic contraction of the muscles in its walls that pushes the food ahead like a surfer on a wave.

☐ **14** *(b)*
The oesophagus, or gullet, carries food from the mouth to the stomach.

☐ **15** *(d)*
The stomach receives food from the gullet, or oesophagus.

☐ **16** *(e)*
The stomach helps to break the food up into small particles by churning it (part of mechanical digestion) and by adding

enzymes and acids, which begin chemical digestion of the food molecules.

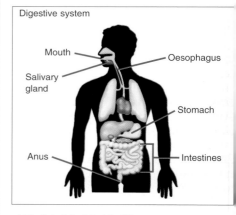

A13, 14, 15, 16, 17, 22

☐ **17** *(a)*
The small intestine receives food from the stomach and then passes the food onto the large intestine. It is in the intestines that most of the food is broken down by enzymes and absorbed into the bloodstream.

☐ **18** *(d)*
Food passes from the stomach to the intestine, where digestion is completed and the useful products of this digestion are absorbed into the bloodstream. The human intestine is approximately seven metres long, tightly folded inside the body, and this great length allows the food to be thoroughly processed.

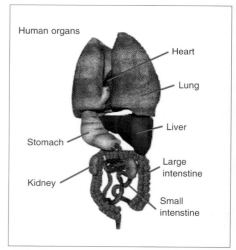

A18, 19

☐ **19** *(e)*
The large intestine is part of the alimentary canal, or gut. The small intestine leads to the large intestine, which is responsible for absorbing water into the body from the food that passes through it. The food, including fibrous roughage, that remains in the gut after it has passed through the large intestine is egested through the rectum and anus.

20 *(d)*
The villi are the millions of infoldings of the wall of the small intestine.

21 *(a)*
The villi provide a huge surface for the absorption of the products of digestion. Most of these, such as glucose, from carbohydrate digestion, or amino acids, from protein digestion, are absorbed into the blood capillary inside each villus. The products of fat digestion, however, are absorbed into the lacteal vessel of each villus.

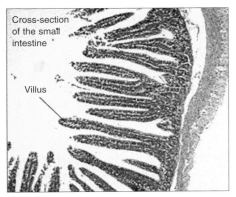

A20, 21

22 *(a)*
In mammals, undigested waste is expelled from the alimentary canal through the anus in the form of faeces.

23 *(e)*
The pancreas secretes enzymes, which help digestion, into the duodenum. It also produces the hormones responsible for maintaining the blood sugar level.

24 *(c)*
The gall bladder produces bile, which contains mineral and bile salts. Bile juice is carried to the intestine by the bile duct.

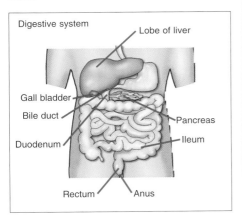

A23, 24

25 *(d)*
When carrying out a Biuret test, the solution added is a mixture of potassium hydroxide solution and copper sulphate solution. This solution is either clear or a very light blue. When it is added to a food solution, the presence of protein is indicated by a mauve-purple colour. If no protein is present there is no colour change.

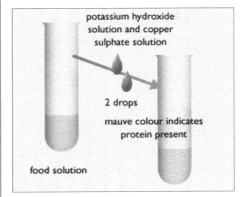

A25

26 *(e)*
When water is added to a food solution after ethanol, which is also a clear liquid, a milky suspension is formed if the solution contains fat. If the solution does not go milky, it does not contain fat.

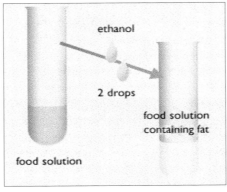

A26

27 *(d)*
Teeth carry out mechanical digestion. They break up the food so that it has a greater surface area upon which enzymes can act, and therefore help to speed up the rate of chemical digestion by the enzymes.

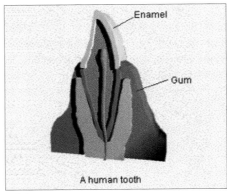

A27

28 *(b)*
Peristalsis is the rhythmical and co-ordinated contraction of muscles in the wall of the oesophagus that pushes food from the back of the mouth to the stomach in preparation for digestion.

29 *False*
Peristalsis is the movement of food down the gullet, but the circular muscles contract behind the food pushing it along in front.

30 *(c)*
The rhythmic contractions of the circular and longitudinal muscles work their way down the oesophagus forcing food down at the front of the wave. This is peristalsis.

31 *(a)*
Digestion is the breaking down of complex foodstuffs to smaller molecules, which can be absorbed into the bloodstream. Digestion is mechanical, by the teeth or stomach, and chemical, by enzymes.

32 *(b)*
Enzymes speed up the reactions that occur in the body without being permanently altered in the reactions themselves, so they are defined as biological catalysts.

33 *(b)*
The later stages of digestion are chemical, as special types of proteins called enzymes are used to break the chemical bonds holding large molecules together.

34 *(e)*
Food is stored in the stomach for several hours after a meal.

35 *(c)*
In the stomach, food is stored, mixed up and broken down mechanically into a smooth paste. The acid pH and the presence of the enzyme pepsin begin the chemical digestion of proteins in the food.

36 *(d)*
The hydrochloric acid produced by the stomach kills most of the bacteria consumed with your food. The enzymes produced by your stomach also work most effectively in the acidic conditions produced by the acid. The acid can wear away the lining of your stomach causing indigestion.

☐ **37** *(b)*
Food passes from the stomach to the intestine, and here digestion is completed and the useful products of this digestion are absorbed into the bloodstream. The intestine is a tube approximately seven metres long, and is tightly folded inside the body. This length gives it more time to carry out its functions of digestion and absorption.

☐ **38** *(a)*
Amylase, present in saliva and intestinal juices, breaks down starch. The amylase enzyme works best in slightly alkaline conditions.

☐ **39** *(b)*
Each starch molecule is broken down to hundreds of maltose molecules, and each maltose molecule is broken down to just two glucose molecules.

☐ **40** *(e)*
The enzyme amylase breaks every other bond in a starch molecule, turning starch into maltose, which is, in turn, broken down to glucose by the enzyme maltase.

☐ **41** *(a)*
Carbohydrases are enzymes that take part in the digestion of large carbohydrates. They are used in the digestion of carbohydrate foods, releasing sugars that are absorbed into the bloodstream.

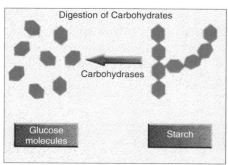

A41, 47

☐ **42** *(b)*
Proteases are enzymes that take part in the breaking down of proteins.

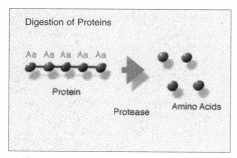

A42

☐ **43** *(d)*
Lipases are enzymes that take part in the digestion or breaking down of lipids, also known as fats. The substrate lipids are eventually broken down to their fatty acid and glycerol components, and these simpler components may then be used by the body.

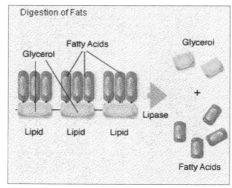

A43

☐ **44** *(e)*
In digestion, proteins are broken down to smaller amino acids, which can be absorbed into the bloodstream. Digestion, in this case, is chemical, with enzymes breaking the chemical bonds holding the protein together.

☐ **45** *(a)*
When proteins are digested their long chains are broken down by enzymes into their constituent amino acids.

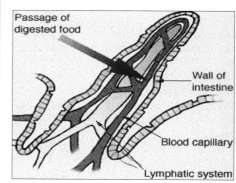

A44, 45

☐ **46** *(e)*
Starch is a large molecule consisting of many glucose sugars bonded together in a chain. Digestion breaks the bonds of this chain, releasing individual glucose sugars that can be absorbed into the bloodstream. Digestion, in this case, is chemical, with enzymes breaking the chemical bonds holding the starch together.

☐ **47** *(b)*
Carbohydrase enzymes are produced in the salivary glands, pancreas and small intestine. Protease enzymes (of which pepsin is one) are produced in the stomach, pancreas and small intestine, whilst lipases are produced by the pancreas and small intestine only. Carbohydrases catalyse the breakdown of complex carbohydrates, such as starch, to simple sugars.

☐ **48** *(a)*
Carbohydrase, protease and lipase enzymes are all produced in both the pancreas and small intestine.

☐ **49** *(d)*
The products of digestion must be available to all parts of the body, so they are transported around in the blood. The blood plasma is water-based, so foods that are not water soluble, such as starches, must therefore be digested into water-soluble components if they are to be useful to the body.

☐ **50** *(c)*
The useful products of digestion are molecules that are small enough to pass through the cells of the walls of the intestine, then through the walls of the capillaries into the bloodstream. Some of the products of fat digestion are not water soluble, and so are absorbed into, and transported by, a special system called the lymphatic system. Once in the bloodstream, the products are transported to where they are needed in the body.

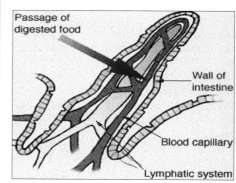

A50, 51, 52

☐ **51** *(b)*
The useful products of carbohydrate digestion, such as monosaccharides, are actively transported across the wall of the intestine and into the capillary that penetrates each of the villi. Since monosaccharides are water soluble this poses no problems, but some of the less soluble products of fat digestion must leave the villus by means of the lacteal vessel.

☐ **52** *(b)*
The soluble amino acids are absorbed into the blood capillary found in each of

the tiny villi in the intestine. From here they will be transported around, and assimilated into, the body.

☐ **53** *(c)*
Bile salts, secreted in bile into the intestine, help with the digestion of fats to fatty acids and glycerol, by breaking large fat droplets into smaller ones. This process is called emulsification. They also help the absorption of the fatty acids from the small intestine into the bloodstream across the outer cells of the villi.

☐ **54** *(b)*
Bile is a yellow-green liquid, made in the liver, that contains bile salts. These salts are released into the small intestine and help the process of digestion by emulsifying fats. Emulsification is the breaking down of fats into small droplets, and this process provides a greater surface area for the lipase enzymes.

☐ **55** *(a)*
The gall bladder stores bile that contains mineral salts, which help to neutralise the acid from the stomach, and bile salts, which emulsify, or break down, lipids into tiny, easily digested droplets.

Human circulation

☐ **56** *(a)*
The heart is located in the chest cavity. It is responsible for pumping blood to the lungs, and receiving this blood back before pumping it to the rest of the body. In this way, the blood is circulated so that all parts of the body can receive oxygen and nutrients, and dispose of waste carbon dioxide.

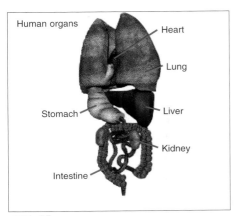

A56, 57

☐ **57** *(e)*
The heart is a four-chambered organ located in the chest cavity. One chamber is responsible for receiving blood from the whole body, except the lungs. From

here the blood is pushed into the next chamber, which pumps blood to the lungs. The blood is returned from the lungs into the next chamber, which pushes it to the next chamber, from where it is pumped around the body.

☐ **58** *(b)*
The left atrium receives oxygenated blood from the lungs via the pulmonary vein. When the atrium contracts, it pushes the blood through a valve to the left ventricle.

☐ **59** *(e)*
The valves present in the heart, sometimes called the atrio-ventricular valves, prevent blood from flowing back into the two atria when the ventricles contract, and so the blood is forced into the arteries leaving the heart.

☐ **60** *(d)*
The left ventricle receives oxygenated blood from the left atrium and pumps the blood into the aorta, the main artery of the body, which curves over the top of the heart before descending.

☐ **61** *(d)*
The right ventricle receives deoxygenated blood from the right atrium, and then pumps the blood to the lungs, through the pulmonary artery.

☐ **62** *(b)*
The right atrium receives deoxygenated blood from the body via the large vein called the vena cava. The atrium then contracts and pushes the blood through a heart valve, called the tricuspid valve, to the right ventricle.

☐ **63** *False*
When looking at a diagram of a heart, it is important to remember that it is as though you had someone lying down with their heart on view. Therefore, the right side of the diagram is actually the left side of the heart. The left ventricle of the heart has the thickest muscular walls of the heart because it has to pump blood furthest round the body.

☐ **64** *False*
The only reliable difference between arteries and veins is that arteries carry blood away from the heart whilst veins carry it towards the heart. Most arteries do carry oxygenated blood; however, the pulmonary artery carrying blood away from the heart to the lungs carries deoxygenated blood, and the pulmonary vein then carries oxygenated blood from the lungs back to the heart.

☐ **65** *(d)*
The pulmonary vein carries oxygenated blood from the lungs back to the heart before the blood is sent to other parts of the body. It is the only vein to carry oxygenated, rather than deoxygenated, blood.

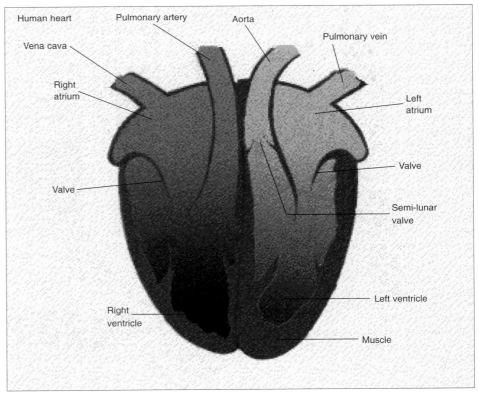

A58, 59, 60, 61, 62, 63

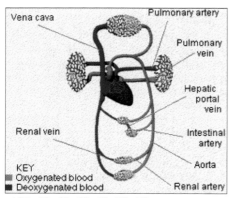

A65, 66, 67, 68, 69, 70, 71

☐ **66** *(a)*
The aorta, which is sometimes called the 'dorsal aorta', is the main artery of the body, running close to the backbone, and carrying oxygenated blood from the heart to all other arteries.

☐ **67** *(e)*
The vena cava is the major vein of the entire body. It receives blood from many smaller veins derived from almost all the body's organs, for instance, the liver and kidneys. It then returns the blood to the right atrium of the heart where the blood will be pressurised and sent to the lungs for re-oxygenation.

☐ **68** *(c)*
The pulmonary artery carries deoxygenated blood from the heart to the lungs so that it can be loaded with oxygen before being sent round the rest of the body. It is the only artery to carry deoxygenated blood.

☐ **69** *(d)*
The renal artery carries oxygenated blood from the aorta, the main artery, to the kidneys where this blood is filtered and any waste materials are removed.

☐ **70** *(a)*
The renal vein carries filtered blood from the kidneys to the vena cava, the main vein, which then returns the blood to the heart. As this blood has also had its oxygen removed by the kidney's respiring tissues, it needs to be loaded again with oxygen as it goes through the lungs.

☐ **71** *(a)*
The hepatic portal vein carries blood from the intestines to the liver. The blood carried in this vein will be rich in nutrients, as the products of digestion are absorbed into the bloodstream at the intestines. Some of these nutrients will be processed or stored in the liver.

☐ **72** *(c)*
The left ventricle of the heart pumps blood at high pressure into the aorta. These pulses of high pressure blood are passed into the other arteries. Arteries have thick elastic walls that stretch when this ripple of pressure passes along. When an artery passes near the surface of your body, its stretching can be felt as your pulse.

☐ **73** (b)
Arteries receive blood from the heart at a high pressure, and so they need thick walls to prevent them bursting. The blood in veins is under a lower pressure, and so the veins do not need thick walls.

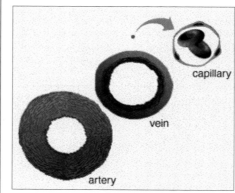

A73

☐ **74** *(a)*
The pressure in veins is so low that they need semi-lunar valves to prevent blood flowing backwards rather than forwards towards the heart. Arteries, on the other hand, receive blood directly from the heart so that the blood is under sufficient pressure to carry it to its destination without any back-flow.

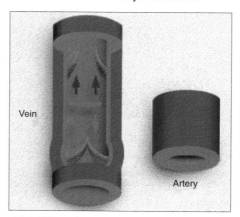

A74, 76

☐ **75** *(e)*
Arteries always take blood away from the heart to the organs, whilst veins always return blood back to the heart from the organs, where oxygen and food have been used in respiration.

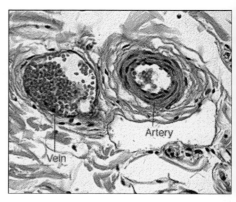

A75

☐ **76** *(c)*
Arteries have thicker walls than veins, to cope with the higher pressure of the blood when it leaves the heart, but veins need valves to stop the blood flowing backwards under low pressure. All arteries, except the pulmonary artery, carry oxygenated blood. All veins, except for the pulmonary vein, carry deoxygenated blood.

☐ **77** *(d)*
During exercise, the muscles are working harder than normal and they require more energy. Respiration provides this energy, but oxygen and glucose are vital to this process, and both are provided by the blood. Therefore, the body must adjust the amount of blood flowing to the tissues in response to how much work those tissues are doing – more work means greater blood flow.

☐ **78** *(b)*
A fatty substance called cholesterol, along with several other types of fat, seems to increase the chance that a person will develop an atheroma blockage in their arteries. If the blockage forms in the coronary artery, it may cause the heart to stop beating, and death will result. If the blockage develops in the brain, it may cause a 'stroke' and part of the brain may be disabled. Smoking may also trigger atheroma blockages to form, contributing to heart disease.

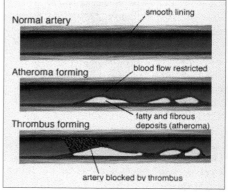

A78

☐ **79** *(b)*
Main arteries divide to form arterioles, which, in turn, divide to form capillaries whose walls are only a single cell thick. It is through these thin capillary walls that the exchange of substances between the blood and the tissues occurs. Several capillaries from the tissues join to form a venule and several venules, carrying blood away from the tissues, join to form a vein, which will take blood to the heart.

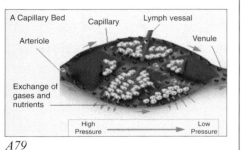
A79

☐ **80** *(d)*
The heart is divided into two halves with each half having two chambers. If we start with a red blood cell travelling from the lungs to the heart, it will go through the left half of the heart, then round the rest of the body, then back to the right side of the heart, and then back to the lungs.

Composition and function of blood

☐ **81** *(e)*
The major constituents of blood are plasma, which is the liquid that suspends the blood cells, red blood cells, which are responsible for oxygen transport, and white blood cells, which help the body fight disease in a number of ways.

☐ **82** *True*
Blood consists of a fluid, plasma, which contains many dissolved substances. Red and white blood cells float about in this fluid. Platelets are small fragments of bone marrow cells that help to form blood clots.

☐ **83** *True*
Blood plasma consists mainly of water, which has many things dissolved in it. Nutrients are carried from the digestive system to the liver and then on to the rest of the body. Carbon dioxide is carried from respiring cells to the lungs where it is released from the body. Urea is taken from the liver to the kidneys, which remove it from the blood and

make urine, which is then released from the body. Hormones are chemical messengers transported by the blood.

☐ **84** *(c)*
Red blood cells are 'biconcave' in shape, which means they are like a ring doughnut with a solid middle.

☐ **85** *(d)*
White blood cells are part of the immune system of the body, allowing us to defend ourselves against invasion by bacteria, viruses and other parasites. There are many different types of white blood cell, with some of the larger ones ingesting and digesting bacteria, while some of the smaller ones make antibody proteins to help kill disease organisms by other methods.

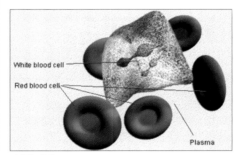
A85, 86

☐ **86** *(a)*
Red blood cells are 'biconcave' in shape. This shape gives them both a large surface area and the ability to expand and shrink in volume without undue damage.

☐ **87** *(c)*
Plasma is the liquid part of blood, containing 90% water and 10% plasma proteins, hormones and minerals.

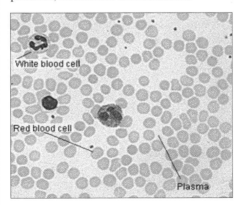
A87

☐ **88** *(b)*
Platelets are a part of blood. They are small fragments of cells that do not have a nucleus. They help blood to clot at the site of a wound.

☐ **89** *(a)*
They all are components of mammalian blood, except for chloroplasts, which are found in plant cells.

☐ **90** *(c)*
Human blood is a mixture of plasma, red and white blood cells, and platelets.

☐ **91** *(d)*
Red blood cells are filled with millions of molecules of a red protein called haemoglobin, which carries oxygen molecules.

☐ **92** *(a)*
Blood clots in areas where it is exposed to the air or in damaged tissues, such as a cut finger. The clot forms due to chemical reactions in the exposed blood, and seals each bleeding capillary quickly so stopping any harmful microbes entering the body. Fresh skin will eventually reform over the cut, but this does not happen as quickly.

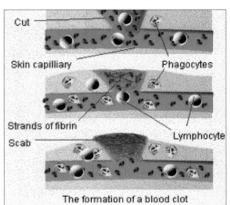
A92

☐ **93** *(c)*
If a blood vessel is cut, the platelets start off a chain of events that leads to the formation of the insoluble fibrin fibres from the soluble precursor fibrinogen. These fibres then cover the ruptured area and act like a net capturing red blood cells. When these red blood cells dry, they form a protective clot beneath which the repair of the wound takes place.

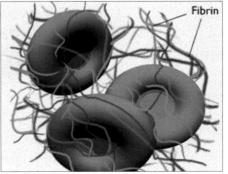
A93

94 *(d)*
White blood cells are very important in the defence of the human body against disease. They not only have the ability to ingest bacteria and produce antibodies, but also produce chemicals called antitoxins that can neutralise the toxins produced by bacteria.

Human breathing

95 *(b)*
The lungs are located in the chest cavity along with the heart.

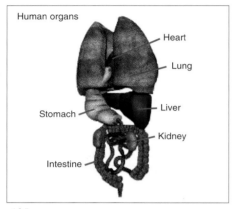

A95

96 *(b)*
Mammals possess two lungs, which are responsible for getting oxygen into the bloodstream from the surrounding air. They also get rid of carbon dioxide, produced as a waste product of respiration, by passing it from the bloodstream into the air.

97 *(d)*
The lungs are located in the chest cavity. Lungs are designed to extract oxygen efficiently only from air. For animals needing to extract oxygen in water, such as fish, gills are necessary.

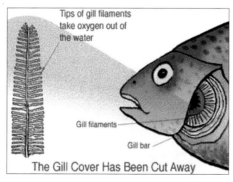

A97

98 *(e)*
The trachea, or windpipe, carries air from the nose and mouth to the bronchi, which supply the lungs. It is reinforced by rings of cartilage to keep it open at all times, even when lumps of food are swallowed down the adjacent oesophagus.

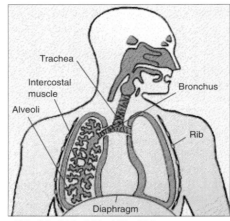

A98, 99, 100, 101, 102, 103

99 *(c)*
The trachea divides into the two bronchi tubes so that air can be carried to both lungs through many smaller bronchioles. As with the trachea, the bronchi are reinforced with rings of cartilage to keep them open at all times, even through vigorous chest movements.

100 *(a)*
Air passes from the bronchioles to the alveoli and it is from these tiny sac-like structures that oxygen is picked up, and carbon dioxide is dropped off, by the bloodstream.

101 *(e)*
The ribs help to protect the vital organs, the heart and the lungs, contained within the ribcage. They are also vital to the process of breathing, for their movement, controlled by the intercostal (rib) muscles, changes the volume within the thoracic cavity, which is the volume enclosed by the ribcage and diaphragm.

102 *(b)*
The intercostal (rib) muscles are located between the ribs and are important in making the breathing movements of the chest. When inhaling, the intercostal muscles contract, and when exhaling, these muscles relax.

103 *(a)*
The diaphragm is a sheet of muscle that is very important in breathing. It divides the abdomen from the chest.

104 *False*
During inhalation the chest cavity needs to increase in volume, so drawing air into the lungs. To do this, the external intercostal muscles contract, pulling the ribcage up and out. Meanwhile the diaphragm also contracts, which changes it from a dome shape into a flatter shape. Both of these actions cause the volume of the chest cavity to increase and air is drawn into the lungs.

105 *False*
The lungs have a very large surface area, which is in close contact with many capillaries carrying blood that has been all round the body. Oxygen diffuses from the air into the blood, whilst carbon dioxide, which is a waste product produced by respiring tissues, diffuses out into the air. Urea is another waste product but it is removed from the blood in the kidneys.

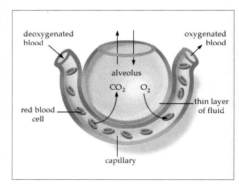

A105

106 *(e)*
The trachea carries air from the nose and mouth to the bronchi. It is lined with hair-like cilia and mucus, so that any dust particles breathed in are trapped in the mucus and carried upwards to the throat to be swallowed and digested. This upward movement is known as the 'ciliary escalator', and is stopped by tobacco smoke.

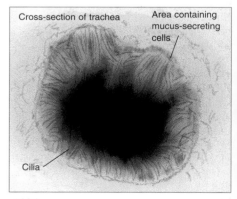

A106

107 *(b)*
The trachea splits into two bronchi so that air can be carried to both lungs at the same time and at the same pressure. The bronchi carry air from the trachea to the smaller bronchioles from which the air moves into the alveoli. Bronchitis

is an infection of the bronchi and bronchioles.

□ 108 (c)
In breathing, the contraction of the diaphragm muscles lowers the floor of the chest and causes an increase in chest volume. At the same time, some of the intercostal muscles, between the ribs, contract and lift the ribs upwards and outwards causing a further increase in chest volume.

□ 109 (a)
During human breathing, both the intercostal muscles and the diaphragm act in a co-ordinated manner that changes the volume of the chest cavity. To draw air into the lungs, the ribs are moved upwards and outwards by the intercostal muscles, while the diaphragm pulls the floor of the chest cavity downwards. This increases the volume of the chest, lowers the air pressure within the chest, and atmospheric air at a higher pressure rushes into the lungs.

□ 110 (a)
When the lungs are full, millions of elastic fibres in the alveoli are stretched, and the chest is higher than in its relaxed position. So, to breathe out, the intercostal muscles and the diaphragm must simply relax and allow the chest weight and lung elasticity to pull the chest back to resting position. During forced breathing, for example when blowing out candles, a special set of intercostal muscles act in an opposite manner to the normal direction, and expel air very rapidly when they contract.

□ 111 (d)
When inhaling, the diaphragm and the intercostal muscles contract, moving the ribcage upwards and outwards. This increases the volume of the chest cavity and lungs, decreasing the pressure to less than atmospheric so that air enters the lungs from outside.

□ 112 (a)
When breathing out, the diaphragm and the intercostal muscles relax, and the ribcage moves inwards and downwards due to gravity, and to the elasticity of the lungs. This decreases the volume of the chest cavity, decreases the volume of air in the lungs, and increases the internal pressure to more than atmospheric so air leaves the bronchi and is exhaled.

□ 113 (c)
As the blood flows past the tissues, it provides them with oxygen and glucose whilst picking up carbon dioxide by diffusion. The tissues need oxygen and glucose for respiration whilst carbon dioxide is the waste product of this process. From here, the blood is taken to the lungs, where the carbon dioxide is excreted into the atmosphere and more oxygen picked up.

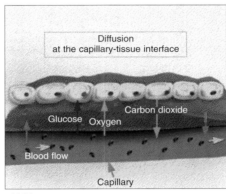

A113

□ 114 (a)
Diffusion of carbon dioxide out of the blood and into the lungs is helped by the very thin, moist walls of the microscopic alveoli. In each lung there are about 150 million alveoli, which provide an enormous surface area through which gas exchange can occur. Oxygen uptake also takes place across the alveoli.

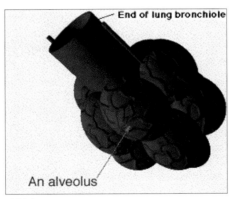

A114

□ 115 (c)
Oxygen moves into the blood and carbon dioxide moves out of the blood by diffusion, each type of molecule moving towards the region of its lowest concentration.

□ 116 (c)
Mucus-secreting cells help to trap particles entering the lungs and so keep the lungs clean. The other four features

are all directly related to increasing the uptake of oxygen.

□ 117 (d)
The great majority of the oxygen carried by the blood is transported, attached to a very special protein called haemoglobin. There are millions of molecules of this protein within each red blood cell, and each molecule of haemoglobin can temporarily hold four molecules (eight atoms) of oxygen as it hurtles around the blood system. When the haemoglobin arrives at a location where the concentration of oxygen is low, such as respiring tissues, it releases some of its oxygen into solution in the plasma and this can then be used by the respiring cells.

□ 118 (d)
Some carbon dioxide is carried within the red blood cells but a large proportion is carried in solution in the plasma.

□ 119 (a)
Feeling the pulse checks that the heart is beating, not that breathing is still functional. It is quite possible for the heart to continue to pump after breathing has stopped, though eventually the heart will run out of oxygen and will die. Any of the other four methods canbe used to check that breathing is still happening.

□ 120 (c)
Differences occur between inhaled and exhaled air because the body needs to take oxygen from the air for the process of respiration.

□ 121 (d)
Differences occur between inhaled and exhaled air because the waste products of respiration, carbon dioxide and water, are excreted in the exhaled air.

□ 122 (c)
Nitrogen and the noble gases are not needed or produced by respiration, so their percentages in inhaled and exhaled air do not change.

Gas	Inhaled air (%)	Exhaled air (%)
Nitrogen	78	78
Oxygen	21	16
Noble gases	0.97	1
Carbon dioxide	0.03	4
Water vapour	0	1

A120, 121, 122

Human respiration

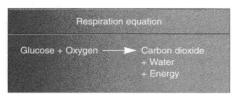

Respiration equation

Glucose + Oxygen → Carbon dioxide
+ Water
+ Energy

A123, 124, 126, 127, 130, 131, 132

☐ **123** *(d)*
In aerobic respiration, oxygen is needed to oxidise the food of the organism and energy is released during this reaction.

☐ **124** *(d)*
Aerobic respiration requires oxygen to oxidise the food of the organism. This food is often glucose from photosynthesis in green plants.

☐ **125** *(d)*
Respiration is the process by which living organisms produce the energy they need to survive. Most organisms use oxygen when they respire. A form of respiration called anaerobic uses no oxygen but yields far less energy and so is not the preferred form in most organisms. Humans can respire anaerobically for short periods, for example, in a sprint race.

☐ **126** *(b)*
In aerobic respiration, food (usually glucose) is oxidised in the presence of oxygen. The carbon atoms in foods, which are attached to other carbons, hydrogens, and some oxygens, now have even more oxygen atoms attached until they become molecules of carbon dioxide, that is one carbon and two oxygen atoms. This gas is then expelled as waste through the lungs in mammals.

☐ **127** *(a)*
Respiration uses oxygen and food, combined in a type of reaction called oxidation, to yield useful energy plus water and carbon dioxide. The water produced is useful to all cells. The carbon dioxide may be useful in photosynthesis within plant cells, but energy is the only useful product listed here.

☐ **128** *(b)*
Oxygen is transported around the body attached to the carrier protein haemoglobin, which is found in the red blood cells. The majority of carbon dioxide is carried in the blood plasma as hydrogen carbonate ions, though some is also carried in the red blood cells.

☐ **129** *(d)*
Muscle cells need energy from respiration to create movements. Respiration uses up oxygen and produces carbon dioxide, so the cytoplasm of a working muscle cell contains a low concentration of oxygen and a high concentration of carbon dioxide. Blood in capillaries has a high oxygen concentration and low carbon dioxide concentration. Therefore, oxygen diffuses into, and carbon dioxide out of the muscle cells down each diffusion gradient.

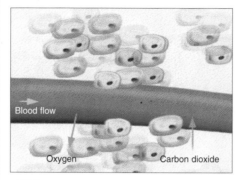

Blood flow

Oxygen   Carbon dioxide

A129

☐ **130** *(e)*
Aerobic respiration is the process by which cells release energy from foods using oxygen. Respiration without oxygen is termed anaerobic and does not release as much usable energy as aerobic respiration.

☐ **131** *(b)*
Glucose is the usual fuel for respiration, though some cells are able to respire some other substances, such as fatty acids from digested lipids.

☐ **132** *(a)*
All mammals are endothermic to some extent, which means that they use some of the energy from respiration to keep their internal body temperature constant within reasonable changes in environmental temperature. Ectothermic organisms, such as lizards or plants, have body temperatures that merely follow the temperature of the environment, though many use behaviour, such as sunbathing, to try to keep as warm and stable as possible.

☐ **133** *(e)*
Respiration, sometimes called cell respiration, is the chemical process by which energy is transferred from food substances into a form usable by the cell. It is the central process of metabolism and must work harder to

supply the cell with energy when the cell is doing more work, as in an active, contracting muscle cell. Some people use the word 'respiration' to mean 'breathing' but this is best avoided. The words 'breathing' or 'ventilation' can be used interchangeably.

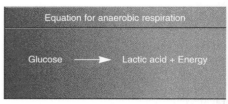

Equation for anaerobic respiration

Glucose → Lactic acid + Energy

A134, 135, 141

☐ **134** *(b)*
Muscles may sometimes have to respire without sufficient oxygen, such as during strenuous exercise. Anaerobic respiration does not produce as much energy as aerobic respiration.

☐ **135** *(e)*
Anaerobic respiration produces a waste product called lactic acid. The shortfall in oxygen is made up as soon as possible, by increased breathing and heart rates, and oxygen is then used to break down the lactic acid. Until all the acid has gone, the body is said to be in 'oxygen debt'.

☐ **136** *(c)*
The recovery period is the period of time it takes for a pulse to recover to its normal rate. From this you can quickly check the level of fitness of an individual.

☐ **137** *(a)*
One simple measure of fitness, called the recovery time, is the time it takes for a pulse to recover to its resting rate. From this you can assess that Phil is the fittest, Trevor next, and Angus the least fit. Other factors such as physical health at the time of testing can obviously have a significant effect, so the tests should not be done on someone who is ill.

☐ **138** *(d)*
The process of fermentation is used in both the brewing and baking industries. In baking, the carbon dioxide causes bread to rise and the alcohol is removed by the heat in the ovens.

☐ **139** *(a)*
As with the anaerobic respiration that occurs in humans, fermentation does not produce as much energy per glucose molecule as aerobic respiration.

☐ **140** *(c)*
All the processes listed, except diffusion, require energy produced by respiration. Diffusion is a passive process, resulting in a general movement of molecules to the area of their lowest concentration, and it does not need respiration energy.

☐ **141** *(d)*
During anaerobic respiration, the incomplete breakdown of glucose produces lactic acid. As this breakdown is incomplete much less energy is produced than during aerobic respiration. The lactic acid that builds up is toxic, so must eventually be broken down.

☐ **142** *(c)*
The lactic acid built up during anaerobic respiration is broken down to carbon dioxide and water. The oxygen required to do this is known as the 'oxygen debt'.

Human nervous system

☐ **143** *True*
The body has senses so that it can respond to its surroundings. These five senses are hearing, sight, sense, taste and touch.

☐ **144** *False*
The nervous system as a whole consists of the central nervous system and all the peripheral nerves, which connect it to the sense and effector, or response, organs. The central nervous system (CNS) consists of two parts, the brain and the spinal cord. The job of the CNS is to co-ordinate senses relayed to it from the sense organs via the peripheral nerves, and to initiate reactions to those senses by the muscles and organs of the body.

☐ **145** *False*
The central nervous system (CNS) only consists of the brain and the spinal cord. The eye is one of the sense organs, which send information to the CNS. The eye sends information about the light that enters it.

☐ **146** *(d)*
Through the five senses we can understand what is going on in the world around us. Happiness and sadness are examples of emotion, not senses.

☐ **147** *(b)*
Indigestion is a pain in the stomach. It does not help us to understand what is going on in the world around us.

☐ **148** *(a)*
The dermis layer of the skin contains a variety of sensory receptors. There are different receptors to detect touch, pressure, pain and temperature (but not humidity). It is through these receptors that many of our actions are determined.

☐ **149** *(a)*
Your skin is not sensitive specifically to acids, though strong acids may cause pain by damaging tissue.

☐ **150** *(a)*
There is not a sensory receptor that detects light, although there is a pigment in the skin that reacts to light.

☐ **151** *(a)*
The brain is located in the head and is protected by the bony skull.

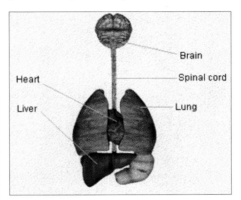

A151, 152

☐ **152** *(d)*
The spinal cord and the brain make up the central nervous system. The spinal cord carries many messages from the nerves all over the body to the brain where the messages are co-ordinated and sent to the effectors.

☐ **153** *(d)*
The brain is the main nervous control centre for the body, all conscious, and most unconscious, decisions about your behaviour are made here.

☐ **154** *(e)*
Your nervous system is made up of your sense organs, nerves, spinal cord and brain. The brain and spinal cord together are termed the central nervous system (or CNS), while the remaining parts are known as the peripheral nervous system.

☐ **155** *(d)*
The skull is not part of the nervous system but is a series of fused bones. It protects the brain inside from damaging shocks and infections.

☐ **156** *(a)*
The backbone is a series of small bones, joined together by ligaments, that enclose and protect your delicate spinal cord nerves against physical damage and infection.

☐ **157** *(a)*
There are receptors in your ears that are highly sensitive to vibration, and this is the way in which you sense sounds.

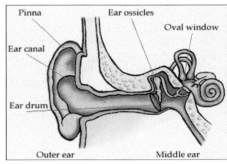

A157

☐ **158** *(b)*
Nerve impulses are not to be confused with hormones. Both will help to co-ordinate the body but hormones are slower, longer lasting and mostly carried in the blood.

☐ **159** *False*
A reflex action is an immediate response to a stimulus. An example is to pull your hand away from a hot object. It may involve the brain, but the large majority of reflexes, including this example, are co-ordinated through the spinal cord. It is not a learned reaction, it is an automatic reaction.

☐ **160** *(e)*
A reflex action is a response of the body that is unconscious, automatic and involuntary. To gain speed and simplicity, these reactions involve the central nervous system as little as possible. Some reflexes of the arms and legs, for example, involve only two nerve cells. Many reflexes occur as a response to stimulus that may cause damage to the body.

☐ **161** *(a)*
The sensory receptors are stimulated by the hot object, and this causes a nerve impulse to be sent along the sensory nerve towards the spinal cord. The impulse is passed either straight to a motor nerve cell, or sometimes via a relay nerve cell, and then on to the effector. In this case, the impulse causes the biceps muscle (the effector) to contract, which pulls the hand away.

☐ **162** *(c)*
The sensory neurone carries the impulse towards the spinal cord from the receptor. It is sometimes called the afferent cell. The cell body of the nerve sits outside the nerve cord, in a location called the dorsal root ganglion ('ganglion' means 'swelling'). At the same time, the other end of the sensory neurone synapses with a relay neurone in the spinal cord.

☐ **163** *(e)*
At the synapse, or junction, between two adjacent nerve cells, the electrical signal carried by the nerve cell cannot cross the gap between the cells, and has to be converted into a chemical signal called a neurotransmitter. The particular synapse shown in the diagram is between a relay neurone and a motor neurone.

☐ **164** *(c)*
The motor neurone takes an instruction from the central nervous system (in this case the spinal cord) to a muscle (the biceps) that will contract in response to the instruction. The body of the motor neurone is located inside the spinal cord. Motor neurones are different from sensory neurones and can suffer a dreadful disease, called motor neurone disease, which is when motor functions are gradually lost until death occurs.

☐ **165** *(c)*
The effector structure, the biceps muscle in this case, carries out the instructions of the central nervous system in response to the painful stimulus. Muscles contract in response to signals arriving from nerves, and when the biceps muscle contracts, it raises the lower arm towards the upper arm so pulling the hand away from harm. The triceps muscle is antagonistic to the biceps, and straightens the arm again when the danger is avoided.

☐ **166** *(d)*
Motor neurones carry nervous messages, or impulses, from the brain and spinal cord to the muscles around the body. They are very long and thin so that they can carry the message quickly. They are also surrounded by a fatty material that ensures the message is passed very quickly along the neurone itself.

☐ **167** *(c)*
Motor neurones stimulate effectors to respond. Often, as in this case, the effector in a reflex is a muscle, but it might also be a gland secreting hormones in some types of reflex.

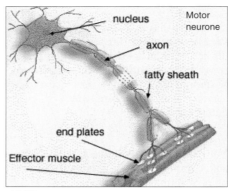
A167

☐ **168** *(d)*
If the nervous system is to work, it is vital that the nerves can pass messages to each other, but electrical signals, or impulses, cannot travel across the synapse between two nerve cells. Instead, the signal is transferred into chemical form, and a pulse of a special chemical, called neurotransmitter, crosses the synaptic gap and restarts the electrical impulse when it reaches the far side.

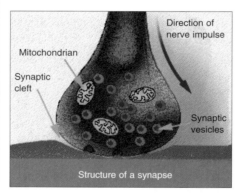
A168

Human eye

☐ **169** *(d)*
The cornea is the front part of the sclera and is transparent. It allows light to enter the eye and pass through the pupil.

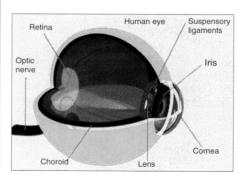
A169, 170, 171, 172, 173

☐ **170** *(c)*
The lens' shape is controlled by the ciliary muscle, which surrounds the lens and is connected to the lens by the suspensory ligaments.

☐ **171** *(a)*
The iris controls the amount of light that enters the eye.

☐ **172** *(b)*
On the retina are light sensitive cells called rods and cones, but the retina is not equally sensitive across its entire area. There is an area in the centre called the 'fovea' where there is a higher density of light-sensitive cells, especially the cells sensitive to colour.

☐ **173** *(d)*
The nervous messages from the light sensitive cells on the retina are sent from the eye to the brain through millions of nerve cells that make up the optic nerve.

☐ **174** *(a)*
Light rays bend whenever they pass from a substance of one optical density, the 'refractive index', into a substance of a different optical density. When light rays pass from the air into the cornea they bend, and when they pass from the cornea into the liquid behind the cornea they bend again. This bending of the light is considerable because the cornea has such a curved surface.

☐ **175** *(b)*
The lens controls the fine focusing of the light onto the retina, changing shape according to the distance to the light source.

☐ **176** *(b)*
The curved surface of the cornea bends the light entering the eye so as to form a fuzzy image on the retina.

☐ **177** *(c)*
The lens changes shape according to how near the light source is. It is thicker when the source is closer, because diverging light rays from the source have to be bent more to be focused on the retina, whilst it is thinner when the source is further away.

☐ **178** *(e)*
Once an image falls on the retina, the light-sensitive cells are stimulated and send a message via the optic nerve to the brain, where the message will be interpreted and perceived. The fovea is the central area on the retina, where there is the highest density of

light-sensitive cells, and vision is most acute at this point. Whilst reading this sentence, the light from the words is focussed on the fovea. You can see the rest of the page, but you cannot identify the words. Light from these words is falling on the rest of the retina.

□ **179** *(d)*
The cornea and lens focus light onto the retina, where the light sensitive cells are stimulated to send a message through the optic nerve to the brain. By movements of your head and eyes, you try to keep the interesting part of an image, for instance, a person in a landscape, focussed on the central part of your retina, the fovea.

□ **180** *(e)*
The light that enters the eye stimulates the light-sensitive cells on the retina, and these cells then send a message to the brain, where the nervous signals are interpreted and understood.

□ **181** *(b)*
If the light is bright, certain muscles in the iris contract causing the size of the pupil to be reduced so that less light enters the eye. This avoids damage to the highly sensitive tissues in the retina of the eye. In dim light a different set of muscles in the iris contract, which makes the pupil bigger and allows more light onto the retina to form a brighter image.

□ **182** *(b)*
The iris consists of two sets of muscles, one arranged in rings around the pupil and the other arranged like the spokes of a wheel radiating out from the centre of the pupil. By co-ordinating the contractions of these two muscle groups, the iris can control the width of the pupil to let in less light in bright conditions and more light in dim conditions.

□ **183** *(a)*
In bright light, the circular muscles of the iris contract whilst the radial muscles relax. This causes the iris to enlarge leading to a decrease in size of the pupil. This is important because it means not too much light will enter the eye and damage the retina.

□ **184** *(a)*
In dim light, the radial muscles of the iris contract whilst the circular muscles relax, and this causes an enlargement in the size of the pupil. This is important because it means a brighter image can be formed on the retina.

□ **185** *(d)*
In bright light, the circular muscles of the iris contract whilst the radial muscles relax, this causes the iris to enlarge so the pupil gets smaller.

□ **186** *(d)*
The response of the iris to light intensity is an automatic reflex and does not require conscious thought.

□ **187** *(b)*
Rods and cones are types of light-sensitive cells and are located in the retina of the eye. Rods are sensitive only to different intensities of light, and so are able to form a black and white image to send to the brain. They are most important for seeing at night or when there is not very much light.

□ **188** *(a)*
Cones enable us to distinguish different wavelengths, or colours, of light. There are three different types, which are each sensitive to either red, blue or green, rather like the sensors in a colour video camcorder. Cones are comparatively rare in the animal kingdom – most vertebrates have only rods and see only in black and white.

□ **189** *(a)*
The lens in your eye has to be able to change shape, or accommodate, so that you can focus on objects of varying distances away from you. Your lens will be long and thin when you are looking at something far away whilst it will be short and fat when you are looking at something that is close to you.

□ **190** *(e)*
The suspensory ligaments connect the ring of ciliary muscle to the lens.

Human hormones

□ **191** *(a)*
Co-ordination can be either by the nervous or endocrine system. The endocrine system is made up of endocrine, or ductless, glands that release hormones into the bloodstream. These hormones will affect the activity of a target organ or organs.

□ **192** *False*
Hormones are chemicals produced by special glands in the body. Their release may be triggered by nervous impulses but they are themselves released into the bloodstream, which carries them to their target organs. For example, the pancreas produces a hormone, called insulin, that can be released into the blood. When the insulin reaches the liver, it causes the liver to convert glucose into glycogen, so helping to control blood sugar levels.

□ **193** *(d)*
The endocrine system is made up of endocrine glands that release chemicals, called hormones, into the bloodstream. These hormones affect the activity of certain target organs.

□ **194** *(c)*
Hormonal messages are generally slower-acting, longer-lasting and less specific in their targets than nerve impulses. This suits them to controlling aspects of the organism, such as growth, changes in metabolic rate, and mood changes, whereas the nervous system is best suited to rapid reactions to rapidly changing events.

□ **195** *(e)*
Testosterone is produced by the testes in the male. Smaller concentrations of this hormone are also present in women's bodies.

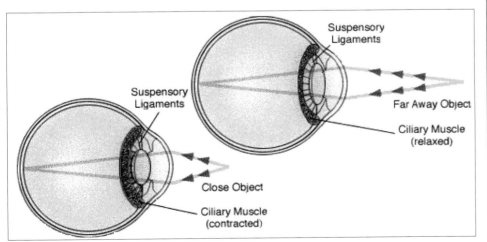

Suspensory Ligaments

Suspensory Ligaments

Far Away Object

Ciliary Muscle (relaxed)

Close Object

Ciliary Muscle (contracted)

A174, 175, 176, 177, 189

☐ **196** *(d)*
The hormone testosterone is responsible for the development of the following physical characteristics: enlargement of the sex organs, muscle enlargement, development of body hair, and the voice 'breaking' or deepening.

☐ **197** *(a)*
Testosterone causes an increase in body hair, especially on the 'secondary sexual sites', such as chest and pubic regions, and not a decrease in body hair. It also causes a lowering of the voice, an increase of the musculature, an increase of the sex drive, and an enlargement of the penis and testicles at puberty.

☐ **198** *(b)*
The ovary produces oestrogen, which causes the growth of a new uterus lining in days 0 - 14 of the menstrual cycle. It also produces progesterone after day 14 of the cycle, which causes the uterus to prepare itself to receive a fertilised ovum. If fertilisation happens, the placenta eventually takes over progesterone production, stopping menstruation during pregnancy. If fertilisation does not occur, then progesterone production slows and menstruation occurs.

☐ **199** *(d)*
The ovary produces oestrogen, which triggers the preparation of a thicker uterus lining during the first few days of the menstrual cycle. This thick lining is well supplied with capillaries and is essential if the fertilised egg is to implant and begin to grow in the uterus.

☐ **200** *(b)*
The oral contraceptive pill contains manufactured chemicals similar to progesterone and oestrogen. The combination of these two hormones inhibits ovulation – the release of the ovum in the middle of the menstrual cycle.

☐ **201** *(e)*
The oral contraceptive pill contains chemicals similar to the human hormones, progesterone and oestrogen. These two hormones, in the correct concentrations, inhibit hormones that are responsible for ovulation. If no egg is released, then fertilisation and pregnancy cannot occur.

☐ **202** *(d)*
Testosterone, produced in the testes, is responsible for stimulating sperm production. If a man is infertile because

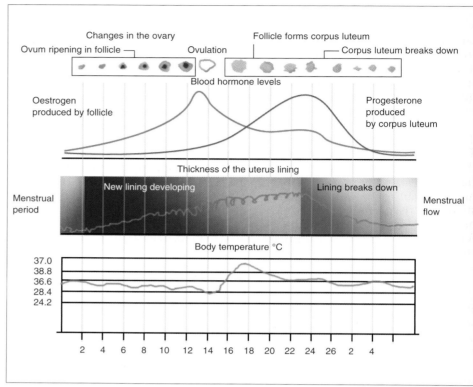

A199, 204

he is not making sperm, testosterone could help.

☐ **203** *(d)*
Female sex hormones, such as progesterone and oestrogen, are often used in the hormone replacement therapy (HRT) used by some women going through menopause. Menopause stops production of these two hormones, and this may have uncomfortable effects on the woman's body; artificial hormones may decrease the discomfort and provide stronger bones.

☐ **204** *(c)*
As the menstrual cycle 'begins', the lining of the uterus breaks down in readiness to re-build the wall of the uterus for the arrival of a fertilised egg.

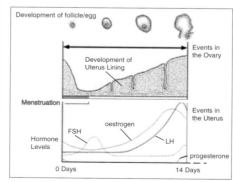

A205, 206, 208, 209,

☐ **205** *(c)*
The follicle stimulating hormone (FSH) causes the maturing of an egg in one of the ovaries, and stimulates the ovaries to produce oestrogens. FSH is also used as a fertility drug for women whose own levels of FSH are too low to stimulate the maturing of eggs.

☐ **206** *(b)*
The follicle stimulating hormone (FSH) is secreted by the pituitary gland. It stimulates the ovaries to produce oestrogens, and causes the maturing of an egg in one of them.

☐ **207** *(a)*
The pituitary gland is located on the floor of the brain. It is sometimes known as a 'master' gland as it produces many hormones that trigger or affect others, so having a very important impact on the body's metabolism.

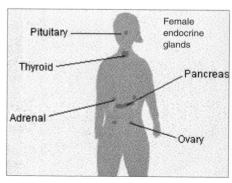

A207, 211

208 (c)
The oestrogens produced by the ovaries inhibit further production of FSH and stimulate the pituitary gland to produce luteinizing hormone (LH). LH stimulates the release of the egg, or ovulation, on about day 14 of the menstrual cycle.

209 (c)
There are several hormones involved in the menstrual cycle of a woman. Initially FSH stimulates an egg to mature in one of the ovaries and stimulates the ovaries to produce oestrogens. The oestrogens inhibit further production of FSH and stimulate the pituitary gland to produce LH.

210 (a)
FSH (follicle stimulating hormone) is secreted by the pituitary gland causing an egg to mature in one of the ovaries. It is not surprising, therefore, that FSH is used as a fertility drug for women whose own levels of FSH are too low to stimulate the maturing of eggs.

211 (c)
The adrenal glands are found on top of the kidneys in men and women.

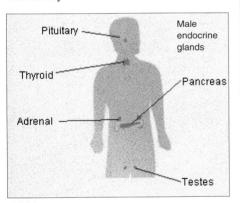

A211

212 (a)
The adrenal gland produces adrenalin, a hormone that prepares the body for a suitable response in emergency situations. Adrenalin causes the heart to beat faster, causing more blood to flow to the vital organs and muscles. It also increases breathing rate and depth, and releases glucose from glycogen reserves in muscles and liver.

213 (a)
Adrenalin is released by the adrenal gland in response to a stressful situation in all humans. Suitable responses prepare an animal's body for 'flight or fight', whichever is more appropriate in the circumstances.

214 (b)
Adrenalin prepares the muscles, starts to mobilise glucose for rapid respiration, and makes preparations for greater oxygen demand. Lowering the body temperature under these circumstances would not increase the chances of escape; probably the opposite would happen.

215 (d)
Homeostasis is the maintenance of a constant internal environment, and one of the many things to be kept constant is the blood glucose level. If the level has risen, the pancreas releases insulin that converts glucose to glycogen, which can then be stored in the liver.

216 (a)
If there is any change from the normal blood glucose level, it is detected by special cells in the pancreas. If the level has risen, the pancreas releases insulin that converts glucose to glycogen.

217 (b)
Levels of glucose too high or too low can be life-threatening to humans. If there is any change from the normal level, it is detected by special cells in the pancreas. If the level drops too low, the pancreas secretes the hormone glucagon that converts the stored glycogen to glucose, which then enters the bloodstream

218 (e)
If there is any deviation in the concentration of blood glucose from the normal level, it is detected by special cells in the pancreas. These cells then prompt the release of either insulin or glucagon, hormones that will restore the concentration of glucose to the proper level by controlling the balance of glucose in the blood.

219 (a)
If the level of blood glucose rises, the pancreas releases the hormone insulin, which converts soluble glucose to a less soluble polymer glycogen, which can then be stored in the liver.

220 (d)
If the level of blood glucose drops below the correct level through exercise or lack of food, the pancreas secretes glucagon, which converts the stored chains of glycogen into soluble glucose.

Importance of homeostasis

221 *True*
It is important to keep conditions inside the body, such as temperature and sugar levels, constant. This is because for each of our cells to work efficiently, the enzymes that do the work need to be in their optimal conditions. This means that the body temperature must be constant, and that the blood, which supplies the cells with their needs, must have the right amounts of sugar and water, and be at the right pH.

222 *True*
Sweating can occur when someone is nervous but its main role in the body is to help keep the internal temperature constant. If the core body temperature (the temperature right inside the body) gets too high, the sweat glands will release sweat onto the skin surface via tiny pores. The sweat will then evaporate using heat from the body, so cooling the body back down to its normal body temperature.

223 (b)
It is important that the conditions within the body remain constant, so that enzymes function as efficiently as possible. The process of keeping the body in a more or less constant internal environment is called homeostasis. Water and sugar concentrations in the blood are regulated within tight limits, in spite of water losses due to breathing and sugar fluctuations due to feeding. Our body temperature is also regulated but at 37°C, not 47°C.

224 (e)
The placenta is connected to the mother's womb. In the placenta, food and oxygen leave the mother's blood and pass into the blood of the fetus.

225 (a)
All these substances need to be controlled in the body, but only water and carbon dioxide are removed by the lungs. However, water is not kept at a low level and is controlled by the kidney.

☐ **226** *(b)*
As the blood flows past the tissues, it provides them with oxygen and glucose whilst picking up carbon dioxide. The tissues need oxygen and glucose for respiration whilst carbon dioxide is the waste product of this process, and is taken from the tissues into the blood by diffusion. This blood is then taken to the lungs, where the carbon dioxide is excreted and more oxygen is picked up.

☐ **227** *(b)*
Carbon dioxide is carried as hydrogen carbonate ions in the blood plasma and attached to haemoglobin. If the level of carbon dioxide in the blood rises, it means the level of oxygen has fallen. The rise in carbon dioxide concentration causes a lowering of blood pH, which is detected in the brain. The part of the brain called the medulla then causes an increase in breathing rate, which returns carbon dioxide and oxygen levels to normal.

☐ **228** *(d)*
Oxygen is picked up by the blood from the alveoli, after dissolving in the moisture inside the lungs and then diffusing through the thin wall of the lung alveoli. Carbon dioxide moves in the opposite direction. The dissolved oxygen then moves into the haemoglobin of the red blood cells, and carbon dioxide moves out of the red blood cells and plasma and into the lung air space. This happens by diffusion – each molecule moving down its diffusion gradient towards the region of lowest concentration.

☐ **229** *(e)*
The two kidneys are responsible for removing the waste products from our blood, and for regulating the amounts of salts and water in our bloodstream. These waste products pass out of the body as urine, which is formed in the kidney and stored temporarily in the bladder.

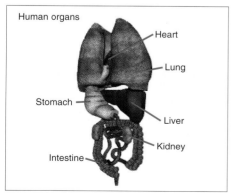
A229, 230, 231

☐ **230** *(b)*
The two kidneys regulate the salt and water content of our bodies and remove any waste products from our blood. These waste products pass out of the body as urine, which is a mixture formed from urea, excess body water, and various mineral salts. The colour of urine does not come from any of these but from various plant and animal pigments that find their way into your urine.

☐ **231** *(b)*
The two kidneys are responsible for removing the waste products from our blood. They do this by a very fine filtering of the blood, so that all unwanted substances flow out of the blood into the kidney tubules. This is followed by a reabsorption of those substances the body needs.

☐ **232** *(e)*
Water is a liquid in which all of the substances that have to be transported around the body must be dissolved. Also it provides a medium for all the chemical reactions of cells to take place; it takes part in the reactions; it helps to remove waste products in urine; it aids temperature control when sweating.

☐ **233** *(d)*
All our food and drink contains water. Even foods we consider as being very dry, such as cereals, contain significant amounts of water, while most of our drinks are well over 90% water, so most water enters our body by ingestion. However, some water is also released when foods, even totally 'dry' ones, are respired because water is liberated along with carbon dioxide. This is called 'metabolic water'.

☐ **234** *(e)*
Water, a vital constituent of our bodies, is lost in urine, sweat, faeces and exhaled air. All the water that is lost must be replaced, otherwise vital chemical reactions in the body will be unable to take place. During exercise we sweat more, so we have to take more water in to keep the balance right.

☐ **235** *(e)*
Humans are endothermic, which means they can keep their internal body temperature stable at 37°C no matter what the external conditions (within reason). The body uses a lot of respiration energy, from oxygen and food (generally glucose), in order to be able to do this.

☐ **236** *(b)*
Water, a vital constituent of our bodies, is lost in the excretion of urine and faeces, in perspiration as sweat, and in exhaled air when we breathe out. In hot weather, when we sweat more, we need to take in more water to keep the water balance correct.

☐ **237** *(d)*
The sensors that control responses, such as sweating, are located deep within the body (the most important being within the brain itself), so that they respond to changes in core body temperature and not to changes in environmental temperature. In your skin, temperature sensors make you aware of outside changes but these do not have a large effect on your body's responses.

☐ **238** *(d)*
Water is lost in urine, sweat, faeces and exhaled air, and any water lost must be replaced otherwise death may result. An increase in air temperature would increase the water lost through sweating; suntan lotion would have no effect on losses; cool watery drinks would increase urination and perhaps sweating. The salt in the meal, however, would quickly reduce the water lost from the kidney and urination would slow down for several hours.

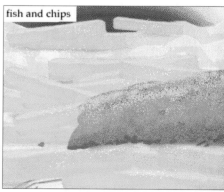
A238

☐ **239** *(c)*
Sweat is produced by the sweat glands, located below the surface of the skin, to cool the body down. The sweat reaches the surface of the skin through pores, and when it evaporates to the surface it takes some of the body heat, so cooling the body.

☐ **240** *(e)*
When sweat evaporates from the surface of the skin, it uses some of the body's own heat to cause the evaporation, and takes this heat away from the surface of the skin in water vapour, so cooling the body's outer layers.

☐ **241** (*c*)
Sweat, more politely called perspiration, is secreted from the surface of the skin and is allowed to evaporate into the atmosphere. This evaporation uses some of the body's own heat and so the surface temperature and the core body temperature fall. Also, blood flowing through the cooler skin will return to the body core and help to cool it.

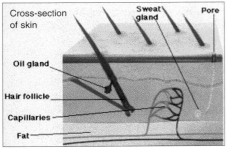
A241, 242, 243

☐ **242** (*d*)
If the internal body temperature rises above its normal temperature, the brain detects this and controls the body's responses to cool itself down. One response is for the sweat glands to produce sweat, which is then secreted onto the skin via pores.

☐ **243** (*d*)
When water evaporates from a warm surface, it takes some of the heat of that surface away with it in the vapour. Your body uses this property to lower its core temperature when overheating. This is not particularly effective in very humid atmospheric conditions when sweat will not evaporate from your skin into the saturated air.

☐ **244** (*a*)
If the internal temperature of a mammal rises, the hair on its skin lies flat, allowing cooler air to flow closer to the surface of the skin. This accelerates the evaporation of sweat, at least in those mammals that sweat. If the body temperature drops, the hair stands erect, producing an extra insulatory layer of air pockets for the mammal.

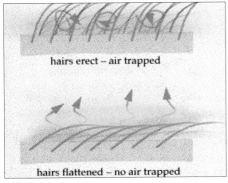
A244

☐ **245** (*b*)
If your core temperature falls below about 37°C, then your brain brings in a series of responses to prevent damage or even death occurring. One of these is shivering, a series of rapid, involuntary contractions that generate heat through muscle respiration. Humans are not the only organisms to perform shivering; many moth species use this trick at the beginning of the evening to warm up their muscles for flight.

☐ **246** (*a*)
Shivering is best defined as rapid involuntary muscle contractions in response to a drop in the core body temperature. These temperature changes are detected by sensors deep within the body and relayed to the brain where the appropriate action to warm the body is decided.

☐ **247** (*b*)
If the brain detects a decrease in the temperature of the body fluids in the body core, it will put into effect several responses to try to increase the body temperature. One of these is shivering, where rapid muscular contractions are performed to try to generate heat that will warm the body. It never seems very effective in humans.

☐ **248** (*e*)
Behavioural responses to low temperatures include changing the clothes you wear, changing location or sunbathing, moving around actively, and changing your posture, so that you lose more or less heat from your body surface. Under-arm deodorants do not change your temperature, they simply alter your smell.

☐ **249** (*e*)
Any rise in temperature is detected by the brain, which causes changes to bring the temperature back to normal, a process known as 'negative feedback'. Vasodilation is a response to the core body temperature being too high. It is when the vessels in the skin widen or 'dilate', allowing more blood to flow through them. Heat is lost from the blood directly to the environment by convection, conduction and radiation, so if more blood flows close to the surface more heat will be lost

☐ **250** (*c*)
Vasoconstriction is a response to the body temperature being too low. It is when the tiny blood vessels in the skin narrow, allowing less blood to flow through them.

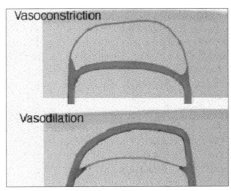
A249, 250

Excretion in the kidneys

☐ **251** (*d*)
The kidneys are responsible for removing and excreting most waste products from the blood, but the lungs also have a specialised role in removing and excreting carbon dioxide, a waste product of respiration, from the blood.

☐ **252** (*c*)
The kidney helps to maintain the correct balance of substances in the blood. It starts by filtering the blood and then taking back any substances the body will need. Any unwanted substances are excreted.

☐ **253** (*c*)
Urine is produced by the kidneys then passed to the bladder where it is stored until the person is ready to excrete it by urination. It is necessary to excrete urine as it contains the poisonous waste product, urea, as well as waste salts and some water. Although the water may be needed by the body, some has to be lost because the other waste products can only be excreted in solution.

☐ **254** (*d*)
Urea is a nitrogen-containing waste produced when proteins need to be converted for respiration, and is often excreted in the urine. Waste salts, such as sodium chloride, will be excreted whenever the salt intake is too high, and the water content of the urine will vary widely, depending on whether or not our bodies are dehydrated. The colour of urine is not produced by the urea, which is colourless, but by tiny amounts of other wastes excreted by the kidneys.

☐ **255** *(c)*
The kidneys are responsible for removing waste products from the blood and for maintaining the correct amount of water in the body, called the water balance of the body. The amount of water in the blood is monitored by the body as part of a homeostatic system. If the blood is too dilute, the kidneys will ensure more water is excreted, and if the blood is too concentrated, the kidneys will excrete less water and keep more within the body.

☐ **256** *(b)*
Patients may have to wait a long time to get a kidney that is compatible with their body cells. A dialysis machine will keep them alive until a transplant is possible. The other answers are all advantages of having the transplant.

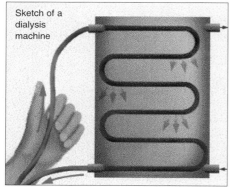

A256

☐ **257** *(c)*
Urea can be poisonous at high levels, so it is transported from the liver to the kidneys where it is filtered out of the blood to be excreted in dilute solution.

☐ **258** *(a)*
The amino acids not needed for producing proteins are processed in the liver. The amino group of each amino acid is removed by enzymes during this process, and then modified to form ammonia, but this is very poisonous and so is converted to urea almost immediately.

☐ **259** *(d)*
Surplus amino acids, not needed for producing proteins, are converted to glycogen and other necessary substances in the liver. Nitrogen and hydrogen atoms are removed from the amino acid during this process and are combined to form urea.

☐ **260** *(a)*
The glomerulus is a bundle of capillaries in the renal or Bowman's capsule. The blood enters the glomerulus from an arteriole under high pressure. Due to

this pressure, small molecules, such as glucose, urea and water, are pressure-filtered out of the glomerulus into the Bowman's capsule. Any molecules too large to pass through the glomerular walls cannot be filtered and remain in the blood.

☐ **261** *(a)*
The Bowman's capsule gathers filtrate from the tight knot of capillaries, the glomerulus, fed by the renal artery.

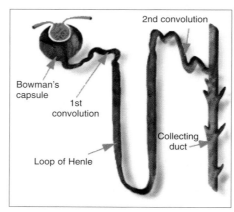

A261, 262, 263, 264, 265

☐ **262** *(e)*
The collecting duct transports urine from the kidney cortex (the outer layers), through the medulla, and into the ureter leading to the bladder.

☐ **263** *(c)*
The loop of Henle allows the kidney to concentrate the urine.

☐ **264** *(b)*
The first convoluted tubule handles all substances that are pressure-filtered out of the blood by the Bowman's capsule.

☐ **265** *(d)*
The distal part of the tubule is located after the loop of Henle, and helps to ensure the levels of sodium chloride and water in the blood are kept at the correct levels.

☐ **266** *(a)*
Blood moves through the glomerulus under high pressure forcing the smaller molecules out of the leaky capillary wall and through the leaky capsule wall into the Bowman's capsule. This process is called 'ultrafiltration' because neither the larger blood molecules, such as proteins, nor the red and white blood cells, can leak through the walls. Most smaller molecules, such as urea, salts, glucose, water, vitamins and amino acids, are filtered into the capsule.

☐ **267** *(c)*
The first convolution of the nephron tubule receives all of the substances that have been filtered out of the blood by the Bowman's capsule, and this is where the majority of molecules are reabsorbed. All of the glucose, vitamins and amino acids, and most of the water and sodium chloride are brought back into the bloodstream in the first convolution. Urea will not be reabsorbed, but will remain in the kidney filtrate and travel on to the remaining sections of the nephron.

☐ **268** *(d)*
Most of the substances needed from the filtrate have already been reabsorbed by the first convoluted tubule, so the filtrate at the loop of Henle is made up of water, urea and sodium chloride. By a complicated mechanism the loop of Henle allows the kidney to concentrate the urine. It is for this reason that desert animals have long loops.

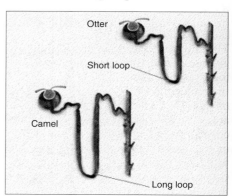

A268

☐ **269** *(e)*
The second convolution helps to ensure the levels of sodium chloride and water in the blood are kept at the correct levels. The reabsorption of these two substances into the bloodstream is dependent upon the state of the body: if the body is short of sodium chloride, aldosterone hormones are released that cause more sodium chloride to be reabsorbed into your bloodstream. This region also regulates the blood pH.

☐ **270** *(b)*
Each collecting duct gathers the filtrate from several nephrons and ensures that the concentration of water within the blood is regulated. As the duct passes through the medulla, it is surrounded by an increasing concentration of salt created by the loop of Henle. Water leaves the collecting duct by osmosis and the body is able to regulate the amount of water, reabsorbed into the body from the duct, by using a hormone to change the nature of the duct wall.

☐ **271** *(c)*
Most of the small molecules, forced out of the glomerular capillaries by the high blood pressure, are useful to the body and are quickly reabsorbed back into the bloodstream from the filtrate. Urea, a small molecule formed from the deamination of amino acids in the liver, is poisonous and, so is not reabsorbed but flows uninterrupted to the bladder and is excreted in urine.

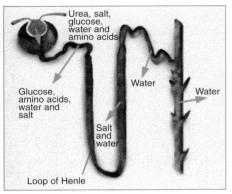

A271, 272

☐ **272** *(e)*
The kidney nephron reabsorbs all the glucose, vitamins and amino acids, and most of the water and mineral salts in the tubule filtrate. Varying amounts of mineral salts and water are reabsorbed at the second convoluted tubule and collecting duct, depending on the state of the body. No urea is reabsorbed. The urine that leaves the kidney, therefore, contains all of the urea, some of the mineral salts, and some of the water originally filtered from the bloodstream.

☐ **273** *(a)*
The kidneys help to maintain the internal environment of your body by filtering the blood; in particular, they maintain a constant level of water in your blood. ADH is crucial in allowing them to do this. If the water content in your blood is too low, ADH is released, which causes more water to be reabsorbed from the filtrate, and results in a more concentrated urine.

☐ **274** *(c)*
Luke will have lost a significant amount of water through sweating. This means the water content in his blood will be low. This will have been detected by his body and ADH will have been released from his pituitary gland, which leads to a relatively high concentration of ADH in his blood. The ADH causes more water to be reabsorbed in his kidneys, which leads to a more concentrated urine. The amount of urea present in his

bloodstream will not be affected by the conditions described in the question.

☐ **275** *(a)*
The situation described in the question means the water content in Jonathan's blood will be high. This will have been detected by his body so very little ADH will have been released from his pituitary gland, which leads to a relatively low concentration of ADH in his blood. The low concentration of ADH means less water will be reabsorbed in his kidneys, which leads to a more dilute urine. The amount of urea present in his bloodstream will not have been affected in this situation.

Defence against disease

☐ **276** *(a)*
Brushing your teeth regularly will help to prevent tooth decay caused by the bacteria that live on your sugary foods, but it will not help you to avoid infection by other bacteria of common diseases. The other behaviours should help you to avoid contamination from animals or other people, and reduce the risks of infection.

☐ **277** *True*
The skin has an outer layer of dead skin cells that make it waterproof and also keep out harmful pathogens, such as bacteria, which may cause diseases.

☐ **278** *(e)*
Many of your body's secretions are designed so that at least part of their role is to prevent the entry of harmful viruses or bacteria. Tears, for instance, contain an enzyme that interferes with the cell walls of bacteria, and prevents them growing on the damp, warm surface of the eye. Even stomach acids help kill germs before they reach the intestines. White blood cells, however, are effective only once an invader has entered your body.

☐ **279** *(d)*
Stomach acids help to prevent living organisms from reaching the intestine; the outer layers of dead skin prevent germs reaching the living layers beneath; mucus helps to prevent germs from reaching living cells in delicate areas; white blood cells help to kill bacteria and viruses. Urine, though, has no direct role in the prevention of infection, being a way in which the body can excrete urea and regulate the water content of body fluids.

☐ **280** *(a)*
The oil gland is situated at the base of the hair follicle. It secretes oil onto the hair, which helps to ensure that the skin is waterproof and helps to prevent microbes entering through the skin.

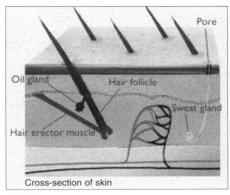

A280

☐ **281** *(c)*
There are many mucus-secreting cells in the lining of the respiratory tract. The mucus they secrete catches tiny bits of dirt, and the cilia also present in the tract sweep the mucus back towards the throat to be swallowed. This way any dangerous micro-organisms can be digested.

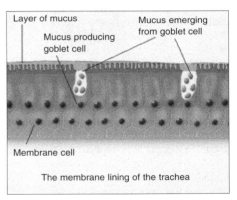

A281

☐ **282** *(b)*
Phagocytes, which are a type of white blood cell, are large and irregular in shape. They can change shape, rather like an Amoeba, to engulf foreign substances, such as bacteria, and digest them. This process is known as phagocytosis and it stops the digested foreign particle damaging its host.

☐ **283** *(a)*
All organisms have complicated mixtures of chemicals, mainly proteins and lipids, in their cell membranes. The white cells of our immune system recognise that the membrane chemicals of an invading organism do not match our own: phagocytes ingest the invader, and lymphocytes begin making antibodies.

284 *(d)*
Antibodies are very complicated molecules made of protein that are produced by a kind of cell called a B-lymphocyte, which is a type of white blood cell. Each antibody molecule can bind to either one, or a small number, of target molecules found in the cell membranes of foreign organisms or particles. This binding reduces the ability of the invader to reproduce or infect the host, and also attracts the attention of large phagocytes, which begin to ingest and digest the invading organism.

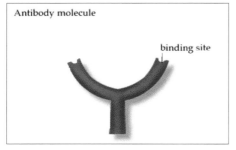

A284

285 *(a)*
Antibodies are special molecules, produced by the immune system, that attach themselves to specific target molecules of the surfaces of germs and help to disable the invaders. Their presence also attracts the white blood cells that will absorb the germs by phagocytosis and digest them into small pieces.

286 *(c)*
After entering the body, bacteria reproduce rapidly so that a few days after infection the body may contain millions of bacteria. Many species produce waste products, known as toxins, that are very poisonous to the body. Fortunately, the body has various immune mechanisms to kill off the bacteria, otherwise many infections would be fatal.

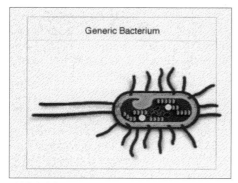

A286, 287

287 *(d)*
After one half-hour there would be two bacteria (2^1), after two half-hours there would be four bacteria (2^2), and after three half-hours there would be eight bacteria (2^3). Since there are 24 half-hours in the 12 hours period, the necessary calculation involves working out 2^{24}, which equals 16,777,216 or over 16 million. An infection is likely to involve thousands or even millions of bacteria even before they begin reproducing.

288 *(d)*
One of the methods of preventing a disease is to vaccinate. The vaccine will prime your immune system so that you will fight any dangerous form of the disease very much more quickly on the second encounter. Research must discover new types of vaccine for each disease.

289 *(a)*
The vaccine injected can contain either a completely harmless relative of the bacteria (the dead or disabled bacterium), or perhaps a small amount of a toxin released by a disease-causing microbe.

290 *(b)*
The first encounter with a disease is often through a vaccination and involves a slow build-up of antibody, low antibody levels, and a rapid decline in the concentration of antibody once the disease is beaten. Secondary responses act faster, generate higher levels of antibody, and keep higher levels of antibody for longer. These are all features that tend to prevent us feeling any symptoms on catching the disease for a second time.

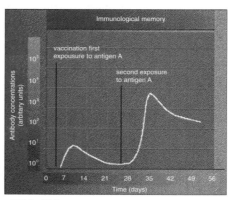

A290, 291

291 *(d)*
On vaccination, the body produces antibodies to fight the vaccine's harmless infection. It also stores, in memory cells, information about the antigen. On the booster vaccination, or after actual infection, the body produces a great many antibodies very quickly because the antigen has been 'remembered' by the memory cells. The steeper upward curve of the antibody concentration curve shows this.

292 *(c)*
The first recorded case of a successful vaccination was carried out by Edward Jenner. The smallpox vaccination was rapidly adopted across the world and Jenner even received a note from the American President, Thomas Jefferson, saying, 'Future nations will know by history only that the loathsome smallpox has existed and by you has been extirpated.'

Use and abuse of drugs

293 *(a)*
Antibiotics are generally produced by soil fungi, and aim to kill any competitor microbes living in the surrounding soil. Antibiotics tend to be chemicals that affect metabolic pathways specific to bacteria, and for this reason can be given to humans safely because our cells are so different to those of bacteria.

294 *(e)*
Antibiotics, such as penicillin, are chemicals used to fight off disease because they can inhibit, or even kill, bacteria in the body. Many different antibiotics exist today, most of them isolated from fungi, which also use them to kill bacteria, but the first discovered was penicillin from the Penicillium fungus (by Alexander Fleming).

295 *(e)*
Analgesics are painkillers, which are drugs that remove the taker's ability to feel pain.

296 *(a)*
Barbiturates, tranquillisers and opiates are depressants, which slow down the actions of the nervous system. Hallucinogens alter your senses producing mental illusions. Amphetamines are stimulants and will speed up the actions of your nervous system. All of these drugs can cause dependence and health problems.

297 *(c)*
Natural changes in moods occur due to changes taking place in the nervous and

endocrine (hormone) systems, so mood-influencing drugs must somehow affect these systems. Many drugs interfere with the transmission of messages between nerve cells at synapses. All drugs can be dangerous if taken without a doctor's help, and can cause the user to become dependent on the drug.

□ **298** *(e)*
All of the drugs listed can have an adverse affect on your nervous system. In particular, they appear to affect the nervous connections in the brain. If taken regularly over a period of time, these drugs can lead to the person becoming addicted, which is a state that leads to distressing emotional and physical changes in the individual concerned.

□ **299** *(d)*
Glue solvents are depressants whilst all the other drugs listed are stimulants. Depressants slow down the action of the brain, leading to a change of mental functions, but glue solvents also damage cells in the liver and kidney. If taken regularly over a period of time, they can lead to poor health and addiction, while an overdose will mean death.

□ **300** *False*
Alcohol is a depressant, which slows down the brain's actions. Alcohol can also damage cells in the liver and the kidney, and can be addictive.

□ **301** *(b)*
Caffeine, found in tea and coffee, is a stimulant. Stimulants accelerate the action of the brain and may help you to conquer mild tiredness during the day.

□ **302** *(e)*
The reasons given are some of the many offered as to why people take mood-influencing drugs. It is important that before any individual takes any drug, he or she knows exactly the effects it will have.

□ **303** *(d)*
Heroin is a highly addictive drug that affects the behaviour of the user, and damages the user's organs, such as the liver, the heart, the brain or the kidneys. It is refined from the opium of poppies and can be used to stop pain in a similar way to morphine.

□ **304** *(d)*
Many diseases can be transmitted on a dirty needle. A bacterium or virus may be present on the needle from a previous user and when the present user injects the drug into his or her body, he or she will also inject the disease-causing microbe. The spread of these dangerous diseases amongst drug users can be reduced if clean needles are always used. Scurvy is caused by a lack of vitamin C in the diet.

□ **305** *(b)*
Love, exercise, and sweet foods may often be metaphorically called drugs but the term is correctly applied only to the alcoholic lager here. The reasons why some drugs are socially acceptable, and others are not, are complex and often historical. Would alcohol be granted a licence for sale if it were 'invented' today?

□ **306** *(c)*
Alcohol is a drug that, in small amounts, causes a decrease in emotional tension and a sense of relative contentment. It increases confidence but decreases physical co-ordination, a combination that can prove lethal among inexperienced drivers of fast cars. Many drunk drivers questioned after accidents thought they had been driving particularly well. Alcohol causes unconsciousness in a concentration of 500 mg per 100 cm blood, and any higher concentration can cause death.

□ **307** *(b)*
Long-term alcohol abuse can have detrimental effects on many organs. It affects the liver by causing cirrhosis, a disease in which the liver cells die and are replaced by useless fibrous tissue, which causes the liver eventually to stop working. Many alcoholics die because of cirrhosis.

□ **308** *(d)*
If a pint of bitter contains 2 units of alcohol, four and a half pints would equal 9 units (4.5 x 2). This would place a driver well above the legal limit for driving in the United Kingdom.

□ **309** *(e)*
The chemicals in cigarette smoke are known to cause many diseases including a variety of cancers, the biggest killer being lung cancer, emphysema – the sufferer finds it very difficult to breathe because the area over which gases can be exchanged between the blood and the air has been reduced – and heart disease.

□ **310** *(d)*
Tar is a substance inhaled into the lungs in cigarette smoke. It contains thousands of chemicals, some of which cause cancer. Tar condenses in the lungs as the smoke cools, and can trigger bronchitis and emphysema in smokers.

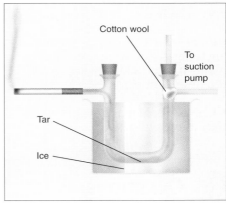

A310

□ **311** *(d)*
A layer of mucus lines the respiratory tract and traps dirt and microbes. The mucus comes from special cells in the lining of the respiratory tract called goblet cells. Rows of fine hair-like structures, called cilia, sweep the mucus, dirt and microbes upwards into the throat where they are swallowed safely.

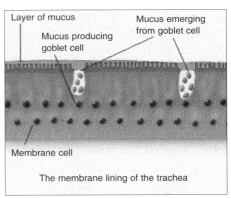

A311

Green Plants as Organisms

Plant structure *(Double Award only)*

The tallest plant ever measured was an eucalyptus tree in Australia standing 132 metres high. The banyan tree can spread out to be 600 metres around its edge. The oldest bristle cone pine is thought to be over 5,000 years old. All of these plants have the same basic structure: roots, stems and leaves. Flowering plants also have flowers.

 KEY FACTS

• **Plant roots** These take water and mineral salts out of the soil, and also anchor the plant in the ground.

• **Plant stem** This carries water and anything dissolved in it around the plant. It also holds the leaves and the flowers in place.

• **Leaves** These make sugars when they photosynthesise.

• **Flowers** These produce pollen and eggs for reproduction. Pollination is when the pollen of one flower is passed to the stigma of another flower.

• **Seeds** These are produced by reproduction and are spread as far away as possible from the parent plant. They germinate to produce new plants.

 QUESTIONS

1 In the diagram of a flowering plant, which letter correctly labels the stem?

- ☐ (a) V
- ☐ (b) W
- ☐ (c) X
- ☐ (d) Y
- ☐ (e) Z

Q1, 2, 3

2 In the diagram of a flowering plant, which letter correctly labels a root?

- ☐ (a) V
- ☐ (b) W
- ☐ (c) X
- ☐ (d) Y
- ☐ (e) Z

3 In the diagram of a flowering plant, which letter correctly labels a leaf?

- ☐ (a) V
- ☐ (b) W
- ☐ (c) X
- ☐ (d) Y
- ☐ (e) Z

4 What, apart from anchorage, is the main function of the roots of a flowering plant?

- ☐ (a) To absorb nitrogen and carbon dioxide
- ☐ (b) To absorb sugar and nitrites
- ☐ (c) To absorb minerals and water
- ☐ (d) To absorb water and carbon dioxide
- ☐ (e) To absorb sugars and minerals

5 Which of the following describes a function of the stem of a flowering plant?

- ☐ (a) To absorb water
- ☐ (b) To absorb oxygen
- ☐ (c) To absorb carbon dioxide
- ☐ (d) To support leaves and flowers
- ☐ (e) To photosynthesise

6 What is the main function of a leaf on a flowering plant?

- ☐ (a) To photosynthesise
- ☐ (b) To absorb water

- ☐ (c) To attract birds or insects
- ☐ (d) To reproduce
- ☐ (e) To balance the plant

7 In a flowering plant, which organ has the function of absorbing water?

- ☐ (a) Flower
- ☐ (b) Fruit
- ☐ (c) Leaf
- ☐ (d) Root
- ☐ (e) Stem

8 In a flowering plant, what is the collective name given to all the structures found above the ground?

- ☐ (a) Hypoterris system
- ☐ (b) Paraterris system
- ☐ (c) Shoot system
- ☐ (d) Stem system
- ☐ (e) Vegetative system

9 In a flowering plant, what is the collective name given to all the structures found below ground level?

- ☐ (a) Peripheral system
- ☐ (b) Root system
- ☐ (c) Tubular system
- ☐ (d) Transpiration system
- ☐ (e) Vascular system

10 The following diagram shows a cross-section through a typical leaf. What type of cell is labelled X?

- ☐ (a) Palisade mesophyll
- ☐ (b) Phloem tube element
- ☐ (c) Spongy mesophyll
- ☐ (d) Stomatal guard cell
- ☐ (e) Xylem vessel element

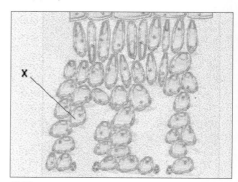

Q10

11 Which substance is moved from the roots to the leaves of a flowering plant, so that photosynthesis can occur?

☐ (a) Carbon dioxide
☐ (b) Glucose
☐ (c) Sucrose
☐ (d) Vitamin C
☐ (e) Water

12 These are small compartments of chemicals, with a membrane around them, that form the building blocks for the bodies of all larger organisms, from worms to elephants, and from seaweeds to oak trees. What are they?

☐ (a) Animals
☐ (b) Cells
☐ (c) Organs
☐ (d) Plants
☐ (e) Tissues

Plant nutrition *(Double Award only)*

What is thought to be the biggest living organism? A tree! The General Sherman tree in California is 84 metres high and 31 metres in circumference. It's trunk is 1,700 cu metres. Most of the tree's structure is made from what you can find in a bottle of Coke – water and carbon dioxide plus a few nutrients. The secret is photosynthesis.

Like all processes, photosynthesis is limited by the supply of its raw materials: light intensity, carbon dioxide concentration, water supply, or by the temperature. If there is not enough carbon dioxide then the rate of photosynthesis is limited and carbon dioxide is said to be the limiting factor.

The first products of photosynthesis are glucose and oxygen. Glucose can be used for a wide range of purposes that are all linked to the growth of a plant. Photosynthesis involves just three elements: carbon, hydrogen and oxygen. Plants require other chemicals to make a wider range of molecules needed for growth. These are the mineral salts, or mineral ions, that a plant collects from the soil through its roots. Mineral uptake requires energy from respiration, which is called active transport.

⬤ KEY FACTS

• **Photosynthesis** This is the process by which plants make their food. Plant leaves are adapted for this process, which uses light energy to combine carbon dioxide from the air and water from the soil to make simple sugars, such as glucose. As well as sugar, oxygen is produced in the reaction.

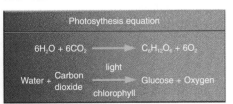

Photosythesis equation
$6H_2O + 6CO_2 \xrightarrow{\text{light}} C_6H_{12}O_6 + 6O_2$
Water + Carbon dioxide $\xrightarrow[\text{chlorophyll}]{\text{light}}$ Glucose + Oxygen

Photosynthesis equation

• **Leaves** These have a large surface area and are thin to allow light to penetrate to all of the photosynthetic cells.

• **Chlorophyll** This is a special green pigment that is kept in tiny packets in the cell, called chloroplasts.

• **Chloroplasts** These are where light is absorbed.

Leaves

• **Stomata** These are where the exchange of gases takes place on the surface of the plant.

• **Xylem and phloem** These bring water and nutrients to the cells and carry away the sugar to the parts of the plant that need it.

• **Temperature** The higher the temperature the quicker the reaction. In biological reactions, there is a maximum temperature above which the reactions slow down. This is because all biological reactions are controlled by enzymes, which are destroyed by too much heat.

• **Light intensity** The amount of light available affects the rate of photosynthesis because the reaction needs light energy to drive it.

• **Carbon dioxide concentration** This also affects the rate of photosynthesis. If there is not enough carbon dioxide then less glucose is produced.

• **Glucose** This may be respired to release energy for other reactions in the plant. It may be stored as starch, which is a large molecule and insoluble, and, therefore, does not affect the concentration inside the cell. Glucose may be combined with nitrates to produce proteins, and may be made into cellulose to make cell walls.

• **Oxygen** This may be used in respiration, or it may be released from the leaves of a plant.

• **Nitrates** These are used for making proteins and DNA. Without nitrates, a plant becomes stunted and the leaves become yellow.

• **Magnesium** This is used for making chlorophyll. Without magnesium, a plant's leaves will go yellow.

• **Potassium** This helps the enzymes controlling photosynthesis to work. Without potassium, the leaves go yellow with dead spots.

• **Phosphate** This is important for respiration and photosynthesis to work. Without phosphate, the roots do not grow properly and younger leaves turn purple.

Experiment to show that a lack of nitrates in plants stunts growth

QUESTIONS

13 In the following diagram of a plant cell, which letter labels the structures responsible for photosynthesis?

- ☐ (a) V
- ☐ (b) W
- ☐ (c) X
- ☐ (d) Y
- ☐ (e) Z

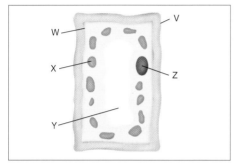

Q13

14 Which of the following lists of resources is needed for photosynthesis?

- ☐ (a) Light, chlorophyll, oxygen and water
- ☐ (b) Light, chlorophyll, carbon dioxide and water
- ☐ (c) Light, chlorophyll, carbon monoxide and water
- ☐ (d) Light, haemoglobin, oxygen and water
- ☐ (e) Light, haemoglobin, carbon dioxide and water

15 Which of the following is not necessary for photosynthesis?

- ☐ (a) Carbon dioxide
- ☐ (b) Chlorophyll
- ☐ (c) Oxygen
- ☐ (d) Sunlight
- ☐ (e) Water

16 True ☐ or false ☐ ?
The gas produced by photosynthesis is carbon dioxide.

17 True ☐ or false ☐ ?
In the dark a plant produces only the gas carbon dioxide.

18 What is produced in photosynthesis?

- ☐ (a) Carbon dioxide and water
- ☐ (b) Carbon dioxide and glucose
- ☐ (c) Oxygen and water
- ☐ (d) Oxygen and glucose
- ☐ (e) Water and glucose

19 Which of the following features is not an adaptation of leaves to perform photosynthesis?

- ☐ (a) High concentration of chlorophyll
- ☐ (b) Large leaf surface area
- ☐ (c) Only a few cells thick
- ☐ (d) Stomatal pores
- ☐ (e) Waxy cuticle on upper surface

20 Which gas is a raw material for photosynthesis?

- ☐ (a) Carbon dioxide
- ☐ (b) Carbon monoxide
- ☐ (c) Nitrogen
- ☐ (d) Oxygen
- ☐ (e) Water vapour

21 The following diagram shows a cross-section through the leaf of a plant. Which letter labels the type of cell where most photosynthesis takes place?

- ☐ (a) V
- ☐ (b) W
- ☐ (c) X
- ☐ (d) Y
- ☐ (e) Z

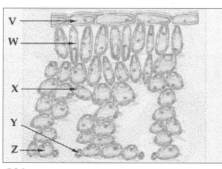

Q21

22 If a plant was given all it needed to photosynthesise, except carbon dioxide, which of the following terms could be applied to carbon dioxide and its relation to the plant?

- ☐ (a) Anti-growth factor
- ☐ (b) Braking factor
- ☐ (c) Limiting factor
- ☐ (d) Photosynthetic factor
- ☐ (e) Stunting factor

23 Which of the following factors might limit the rate of photosynthesis?

- ☐ (a) Humidity of atmosphere
- ☐ (b) Nitrogen concentration in atmosphere
- ☐ (c) Oxygen concentration in atmosphere
- ☐ (d) Temperature of atmosphere
- ☐ (e) Wind speed of atmosphere

24 Which of the following environmental factors might you increase in a commercial greenhouse if you were trying to maximise your yield of tomatoes?

- ☐ (a) The level of atmospheric carbon dioxide
- ☐ (b) The level of atmospheric nitrogen
- ☐ (c) The level of atmospheric oxygen
- ☐ (d) The level of carbohydrate in the soil
- ☐ (e) The level of soluble nitrites in the soil

25 Which of the following factors is unlikely to affect the rate of photosynthesis of a plant?

- ☐ (a) The level of ammonium in the soil
- ☐ (b) The level of carbohydrate in the soil
- ☐ (c) The level of magnesium in the soil
- ☐ (d) The level of atmospheric carbon dioxide
- ☐ (e) The number of herbivores on the plant

26 Which of the following factors does not limit the rate of photosynthesis?

- ☐ (a) The environmental temperature
- ☐ (b) The amount of carbon dioxide available to the plant
- ☐ (c) The amount of light available to the plant
- ☐ (d) The amount of oxygen available to the plant
- ☐ (e) The amount of water available to the plant

27 Photosynthesis produces glucose that is used, in turn, to produce a variety of substances vital to the plant. Any excess glucose is stored. In what form is glucose stored in plants?

- ☐ (a) Cellulose
- ☐ (b) Fructose
- ☐ (c) Saccharin
- ☐ (d) Starch
- ☐ (e) Sucrose

28 Which molecule is produced by photosynthesis, stored as starch and used in respiration?

- ☐ (a) Amino acid
- ☐ (b) Fructose
- ☐ (c) Glucose
- ☐ (d) Lactose
- ☐ (e) Sucrose

68

29 Glucose is produced by green plants during photosynthesis. What is the name of the process in which plants break down glucose to release energy?

- ☐ (a) Breathing
- ☐ (b) Osmoregulation
- ☐ (c) Respiration
- ☐ (d) Translocation
- ☐ (e) Transpiration

30 Which two products of photosynthesis are used in respiration?

- ☐ (a) Glucose and carbon dioxide
- ☐ (b) Glucose and oxygen
- ☐ (c) Glucose and water
- ☐ (d) Water and carbon dioxide
- ☐ (e) Water and oxygen

31 Most organisms need to respire to survive, and most need oxygen from the air to respire. Which biological process replaces this oxygen in the air?

- ☐ (a) Combustion
- ☐ (b) Evaporation
- ☐ (c) Osmosis
- ☐ (d) Photosynthesis
- ☐ (e) Transpiration

32 Which gaseous product of photosynthesis is vital to all animals and plants as a raw material in aerobic respiration?

- ☐ (a) Carbon dioxide
- ☐ (b) Carbon monoxide
- ☐ (c) Nitrogen
- ☐ (d) Oxygen
- ☐ (e) Water vapour

33 Which products of respiration are vital to plants as the raw materials for photosynthesis?

- ☐ (a) Carbon dioxide and nitrogen
- ☐ (b) Carbon dioxide and oxygen
- ☐ (c) Carbon dioxide and water
- ☐ (d) Nitrogen and oxygen
- ☐ (e) Water and oxygen

34 Which product of respiration is taken into plants, via their leaf stomata, and is used for photosynthesis?

- ☐ (a) Carbon dioxide
- ☐ (b) Carbon monoxide
- ☐ (c) Nitrogen
- ☐ (d) Oxygen
- ☐ (e) Water vapour

Higher Level only

35 Plants use the glucose produced in photosynthesis in a variety of ways. How can glucose be used with nitrates from the soil?

- ☐ (a) In respiration to yield energy
- ☐ (b) In osmosis to move water
- ☐ (c) In the loss of water by transpiration
- ☐ (d) In the synthesis of amino acids
- ☐ (e) In the synthesis of starch

36 Name the two raw materials from which plants produce amino acids?

- ☐ (a) Glucose and nitrates
- ☐ (b) Glucose and potassium
- ☐ (c) Glucose and proteins
- ☐ (d) Proteins and nitrates
- ☐ (e) Proteins and potassium

37 Which of the following plant nutrients is required by a plant to make chlorophyll?

- ☐ (a) Magnesium
- ☐ (b) Nitrate
- ☐ (c) Phosphate
- ☐ (d) Phosphorus
- ☐ (e) Potassium

38 A farmer noticed that an area of his field was producing crops with yellow leaves that had dead spots on them. Which of the following minerals might be missing in the soil?

- ☐ (a) Iron
- ☐ (b) Magnesium
- ☐ (c) Nitrate
- ☐ (d) Phosphate
- ☐ (e) Potassium

39 Which of the following nutrients is not required by a plant for healthy development?

- ☐ (a) Iron
- ☐ (b) Lead
- ☐ (c) Nitrogen
- ☐ (d) Phosphorus
- ☐ (e) Sulphur

40 Some sugars are used to build a carbohydrate, which is used by a plant to make cell walls. What is the name of this structural carbohydrate?

- ☐ (a) Cellophane
- ☐ (b) Cellulite
- ☐ (c) Cellulose
- ☐ (d) Chlorophyll
- ☐ (e) Membrane

41 Which of the following statements are true? X: Four guard cells surround a stoma. Y: The cell wall of a guard cell is thicker on the side furthest away from the stoma. Z: Guard cells contain chloroplasts.

- ☐ (a) X, Y and Z
- ☐ (b) X and Y
- ☐ (c) Y and Z
- ☐ (d) Y only
- ☐ (e) Z only

Plant hormones *(Double Award only)*

Plants rely on hormones for co-ordinating their activities. They do not have a nervous system as animals do. Scientists have used plant hormones artificially to control the way in which plants grow. Scientists have also played music to plants to see if it affects their growth! Apparently classical and Indian devotional music produced the best response, whilst rock music seemed to put them in a dying phase!

KEY FACTS

• **Co-ordinating** Plant hormones help to co-ordinate the growth responses of plants to light, moisture and gravity. Plant shoots grow towards light and away from gravity. Plant roots grow towards gravity and moisture, and away from light.

• **Commercial use** Plant hormones are used commercially to stimulate cuttings to produce roots, to control the development of fruit, to produce 'seedless' fruits and to stop normal growth patterns in weeds and kill them.

Growth of a seed

QUESTIONS

42 What do plant shoots grow away from?

- ☐ (a) Gravity
- ☐ (b) Light
- ☐ (c) Nutrients
- ☐ (d) Other plants
- ☐ (e) Water

43 Which of the following is a correct statement about how plant roots and shoots grow?

- ☐ (a) Plant shoots grow towards light and the roots grow away from the stimulus of gravity and towards water
- ☐ (b) Plant shoots grow away from light and the roots grow towards the stimulus of gravity and towards water
- ☐ (c) Plant shoots grow towards light and the roots grow towards the stimulus of gravity and away from water
- ☐ (d) Plant roots grow towards the stimulus of gravity and towards water, plant shoots grow towards light
- ☐ (e) Plant roots grow towards the stimulus of gravity and away from water, plant shoots grow towards light

44 Which of the following controls plant growth?

- ☐ (a) Enzymes
- ☐ (b) Hormones
- ☐ (c) Nerves
- ☐ (d) Nutrients
- ☐ (e) Water

Higher Level only

45 A solution of the plant hormone, auxin, was applied to the area of bean shoot X, shown in red in the diagram below. Bean shoot Y was not treated. If the two shoots are left for two days in conditions of all-round light, what would you expect to happen?

- ☐ (a) X would bend to the left and Y would grow straight
- ☐ (b) X would grow straight and Y would grow straight

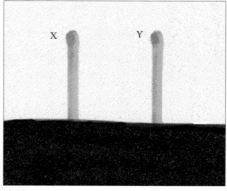

Q45

- ☐ (c) X would grow straight and Y would bend to the left
- ☐ (d) X would bend to the right and Y would bend to the left
- ☐ (e) X would bend to the right and Y would grow straight

46 The left half of a root was smeared with a paste containing the plant hormone, auxin, shown in blue in the following diagram, and then kept in warm and moist soil. Which of the following best describes what would happen to the treated root?

- ☐ (a) It would grow vertically down at a normal rate
- ☐ (b) It would grow vertically down at an increased rate
- ☐ (c) It would grow vertically down at a decreased rate
- ☐ (d) It would grow so that it curved towards the left
- ☐ (e) It would grow so that it curved towards the right.

Q46

47 Which of the following describes an important use for plant hormones in agriculture?

- ☐ (a) To add nitrates in the hormone to the soil
- ☐ (b) To extract genes for genetic engineering
- ☐ (c) To kill insect herbivores that eat crops
- ☐ (d) To improve the structure of the soil
- ☐ (e) To increase the growth of roots on cuttings

48 How might a growing root respond if it enters an area with a lot of water in the soil?

- ☐ (a) The root hairs develop off the main root
- ☐ (b) The main root grows quicker
- ☐ (c) The main root grows slower
- ☐ (d) The main root curls around the area of water
- ☐ (e) The main root doubles back on itself

49 Which of the following procedures would you carry out to get rid of weeds on a football pitch?

☐ (a) Cut the grass
☐ (b) Use a fertiliser
☐ (c) Use a flame thrower
☐ (d) Use a hormone weedkiller
☐ (e) Dig up the weeds

50 Which of the following is not a commercial use for hormones?

☐ (a) Controlling when fruit ripens
☐ (b) Encouraging cuttings to grow roots
☐ (c) Growing plants towards the light
☐ (d) Growing seedless fruits
☐ (e) Killing weeds

Transport systems inside plants *(Double Award only)*

Plants do not have a circulatory system as animals do. They need to transport mineral ions from the soil to all other parts of a plant. The mineral ions are dissolved in water and carried through a plant in a one way trip that ends with the water evaporating from the leaves. The flow of water from the soil into the roots, through the stem and into the leaves is called the transpiration stream.

Sugars, the products of photosynthesis, are needed not just in the leaves but in all parts of a plant. They are transported in solution to where they are needed.

Water moves into the cells by osmosis and increases the pressure inside the cells. Each cell in a plant has a cellulose cell wall that can stretch only a tiny amount. This means that if the cell is full of water, the cell wall is easily stretched to its limit and the cell will feel quite firm (turgid). If all of the cells have plenty of water then they will be turgid and the plant will be erect. If there is not enough water, the plant will wilt.

KEY FACTS

• **Plant roots** These have root hair cells that increase the surface area and, therefore, increase the amount of water and mineral ions the roots can absorb from the soil. Once absorbed, the water moves by osmosis to the centre of the roots where it enters the xylem vessels, which transport the water from the roots to the leaves.

• **Stomata** These are tiny holes through which the water is lost from the leaf as water vapour. Stomata can be closed if the plant is losing more water at the leaves than it is taking up at the roots. Hot, dry and windy conditions increase the rate of transpiration. Most plants have a waxy layer on the top surface of their leaves to reduce water loss.

• **Sugars** These provide the energy and the materials for growth. They can be changed into cellulose for cell walls, or changed into proteins when mixed with nitrates. Therefore, sugars are needed in all parts of a plant. They are made in the leaves and carried away from the leaves in the phloem. Most sugars will go to the parts that are growing the fastest, for example, the shoot, the root tips, the flowers and the fruit. Other sugars may be transported to where they can be stored as starch, which is usually underground, for example, in potato tubers.

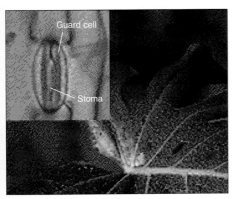
Stoma in a leaf

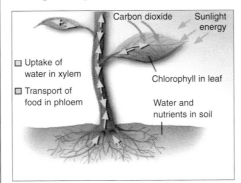
Transport in plants

QUESTIONS

51 Which of the following is vital to the life of a plant?

☐ (a) Gaseous carbon monoxide
☐ (b) Gaseous chlorine
☐ (c) Gaseous nitrogen
☐ (d) Liquid ethanol
☐ (e) Liquid water

52 The following diagram shows a plant in a conical flask of water. It is being kept in normal room conditions (reasonable light level and at room temperature). After an hour, where would you expect the water level to be?

☐ (a) V
☐ (b) W
☐ (c) X
☐ (d) Y
☐ (e) Z

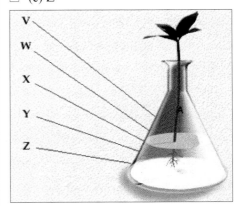
Q52

53 Which tissues of a plant are responsible for absorbing water?

☐ (a) Leaf
☐ (b) Phloem
☐ (c) Root
☐ (d) Shoot
☐ (e) Xylem

54 Where does water enter and where is it lost from a plant?

- ☐ (a) ENTERS: stoma
  LOST FROM: xylem
- ☐ (b) ENTERS: xylem
  LOST FROM: stoma
- ☐ (c) ENTERS: root hair cell
  LOST FROM: shoot hair cell
- ☐ (d) ENTERS: root hair cell
  LOST FROM: stomata
- ☐ (e) ENTERS: stomata
  LOST FROM: root hair cell

55 Which of the following best describes how water moves around a plant?

- ☐ (a) Root hair cell : phloem : leaf for photosynthesis or lost via the stomata
- ☐ (b) Root hair cell : xylem : leaf for photosynthesis or lost via the stomata
- ☐ (c) Stomata : xylem : leaf for photosynthesis or lost via the root hair cells
- ☐ (d) Stomata : xylem : leaf for photosynthesis or lost via the palisade cells
- ☐ (e) Stomata : phloem : leaf for photosynthesis or lost via the palisade cells

56 True ☐ or false ☐ ?
Perspiration is the loss of water from the leaves of a plant.

57 What is the name of the specialised tissues responsible for the transport of water and mineral salts through flowering plants?

- ☐ (a) Cambium tissue
- ☐ (b) Phloem tissue
- ☐ (c) Root tissue
- ☐ (d) Shoot tissue
- ☐ (e) Xylem tissue

58 A freshly cut piece of celery is placed into a beaker containing dilute ink, as shown in the following diagram. Which of the following describes what you would expect to see after about half an hour?

- ☐ (a) Bottom half of celery completely blue
- ☐ (b) Entire celery stalk completely blue
- ☐ (c) Vertical blue lines in the celery stem
- ☐ (d) Celery will have turned flaccid and wilted
- ☐ (e) No change at all in the celery

Q58

59 Which of the following terms best defines transpiration?

- ☐ (a) The loss of water by evaporation through the stomata
- ☐ (b) The absorbtion of water from the soil into the root
- ☐ (c) The transport of water from the root cells to the xylem
- ☐ (d) The transport of water around the plant by the xylem
- ☐ (e) The transport of water from the xylem to the cells of the leaf

60 Which of the following terms is used to describe the loss of water vapour from the leaves of a plant?

- ☐ (a) Transferation
- ☐ (b) Transpiration
- ☐ (c) Transportation
- ☐ (d) Xylematics
- ☐ (e) Xylemation

61 What is the process that makes the transport of water from the roots to the leaves possible, even in the very tallest species of tree?

- ☐ (a) Flocculation
- ☐ (b) Sedimentation
- ☐ (c) Transpiration
- ☐ (d) Transportation
- ☐ (e) Ultrafiltration

62 What is the correct scientific name for the structures through which water is lost from a plant in the process of transpiration?

- ☐ (a) Holes
- ☐ (b) Pores
- ☐ (c) Punctures
- ☐ (d) Sieve plates
- ☐ (e) Stomata

63 What is a stoma?

- ☐ (a) A cell through which water is transported when a diffusion gradient is created
- ☐ (b) A pore, mainly found on the underside of a leaf, through which gases are exchanged
- ☐ (c) A photosynthetic cell found within a leaf, between the spongy mesophyll and vein
- ☐ (d) A starch-storing root cell whose shape is specially adapted to absorb water
- ☐ (e) One of the two cells that surround the pores, generally found on the underside of leaves

64 Which of the following is mostly made of dead cells?

- ☐ (a) Cuticle
- ☐ (b) Palisade
- ☐ (c) Phloem
- ☐ (d) Roots
- ☐ (e) Xylem

65 True ☐ or false ☐ ?
Phloem tubes transport mineral ions dissolved in water.

66 What is the name of the transport vessel through which sugars are transported from a leaf to a developing fruit?

- ☐ (a) Mesophyll
- ☐ (b) Parenchyma
- ☐ (c) Phloem
- ☐ (d) Stoma
- ☐ (e) Xylem

Higher Level only

67 Which process most accurately describes how water is taken from the soil into the root hairs?

- ☐ (a) Absorption
- ☐ (b) Active transport
- ☐ (c) Diffusion
- ☐ (d) Osmosis
- ☐ (e) Ultra-filtration

68 Which process most accurately describes how mineral ions are taken from the soil into the root hairs?

- ☐ (a) Absorption
- ☐ (b) Active transport
- ☐ (c) Diffusion
- ☐ (d) Osmosis
- ☐ (e) Ultra-filtration

69 In which of the following weather conditions would the rate of transpiration be greatest?

☐ (a) Low wind speed, high humidity
☐ (b) Low wind speed, low humidity
☐ (c) High wind speed, high humidity
☐ (d) High wind speed, low humidity
☐ (e) Medium wind speed, medium humidity

70 In which of the following weather conditions would the rate of transpiration be greatest?

☐ (a) Low temperature, weak light
☐ (b) High temperature, weak light
☐ (c) Low temperature, strong light
☐ (d) High temperature, strong light
☐ (e) Medium temperature, medium light

71 Which of the following factors would immediately cause a stoma to open?

☐ (a) Decrease in surrounding light level
☐ (b) Increase in water entering guard cells
☐ (c) Increase in surrounding temperature
☐ (d) Increase in leaf carbon dioxide level
☐ (e) Increase in rate of leaf transpiration

 ANSWERS

Plant structure

☐ **1** *(b)*
The stem is the main support for the leaves and the flowers. In some unusual species, such as cacti, the leaves are reduced to defensive spines and all photosynthesis occurs in the green stem.

☐ **2** *(d)*
The roots of a flowering plant lie below the surface of the soil.

☐ **3** *(c)*
A leaf is generally a flattened green organ that grows at the end of shoots or branches. There can be many thousands of leaves on a plant. Deciduous plants lose all their leaves every winter and grow new leaves each spring.

A1, 2, 3

☐ **4** *(c)*
The main function of the roots is to absorb water, and the minerals dissolved in this water, into the plant. These substances are then transported to other areas of the plant, for instance, to where photosynthesis is taking place. The roots are, of course, also vital in anchoring the plant into the ground so it does not get blown away by the wind.

☐ **5** *(d)*
The stem is the main structure of the shoot system on which the leaves and the flowers grow. In larger plants, the stem may have branches on which the flowers and the leaves grow. It also contains major transport vessels by which water, nutrients and minerals are transported around a plant.

☐ **6** *(a)*
Leaves are the plant's organs of photosynthesis and are where a plant converts carbon dioxide and water into its own food, carbohydrate.

☐ **7** *(d)*
The main function of the roots is to absorb water, and the minerals dissolved in this water, into the plant, and transport it to other areas of the plant.

☐ **8** *(c)*
In a flowering plant all the structures located above ground level, including the stem, the leaves and the flowers, are known as the shoot system.

☐ **9** *(b)*
In a flowering plant, all the structures usually found within the soil, such as the roots or the root tubers, are known as the root system.

☐ **10** *(c)*
Spongy mesophyll cells are found on the lower side of the leaves just above the stomata. Their many air spaces allow gases, such as carbon dioxide, which is vital for photosynthesis, to diffuse through a leaf and reach other mesophyll layers.

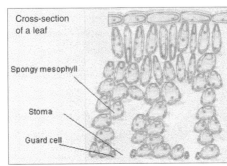

A10

☐ **11** *(e)*
Water is collected from the soil by the roots and is used in photosynthesis. This is because photosynthesis combines hydrogen with carbon dioxide to make carbohydrate, and the hydrogen atoms are stripped from the water molecules using the power of sunlight. Minerals of many kinds are also acquired by the roots, but none are in the list given.

☐ **12** *(b)*
Almost all living organisms are made up of small compartments known as cells. Organisms with only a single cell, such as bacteria, are called unicellular, while those with many cells, such as humans, are called multicellular. The virus is the only type of living organism that does not base its structure on cells.

Plant nutrition

☐ **13** *(c)*
The cells of the leaves, especially the palisade cells close to the surface, are packed with chloroplasts that contain chlorophyll. Photosynthesis takes place in these chloroplasts.

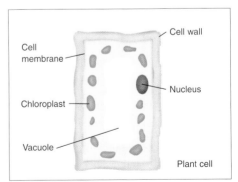

A13

☐ **14** *(b)*
Photosynthesis is the process by which plants produce glucose by combining some of the atoms of carbon dioxide and water. Photosynthesis also needs light energy from the sun, and chlorophyll to absorb light energy.

☐ **15** *(c)*
Oxygen is not needed for photosynthesis because it is a waste product of the process. The atoms of oxygen given off as waste come from molecules of water whose hydrogen atoms have been stripped away by a plant for use in photosynthesis.

☐ **16** *False*
The gas produced by photosynthesis is oxygen, not carbon dioxide. Photosynthesis converts carbon dioxide and water into glucose, which is used by the plant as food, and oxygen, which is released from the plant.

☐ **17** *True*
In the dark a plant cannot photosynthesise. However, whether in light or dark, a plant will always be respiring, and so in the dark it will be producing carbon dioxide.

☐ **18** *(d)*
Photosynthesis is the process by which plants produce glucose that can then be respired by the plant cells. Oxygen is also produced as a waste product of photosynthesis, and escapes from the stomata of the leaves. The glucose may be converted into starch if the plant needs to store surplus energy for long periods.

☐ **19** *(e)*
Leaves do have a waxy cuticle, but this is to avoid excess water loss from the upper surface and is not an adaptation that helps photosynthesis. Their large surface area and thin structure help gather light, and the stomata allow the entry of carbon dioxide.

☐ **20** *(a)*
Photosynthesis is the process by which plants take the hydrogen atoms from water and combine them with molecules of carbon dioxide into a new type of compound, called carbohydrate. Chemists say that the carbon dioxide has been 'reduced' in this reaction, which means that it has accepted atoms of hydrogen to become a different molecule. Hydrogen is said to be a 'reducing agent' in this reaction.

☐ **21** *(b)*
The palisade cells are usually the most active photosynthesising cells in a typical leaf. They are close to the upper surface, and so receive high levels of light, while their lower ends are in contact with the air spaces of the spongy mesophyll, and so receive carbon dioxide. Their long thin shape

and vertical position means that light entering the palisade cell can hit the chloroplasts without having to be weakened by travelling through too many cell walls.

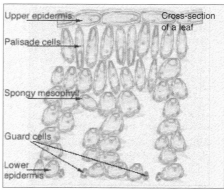

A21

☐ **22** *(c)*
A plant needs light, carbon dioxide, water, chlorophyll and the right temperature to photosynthesise efficiently. If any one of these resources or conditions is lacking whilst the others are in plentiful supply, this one factor will limit the rate of photosynthesis. Such a resource, in short supply, is called a limiting factor.

☐ **23** *(d)*
One of the four main factors that can limit the rate of photosynthesis under ordinary conditions is the environmental temperature. It acts by changing the rate at which the enzymes involved in photosynthesis do their job. Over the longer term, some other factors, such as the supply of essential minerals from the soil, may also limit the rate of photosynthesis.

☐ **24** *(a)*
Four main factors influence the rate of photosynthesis: water supply, atmospheric carbon dioxide, light levels, and environmental air temperature. Other factors, such as soil acidity, can affect photosynthesis by making the plant unhealthy. Atmospheric oxygen and nitrogen would have no effect, and plants cannot directly use carbohydrate in soil. Nitrites are not usually absorbed by plant roots, which prefer nitrates or ammonium as their sources of nitrogen for making proteins.

☐ **25** *(b)*
The level of carbohydrate in the soil will not affect the rate of photosynthesis, since plants can make no use of carbohydrate unless it is decomposed by soil bacteria. Magnesium is needed to make chlorophyll; herbivores will eat

leaves; ammonium is needed to make enzymes and other photosynthetic reactants; carbon dioxide is a raw material of photosynthesis.

☐ **26** *(d)*
There are only four main environmental factors that influence the rate of photosynthesis: the amount of water, carbon dioxide and light available to the plant, and the environmental temperature.

☐ **27** *(d)*
Glucose is produced by photosynthesis, and is the basis from which all substances vital to a plant are made. Any excess glucose molecules are joined together (condensed) into a chain of over 1,000 glucose units, known as starch.

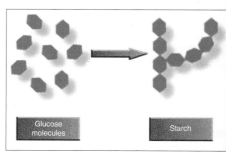

A27

☐ **28** *(c)*
Glucose is produced by photosynthesis, stored as starch, and used as the fuel for respiration.

☐ **29** *(c)*
Glucose is the fuel for respiration, the process that provides a plant with the energy it needs for life. Starch can be broken down (hydrolysed) by enzymes back into glucose for respiration when needed.

☐ **30** *(b)*
Photosynthesis produces oxygen and glucose from carbon dioxide and water, using the energy of light acting on the chloroplasts. The glucose may then act as the fuel for respiration, but respiration may also use some of the oxygen. Respiration releases all the energy the plant needs for such things as growth or reproduction.

☐ **31** *(d)*
Oxygen is produced as a waste product in photosynthesis, although some may be used for respiration by the plant. Plenty of oxygen, however, escapes through the stomata, and allows other organisms to respire and produce energy for themselves.

74

☐ **32** *(d)*
Oxygen, the gaseous product of photosynthesis, is released from green plants and allows other organisms to respire and produce energy for themselves.

☐ **33** *(c)*
Respiration is the process by which animals and plants release energy from carbohydrates and other food molecules. It uses oxygen and glucose as its raw materials and produces carbon dioxide and water as its waste products. These two wastes are the raw materials for photosynthesis and are taken in by plants.

☐ **34** *(a)*
Carbon dioxide and water are the two waste products of respiration but are the raw materials for photosynthesis. Plants take in carbon dioxide through their stomata, and water through their roots. These products combine to form carbohydrates.

☐ **35** *(d)*
Some of the glucose produced by photosynthesis is changed, using the nitrogen atoms from nitrates taken from the soil, to form amino acids. Amino acids are the building blocks of proteins that are used in almost every aspect of a plant's life, especially as they are the enzymes that control cell chemistry.

☐ **36** *(a)*
Amino acids contain carbon, oxygen, hydrogen and nitrogen atoms. The first three of these can be provided by the glucose molecules made in photo-synthesis, but glucose contains no nitrogen atoms and a plant cannot use gaseous nitrogen from the air. Therefore, a plant must obtain nitrogen atoms from nitrate or sometimes ammonium compounds in the soil, and use these in combination with a rearranged glucose molecule to synthesise an amino acid.

☐ **37** *(a)*
All the nutrients listed are important for the successful growth of a plant. Magnesium is part of the chlorophyll molecule and so without it a plant cannot photosynthesise.

☐ **38** *(e)*
A lack of nitrate, magnesium and potassium will produce yellow leaves, but a lack of potassium also produces characteristic dead spots.

☐ **39** *(b)*
Nitrogen, sulphur, iron and phosphorus are among many minerals that are vital to a healthy plant. Some, for instance phosphorus, are required in large quantities while others, for instance molybdenum, are required in only tiny (or 'trace') amounts. Lead, however, is not needed for any metabolic process in plants, but often occurs through pollution.

☐ **40** *(c)*
Sugars produced in photosynthesis may be converted to cellulose for growing cell walls. In this conversion, thousands of glucose sugar units are bonded together in a special way to make a cellulose polymer that is insoluble, strong and indigestible by many animals.

☐ **41** *(e)*
Two guard cells surround a stoma, and they open and close the stoma. The area of cell wall closest to the stoma is thicker than the rest of the cell wall so that when the cell is turgid it bends. If both guard cells are bent the stoma is opened wide. Guard cells possess chloroplasts so they can photosynthesise and power this cell movement.

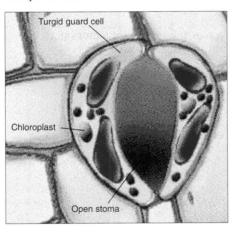

A41

Plant hormones

☐ **42** *(a)*
Plant shoots might grow away from other plants, but the plant is probably in search of more light. Shoots grow away from gravity so that the plant can grow into the air for photosynthesis and reproduction.

☐ **43** *(d)*
Plant roots grow towards gravity, so that the plant can stay in the soil for anchorage, and then they grow towards water. Plant shoots grow towards the light so that the leaves can photosynthesise.

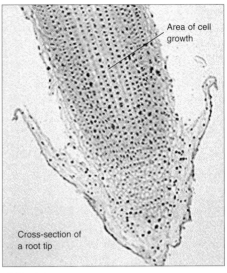

A43, 44

☐ **44** *(b)*
Hormones control plant growth. They can make cells in one region grow faster than in another region, which leads to 'bending'. For example, if there is more hormone on the dark side of a shoot, it will grow faster than the side in the light; the shoot will 'bend' as it grows towards the light.

☐ **45** *(e)*
Auxins are hormones that affect the rate at which cells elongate during the growth of shoots. In all-round light, both plants should have their natural auxins distributed equally at all points around the shoot, and should grow vertically. When additional auxin is applied to the left side of shoot X, it would cause the left side to elongate quicker than the right side, and this would produce a bend towards the right. Shoot Y would continue to grow straight up.

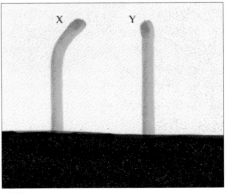

A45

46 (d)

Auxins play a part in the growth responses of plants by causing a change in the elongation or growth rate of cells. When applied to root tissue, auxin causes the new cells to elongate less quickly than usual, unlike in the shoot where auxin accelerates growth. The root will therefore curve towards the left. This is part of a response that allows the root to grow downwards.

A46

47 (e)

Plant hormones are used in agriculture and horticulture in many ways, including the improvement of root growth in cuttings, the regulation of fruit development, and the destruction of some kinds of weeds by disrupting their growth patterns.

48 (a)

As a root grows through areas where the water concentration is high, microscopic root hairs develop off the main root. These root hairs increase the surface area of the root enabling more water and minerals in solution to be absorbed into the plant.

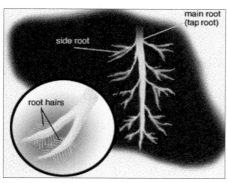

A48

49 (d)

Digging out the weeds seems like a lot of hard work and might not remove any weed seeds. Using a flame thrower is perhaps a little drastic! Using a fertiliser might help if the weeds are growing and competing with the grass for nutrients.

Cutting the lawn may encourage certain weeds, but using hormone weed killers can be selective and can stop the weeds growing normally. The weeds soon die.

50 (c)

Whilst hormones can be used to cause plants to grow towards the light, it is much easier to put the plants in a place that receives plenty of light, such as by a window. All the other examples listed are ways in which hormones are used commercially.

Transport systems inside plants

51 (e)

Water is vital for several reasons: it is crucial in photosynthesis, it provides a liquid base for the cell reactions of a plant, and it helps to keep a plant upright.

52 (d)

A plant needs water to survive and this water is absorbed by the roots. After an hour, the plant shown in the question will have absorbed some of the water but by no means all of it.

53 (c)

Water is absorbed from the soil by the roots of a plant.

54 (d)

Water diffuses from the soil into the root hair cells and is lost through the stomata in the leaves of a plant.

55 (b)

Water is transported round a plant using transpiration – the air surrounding a stoma has a lower concentration of water than the cells behind the stoma so water moves to this area of lower concentration. The cells around the stoma now have a lower concentration than the other leaf cells so water moves into them via osmosis. In this way, diffusion causes water transport through the cells of the leaf, the xylem, the root cells and the root hair cells, into which water diffuses from the soil.

56 *False*

Transpiration is the loss of water from the leaves of a plant. It occurs because the air around the leaves is usually less humid than inside them, so water evaporates from the surface. The underside of a leaf has tiny pores called stomata that can open and close to let the water out or keep it in.

57 (e)

Roots absorb water and mineral salts from the soil, and the water is transported through the cells of the root to the xylem in the centre. The xylem vessels are long, thin tubes that run the length of the plant taking water and minerals from the roots, up through the stem, to all sites where they are used.

58 (c)

The celery absorbs ink from the beaker and transports it up the xylem vessels in the stem. The xylem vessels are vertical tubes running up the stem and so, as the ink is transported up the stem, you would be able to see the blue ink lines go higher.

59 (a)

Water in a leaf is lost to the air via stomata, which are small pores found on the underside of the leaf. This water loss, or transpiration, occurs because the surrounding air has a lower concentration of water than the area immediately behind the stoma in the leaf, and so water vapour will diffuse out of the leaf down its concentration gradient.

60 (b)

Transpiration is the name given to the loss of water vapour from the leaves of a plant, mainly through the stomatal pores on the underside of the leaves. Water loss through transpiration may be very high: an oak tree in high summer may lose hundreds of litres of water through transpiration each day.

61 (c)

Water is transported round a plant as a result of transpiration. The air outside a leaf has a lower concentration of water than the cells within the leaf, so water evaporates from the leaf moving out of it through the stomata. The leaf cells pull in more water from nearby xylem vessels and these, in turn, pull water up the plant from the root tissues; this mechanism is usually known as 'transpiration pull'.

62 (e)

Water is lost to the air from a plant via the pore-like structures called stomata, found mainly on the underside of the leaves. The stomata can open and close to let the water out or keep it in.

63 (b)

Small pores, known as stomata (plural of stoma), are the route by which a leaf takes in carbon dioxide and loses waste gaseous oxygen. Water vapour also escapes from the stomata, though a plant has many features that try to limit the loss, as too much water loss could lead to death.

☐ **64** *(e)*
Only xylem is mostly made of dead cells that have lost their cytoplasm. Xylem vessels are like minute drain pipes!

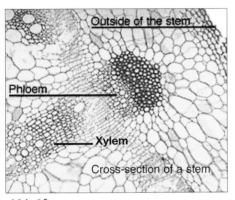

A64, 65

☐ **65** *False*
Phloem vessels transport sugars dissolved in water from the leaves, where they have been made, to other areas in a plant, where they may be used or stored. Phloem tubes allow sugars to move in both directions, up and down a plant. Some of the sugars may have been combined with nitrates to make amino acids and these too are carried in the phloem. Mineral ions are transported dissolved in water in the xylem vessels, which run from the roots to the leaves.

☐ **66** *(c)*
Sugars, the products of photosynthesis, are transported from the leaves to storage organs, such as fruit, in the phloem vessels. These are tubes, made of many 'sieve-tube' cells laid end-to-end, specialised for the transport of the sugar sucrose, though some other substances, such as amino acids, are also carried. The 'sieve-tube' cells are so-called because they have end walls perforated with many small holes, rather like a sieve.

☐ **67** *(d)*
All of the options are terms used to define the movements of materials. Osmosis describes the movement of water molecules from a region of high concentration to a region of lower concentration. This takes place through the partially permeable membrane of a root hair cell.

☐ **68** *(b)*
All of the options are terms used to define the movements of materials. Mineral ions are taken from the soil, where they are in low concentrations, into the root, where they are in higher concentrations. This requires energy and so moves by active transport.

☐ **69** *(d)*
The lower the concentration of water outside a leaf, the faster the rate of transpiration, because there is a greater difference between the water concentrations inside and outside the leaf. Decreasing atmospheric humidity

and increasing wind speed lower the external water vapour concentration in the air, and cause an increase in the transpiration rate.

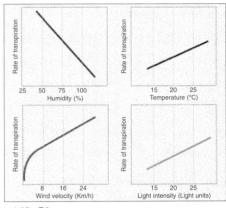

A69, 70

☐ **70** *(d)*
Decreasing humidity, increasing temperature and increasing wind speed lower the external water concentration, so causing an increase in the transpiration rate. Also, more light means that more stomata are open, so increasing the transpiration rate.

☐ **71** *(b)*
The guard cell wall closest to a stoma is thicker than the rest of the cell wall, so when the cell is turgid, from water entering the cell, it bends. If both guard cells bend the stoma opens. Details of stomatal behaviour vary between species of plant, but in all species, water entering the guard cells will cause the stomata to open.

Variation, Inheritance and Evolution

Variation *(Single and Double Awards)*

Each human being is unique. There is nobody on this planet who is the same as you! If you have an identical twin then you might be genetically the same, but at some time in your life you will have experienced something that is different to your twin. Differences demonstrate variation, which can be either genetic or environmental. It follows that if a woman and her partner, who are both unique, have children then they too will be unique. Only half of the genetic code of each parent goes to make up the new child, and that genetic code is chosen at random. Clones are an exception to this but, as yet, a human clone has never been produced.

The word mutation means change. It refers to any change in the structure of a chromosome. Mutations are often harmful, although some are neutral and others are beneficial. Mutations are necessary for evolution to take place.

 KEY FACTS

• **Differences** These occur between individuals of the same species because of differences in the genes they have inherited (genetic causes) and differences in the conditions in which they developed (environmental causes). Identical twins have exactly the same genetic information, so any differences between them must be environmental.

• **Asexual reproduction** This occurs when new individuals are produced by mitosis from parental cells. The new individuals, known as clones, therefore contain identical genetic information to the parents.

Identical twins

• **Sexual reproduction** This helps to increase genetic variation. Sexual reproduction increases variation because genes exist in different forms (alleles), meiosis randomly chooses half of these alleles to produce gametes, and two gametes, one from each parent, fuse at random to produce a combination of genes.

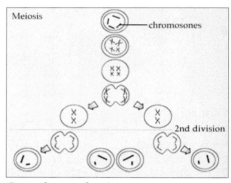
Sexual reproduction

• **Mutation** This produces genetic variation. Mutations can be changes in genes or changes in a chromosome. They can result in new forms of genes. Ionising radiation such as gamma rays, ultra-violet rays and X-rays can cause mutations. Some chemicals called mutagens, which includes some in tobacco smoke, can also cause mutations. The more an organism is exposed to these conditions, the more likely it is to have a mutation. Mutations are beneficial if the genetic variation produced helps the organism to survive.

 QUESTIONS

1 Which of the following characteristics describes an insect?

- ☐ (a) 2 body parts, 4 pairs of legs, endoskeleton
- ☐ (b) 2 body parts, 3 pairs of jointed legs, endoskeleton
- ☐ (c) 3 body parts, 3 pairs of jointed legs, endoskeleton
- ☐ (d) 3 body parts, 3 pairs of jointed legs, exoskeleton
- ☐ (e) 3 body parts, 2 pairs of jointed legs, exoskeleton

2 Harry found an animal in his back yard and saw it had 4 pairs of legs, 2 body parts and no antennae. What has Harry found?

- ☐ (a) An annelid
- ☐ (b) An arachnid
- ☐ (c) A crustacean
- ☐ (d) An insect
- ☐ (e) A myriapod

3 Which of the following best defines the term 'species'?

- ☐ (a) A group of organisms that are able to breed and produce fertile offspring
- ☐ (b) A group of organisms that are related by having at least 99% of their genes identical
- ☐ (c) A group of organisms that are related to each other by descent from an ancestor
- ☐ (d) A group of organisms that look so similar that they cannot be distinguished
- ☐ (e) A group of similar organisms that have identical alleles on all their chromosomes

4 Use the key in the column opposite to identify whether the vertebrate shown is V, W, X, Y or Z.

- ☐ (a) V
- ☐ (b) W
- ☐ (c) X
- ☐ (d) Y
- ☐ (e) Z

5 Use the key in the column opposite to identify whether the vertebrate shown is V, W, X, Y or Z.

- ☐ (a) V
- ☐ (b) W
- ☐ (c) X
- ☐ (d) Y
- ☐ (e) Z

6 Use the key in the column opposite to identify whether the vertebrate shown is V, W, X, Y or Z.

- ☐ (a) V
- ☐ (b) W
- ☐ (c) X
- ☐ (d) Y
- ☐ (e) Z

7 Use the key in the column opposite to identify whether the vertebrate shown is V, W, X, Y or Z.

- ☐ (a) V
- ☐ (b) W
- ☐ (c) X
- ☐ (d) Y
- ☐ (e) Z

8 Use the key in the column opposite to identify whether the vertebrate shown is V, W, X, Y or Z.

- ☐ (a) V
- ☐ (b) W
- ☐ (c) X
- ☐ (d) Y
- ☐ (e) Z

9 Which of the following is not a difference between an ovum and a sperm?

- ☐ (a) A sperm is considerably smaller than an ovum
- ☐ (b) A sperm is mobile whilst an ovum is not
- ☐ (c) A sperm is a male gamete while an ovum is a female gamete
- ☐ (d) Ova are produced by the ovaries whereas sperm are produced by the testes
- ☐ (e) Sperm contain their chromosomes in the nucleus whereas ova contain theirs in the cytoplasm

1a	Animal has fins	V
b	Animal has no fins	2
2a	Animal has fur or feathers	3
b	Animal has no fur or feathers	4
3a	Animal has 2 legs, 2 wings and feathers	W
b	Animal has 4 legs or 2 arms and 2 legs	X
4a	Animal has moist skin without cracks	Y
b	Animal has dry skin with scales	Z
KEY	Answers	Go to

Q4

1a	Animal has fins	V
b	Animal has no fins	2
2a	Animal has fur or feathers	3
b	Animal has no fur or feathers	4
3a	Animal has 2 legs, 2 wings and feathers	W
b	Animal has 4 legs or 2 arms and 2 legs	X
4a	Animal has moist skin without cracks	Y
b	Animal has dry skin with scales	Z
KEY	Answers	Go to

Q5

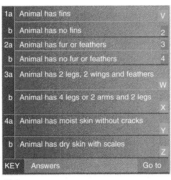

1a	Animal has fins	V
b	Animal has no fins	2
2a	Animal has fur or feathers	3
b	Animal has no fur or feathers	4
3a	Animal has 2 legs, 2 wings and feathers	W
b	Animal has 4 legs or 2 arms and 2 legs	X
4a	Animal has moist skin without cracks	Y
b	Animal has dry skin with scales	Z
KEY	Answers	Go to

Q6

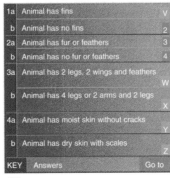

1a	Animal has fins	V
b	Animal has no fins	2
2a	Animal has fur or feathers	3
b	Animal has no fur or feathers	4
3a	Animal has 2 legs, 2 wings and feathers	W
b	Animal has 4 legs or 2 arms and 2 legs	X
4a	Animal has moist skin without cracks	Y
b	Animal has dry skin with scales	Z
KEY	Answers	Go to

Q7

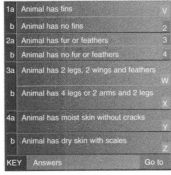

1a	Animal has fins	V
b	Animal has no fins	2
2a	Animal has fur or feathers	3
b	Animal has no fur or feathers	4
3a	Animal has 2 legs, 2 wings and feathers	W
b	Animal has 4 legs or 2 arms and 2 legs	X
4a	Animal has moist skin without cracks	Y
b	Animal has dry skin with scales	Z
KEY	Answers	Go to

Q8

10 What is the best definition of fertilisation in animals?

☐ (a) When the sperm enters the vagina
☐ (b) When the sperm meets the ovum
☐ (c) When the sperm enters the ovum
☐ (d) When the sperm and the ovum nuclei fuse
☐ (e) When the ovum divides to form two cells

11 When fertilisation occurs how many of the (approximately) 500 million sperm emitted in an ejaculation pass through the cell membrane of the ovum?

☐ (a) 1
☐ (b) 10
☐ (c) 100
☐ (d) 1000
☐ (e) 10,000

12 Which of the following terms best describes how parents pass on some of their characteristics to their offspring?

☐ (a) Blood flow
☐ (b) Endocrine system
☐ (c) Gametes
☐ (d) Immune system
☐ (e) Nerve impulses

13 How are identical twins formed ?

☐ (a) One egg is fertilised by two sperm
☐ (b) One egg is fertilised and stored in the uterus, then a month later the same thing occurs and the two fertilised eggs start developing together
☐ (c) One egg is fertilised by one sperm but during the first divisions the embryo splits in two, giving two embryos
☐ (d) Two eggs are fertilised by two sperm
☐ (e) Two eggs are fertilised by one sperm

14 Some inherited characteristics can be modified by environmental conditions. Which of the following has been used to prove this?

☐ (a) Identical twins reared together
☐ (b) Non-identical twins reared together
☐ (c) Separately reared non-identical twins
☐ (d) Separately reared identical twins
☐ (e) Siamese twins

15 Many plants reproduce asexually. Which of the following statements about the offspring of asexual reproduction is true?

☐ (a) They will have only half their father's genes
☐ (b) They will be extremely similar to their mother
☐ (c) They are genetically identical to the parent
☐ (d) They will inherit only poor characteristics
☐ (e) They will inherit only good characteristics

16 Plants can be grown from seed. This is sexual reproduction. Which of the following statements about the young plant is true?

☐ (a) It will be identical with one parent
☐ (b) It will not resemble either parent
☐ (c) It will have only the bad characteristics of the parents
☐ (d) It will have only the good characteristics of the parents
☐ (e) It will have some characteristics of each parent plant

17 Which of the following factors contribute to the final height of an adult plant?

☐ (a) Environmental factors only
☐ (b) Environment and blind chance
☐ (c) Genetic only
☐ (d) Genetic and environmental factors
☐ (e) Genetic and blind chance

18 True ☐ or false ☐ ?
The only differences that might exist between identical twins have to be caused by the environment because they have identical genetic make-ups.

19 Which of the following factors does not influence the weight of a new born baby?

☐ (a) Body temperature of mother
☐ (b) Genetic details of father
☐ (c) Genetic details of mother
☐ (d) Quality of mother's diet
☐ (e) Smoking habits of mother

20 Which of the following populations is likely to show the most variation?

☐ (a) Sexually-reproducing organisms in a variable environment
☐ (b) Asexually-reproducing organisms in a variable environment
☐ (c) Sexually-reproducing organisms in a stable environment
☐ (d) Asexually-reproducing organisms in a stable environment
☐ (e) Vegetatively-reproducing organisms in a stable environment

21 What is the term given to a gene that has been altered from its normal form?

☐ (a) A changeling
☐ (b) A meiosis
☐ (c) A mitosis
☐ (d) A mutant
☐ (e) A syndrome

22 Which of the following increases the genetic variation among the members of a population?

☐ (a) Asexual reproduction
☐ (b) Cloning
☐ (c) Genetic mutation
☐ (d) Mitosis
☐ (e) Seed dispersal

23 Which one of the following can cause a mutation?

☐ (a) Excess fats in the diet
☐ (b) Mental stress
☐ (c) Radiation
☐ (d) Starvation
☐ (e) Undue physical exertion

24 Which of the following will not cause an increased rate of mutation if applied to a group of dividing cells?

☐ (a) Gamma rays
☐ (b) Ultra-violet light
☐ (c) Visible light
☐ (d) X-rays
☐ (e) Some chemicals in cigarette smoke

25 A batch of living cells kept in the laboratory are given daily doses of non-lethal radiation. What is the most likely outcome of this experiment?

☐ (a) More deaths in the cells
☐ (b) More mitosis in the cells
☐ (c) More meiosis in the cells
☐ (d) More mutations in the cells
☐ (e) No change in the cells

Higher Level only

26 Which of the following processes is the most likely to lead to offspring of varying genetic make-up?

☐ (a) Asexual reproduction
☐ (b) Binary fission
☐ (c) Meiosis
☐ (d) Mitosis
☐ (e) Vegetative propagation

27 Which of the following diseases is caused by cells dividing repeatedly and becoming unable to function?

- ☐ (a) AIDS
- ☐ (b) Cancer
- ☐ (c) Herpes
- ☐ (d) Influenza
- ☐ (e) Meningitis

28 Which of the following is known to be a cause of cancer in humans?

- ☐ (a) Argon gas
- ☐ (b) Carbon monoxide
- ☐ (c) Heat stress
- ☐ (d) Ionising radiation
- ☐ (e) Loud music

29 Which of the following best explains why sexual reproduction leads to variation among the offspring of a mating?

- ☐ (a) One quarter of a parent's alleles are contained in a gamete, so any offspring receives half its genetic information from its grandparents
- ☐ (b) Half a parent's alleles are contained in a gamete, so any offspring receives half its genetic information from the mother and half from the father
- ☐ (c) Half a parent's alleles are contained in a gamete, so any offspring receives all its genetic information from the mother and none from the father
- ☐ (d) All a parent's alleles are contained in a gamete, so any offspring receives half its genetic information from the mother and half from the father
- ☐ (e) All a parent's alleles are contained in a gamete, so any offspring receives identical copies of its genetic information from the mother and the father

---

Genetics *(Single and Double Awards)*

Understanding genetics enables us to predict what the offspring of sexual production might be like. In the future, this understanding might help us to avoid genetic disorders. Some people believe that we should not interfere with nature. Knowing some of the important terms and knowing how the genes combine, increases our understanding of genetics and allows us to discuss this amazing topic.

Genetics affects us all. As scientists discover more about human genes, so we learn more about how genetics influences our everyday lives. This is most obvious for people with a recognised genetic disease. It is important that we know of these diseases and are aware of how they could be passed on.

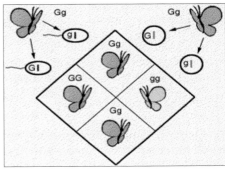
Genetic diagram

 KEY FACTS

• **Sex determination** Gender is two groups of characteristics: male and female. The gender of a human is determined by a pair of chromosomes in body cells called the sex chromosomes. There are two types of sex chromosome, the X-chromosome and the Y-chromosome, so-called because of their shape during mitosis. Males have an X-chromosome and a Y-chromosome (XY), while females have two X-chromosomes (XX). When considering gender, the sperm carries the deciding chromosome as all eggs contain an X-chromosome.

• **Genetics** This describes how our inherited characteristics are expressed. A gene is the unit of inheritance, which controls a particular characteristic, such as eye colour. Genes exist in pairs, one on each of a pair of chromosomes.

• **Alleles** These are the different forms of genes. For example, brown, green or blue eye colour. A dominant allele only needs to be present on one chromosome to control the characteristic. A recessive allele has to be present on both chromosomes to control the characteristic.

• **Phenotype** This is the physical form of a characteristic, which describes what a person actually looks like. For example, when a person has brown, green or blue eyes.

• **Genotype** This describes the combination of alleles for a particular characteristic in an organism. A heterozygous genotype is a combination of two different alleles. A homozygous genotype is a combination of two alleles that are the same.

• **Genetic diagram** This sets out a genetic cross showing the genotypes of the parents and gametes, and how they mix at fertilisation to produce offspring with new genotypes.

• **Hereditary diseases** Some diseases may be inherited, as they are caused by particular alleles of some genes. They can be inherited because they are passed to the offspring in the parents' genetic material. Huntington's chorea is caused by a dominant allele. If one parent has the disorder they can pass it on to their children. Cystic fibrosis is caused by a recessive allele. Therefore, it is possible for two parents, who do not have the disease, to pass it on to their child if they both carry a copy of the recessive allele. Haemophilia is caused by a sex-linked recessive allele. It is possible for a man to have the disease with only one allele because there is no equivalent allele on the Y-chromosome. It is possible for a female to carry the disease allele for haemophilia and pass the disease on to her sons or to pass the allele on to her daughters to carry. Red-green colour blindness is also a sex-linked recessive allele.

QUESTIONS

30 What is usually defined as 'the unit of inheritance'?

- ☐ (a) The chromosome
- ☐ (b) The gene
- ☐ (c) The mitochondria
- ☐ (d) The nucleolus
- ☐ (e) The nucleus

31 Which one of the following statements is incorrect?

- ☐ (a) Different species can have different numbers of chromosomes in the nuclei of their cells
- ☐ (b) Chromosomes are long lengths of DNA coiled and combined with protein
- ☐ (c) Genetic information is carried on the chromosomes in the form of a DNA code
- ☐ (d) Members of the same family have identical alleles on identical chromosomes
- ☐ (e) All members of a species possess the same number of chromosomes, ignoring mutations

32 On examining a photograph of a set of human chromosomes, it is noticed that one of the chromosome pairs has members that are quite different in size and shape. What does this tell us about the 'owner' of the cell?

- ☐ (a) The individual is male
- ☐ (b) The individual is female
- ☐ (c) The individual is a child
- ☐ (d) The individual is an albino
- ☐ (e) The individual has cystic fibrosis

33 What can you tell about the individual whose chromosomes are shown in the following diagram?

- ☐ (a) The individual is male
- ☐ (b) The individual is female
- ☐ (c) The individual is a child
- ☐ (d) The individual has cystic fibrosis
- ☐ (e) The individual has Down's syndrome

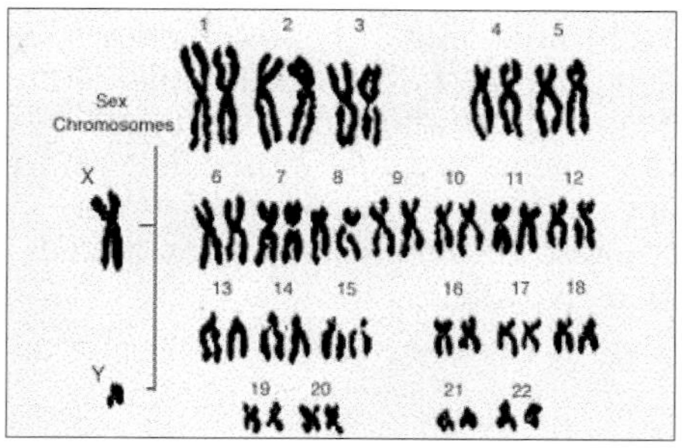

Q33

34 True ☐ or false ☐ ?
Cells of a male human contain an X- and a Y-chromosome.

35 Which sex chromosomes would you find in a cell of a human male?

- ☐ (a) XO
- ☐ (b) YO
- ☐ (c) XY
- ☐ (d) XX
- ☐ (e) YY

36 Which are the correct genotypes to replace letters A, B, C and D in the following diagram?

- ☐ (a) A=Y, B=X, C=XX, D=XY
- ☐ (b) A=Y, B=X, C=XY, D=XX
- ☐ (c) A=X, B=Y, C=XY, D=XX
- ☐ (d) A=X, B=Y, C=XX, D=XY
- ☐ (e) A=X, B=X, C=XY, D=XX

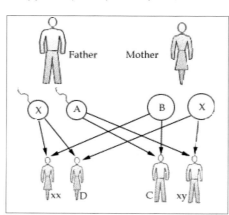

Q36

37 In the following diagram the man with the A-chromosomes mates with the woman with the B-chromosomes. What are the chances of any one of their offspring being female?

- ☐ (a) 0%
- ☐ (b) 25%
- ☐ (c) 50%
- ☐ (d) 75%
- ☐ (e) 100%

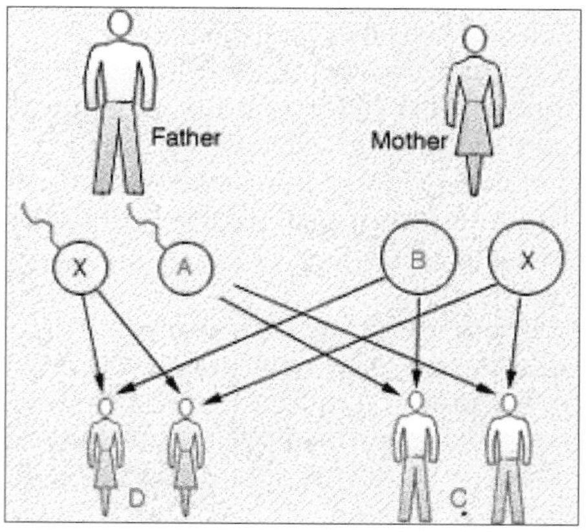

Q37

38 Mr. and Mrs Brown have already had five daughters when they find out Mrs Brown is pregnant again. What is the probability of their sixth child being another daughter as compared to a son?

- ☐ (a) 0%
- ☐ (b) 10%
- ☐ (c) 25%
- ☐ (d) 42%
- ☐ (e) 50%

39 Which of the following diseases can be inherited?

- ☐ (a) Beriberi
- ☐ (b) Cystic fibrosis
- ☐ (c) Measles
- ☐ (d) Tuberculosis
- ☐ (e) Typhoid

40 Which of the following diseases can be inherited?

- ☐ (a) Chicken pox
- ☐ (b) Huntington's chorea (or disease)
- ☐ (c) Mumps
- ☐ (d) Tuberculosis
- ☐ (e) Yellow fever

41 Which of the following diseases can be inherited?

- ☐ (a) Bubonic plague
- ☐ (b) Flu
- ☐ (c) Muscular dystrophy
- ☐ (d) Polio
- ☐ (e) Tetanus

42 Which of the following diseases can be inherited?

- ☐ (a) Gonorrhoea
- ☐ (b) Haemophilia
- ☐ (c) Hepatitis A
- ☐ (d) Pneumonia
- ☐ (e) Rickets

43 Which of the following diseases can be inherited?

- ☐ (a) Rubella
- ☐ (b) Scurvy
- ☐ (c) Sickle cell anaemia
- ☐ (d) Smallpox
- ☐ (e) Syphilis

44 Which of the following statements are true? X: Cystic fibrosis can be inherited even when neither parent has the disease. Y: Huntington's chorea is passed on by one parent who suffers the disease. Z: Haemophilia can be passed on to sons by women who do not have the disease.

- ☐ (a) X, Y and Z
- ☐ (b) X and Y
- ☐ (c) X and Z
- ☐ (d) Y and Z
- ☐ (e) X only

45 Which genetic disease causes the sufferer to produce abnormally thick mucus that may block the lungs and alimentary canal?

- ☐ (a) Cystic fibrosis
- ☐ (b) Haemophilia
- ☐ (c) Huntington's disease
- ☐ (d) Muscular dystrophy
- ☐ (e) Sickle cell anaemia

46 Which of the following diseases is caused by a dominant allele and causes gradual nervous degeneration in the sufferer?

- ☐ (a) Asthma
- ☐ (b) Cystic fibrosis
- ☐ (c) Haemophilia
- ☐ (d) Huntington's disease
- ☐ (e) Sickle cell anaemia

47 Which of the following medical conditions cannot be inherited?

- ☐ (a) Albinism
- ☐ (b) Cystic fibrosis
- ☐ (c) Haemophilia
- ☐ (d) Rubella
- ☐ (e) Sickle cell anaemia

48 Which of the following disorders can be inherited?

- ☐ (a) Colour blindness
- ☐ (b) Influenza
- ☐ (c) Measles
- ☐ (d) Meningitis
- ☐ (e) Salmonella

Higher Level only

49 Which genetic term is defined as '...the condition of an allele, that is always expressed in the phenotype if present in the genotype and cancels the effects of other alleles present'?

- ☐ (a) Full dominance
- ☐ (b) Incomplete dominance
- ☐ (c) Incomplete recessiveness
- ☐ (d) Recessiveness
- ☐ (e) Submisso-dominance

50 True ☐ or false ☐ ?
Dominant alleles have to be present in pairs if they are going to be expressed in a phenotype.

51 What genetic term could be described as '... the characteristic controlled by this allele is expressed in the phenotype only if the genotype is homozygous for this allele'?

- ☐ (a) Egalitarian
- ☐ (b) Fully dominant
- ☐ (c) Fully recessive
- ☐ (d) Incompletely dominant
- ☐ (e) Incompletely recessive

52 Which genetic term might be defined as '...a shortened description of the type of genetic information in a cell'?

- ☐ (a) The chromosome
- ☐ (b) The gene
- ☐ (c) The genotype
- ☐ (d) The nucleus
- ☐ (e) The phenotype

53 Which genetic term could be described as '... characteristics shown by the organism as a result of the type of alleles in the nucleus'?

- ☐ (a) The genotype
- ☐ (b) The phenotype
- ☐ (c) The phenylalanine
- ☐ (d) The phlegmatic
- ☐ (e) The pragmatic

54 What genetic term is defined as '...the condition when the two alleles controlling a character in an individual are identical'?

- ☐ (a) Complete dominance
- ☐ (b) Genotype
- ☐ (c) Heterozygous
- ☐ (d) Homozygous
- ☐ (e) Recessive

55 Which genetic term is defined as '...the condition when the two alleles controlling a characteristic in an individual are not identical'?

- ☐ (a) Abomination
- ☐ (b) Domination
- ☐ (c) Hemizygous
- ☐ (d) Heterozygous
- ☐ (e) Homozygous

56 It is known that, in mice, the allele for a black coat is dominant to that for a white coat. Which are the correct letters to use when representing the black and white coat alleles?

- ☐ (a) B (black) : b (white)
- ☐ (b) b (black) : B (white)
- ☐ (c) B (black) : W (white)
- ☐ (d) b (black) : w (white)
- ☐ (e) B (black) : w (white)

57 The eye colour of Siamese cats is affected by one gene, in which the allele for brown eyes is dominant to the allele for green eyes. Which of the following notations would be unacceptable for describing this situation?

- ☐ (a) Brown = BROWN, Green = brown
- ☐ (b) Brown = B, Green = G
- ☐ (c) Brown = B, Green = b
- ☐ (d) Brown = E, Green = e
- ☐ (e) Brown = EYE, Green = eye

58 In rabbits, the allele for black coat colour is dominant to the allele for white fur. A black male was mated with a white female and the resulting litter contained two white and three black babies. Using suitably selected letters to represent the alleles, what is the genotype of the father?

- ☐ (a) B B
- ☐ (b) b b
- ☐ (c) B b
- ☐ (d) W W
- ☐ (e) w w

59 Angus MacGregor has always been able to roll his tongue but his wife, Jo, cannot. They know the allele for rolling is dominant to that for the inability to roll. Their son, Bob, is unable to roll his tongue. Which of the following describes Angus' genotype?

- ☐ (a) Homozygous : TT
- ☐ (b) Homozygous : Tt
- ☐ (c) Heterozygous : TT
- ☐ (d) Heterozygous : Tt
- ☐ (e) Heterozygous : tt

60 In rats, the allele for black fur is dominant to the allele for brown fur. If two brown rats were mated, which of the following mixtures of offspring phenotypes would you expect?

- ☐ (a) 75% brown : 25% black
- ☐ (b) 50% brown : 50% black
- ☐ (c) 25% brown : 75% black
- ☐ (d) 100% black
- ☐ (e) 100% brown

61 A pea grower was unsure of the genotype of a prize red-flowered plant, so he crossed it with a homozygous-recessive white-flowered plant, and all resulting 224 seeds grew into red-flowered plants. Has he found the answer to his problem and, if so, what is the genotype of his prize pea?

☐ (a) No, because some mutations clearly occurred in the offspring
☐ (b) No, he cannot tell with the information so far supplied
☐ (c) Yes, the genotype of his prize pea is homozygous (R R)
☐ (d) Yes, the genotype of his prize pea is heterozygous (R r)
☐ (e) Yes, the genotype of his prize pea is homozygous (r r)

62 A breeder of butterflies has found that wing-colour is determined by a pair of alleles, with the dominant being green (G) and the recessive yellow (g). If she mates two heterozygotes, what would be the expected ratio of green to yellow butterflies in the offspring?

☐ (a) 75% green : 25% yellow
☐ (b) 50% green : 50% yellow
☐ (c) 25% green : 75% yellow
☐ (d) 100% green
☐ (e) 100% yellow

63 A beetle expert has noticed, in one species, that there is a gene that determines the number of spines on the back leg. The dominant allele F produces four spines, and the recessive allele f produces three spines. Genotype Ff is crossed with another of identical genotype. How many of the 80 offspring would you expect to possess four spines?

☐ (a) 20
☐ (b) 40
☐ (c) 60
☐ (d) 70
☐ (e) 80

64 In fruit flies, straight wing (S) is dominant to curly wing (s). If two homozygous straight-winged flies were crossed, what phenotypic ratio of straight to curly would be expected in the offspring?

☐ (a) 75% straight-winged : 25% curly-winged
☐ (b) 50% straight-winged : 50% curly-winged
☐ (c) 25% straight-winged : 75% curly-winged
☐ (d) 100% straight-winged

☐ (e) 100% curly-winged

65 A species of beetle has either long or short antennae. The characteristic is controlled by a pair of alleles, the allele for short antennae being dominant over long antennae. In one mating, beetles of the two types are crossed and produce a mixture of offspring – some with long and some with short antennae. What proportion of the offspring would you expect to possess long antennae?

☐ (a) 90% with long antennae
☐ (b) 75% with long antennae
☐ (c) 50% with long antennae
☐ (d) 25% with long antennae
☐ (e) 10% with long antennae

66 The presence or absence of a tail in mice is controlled by a pair of alleles, in which the allele for presence of a tail is dominant to the allele for absence. If a heterozygote mouse for this character was crossed with a tail-less mouse, what would you expect to see in the offspring?

☐ (a) 75% with tails, 25% without tails
☐ (b) 50% with tails, 50% without tails
☐ (c) 25% with tails, 75% without tails
☐ (d) 100% with tails
☐ (e) 100% without tails

67 A rat homozygous for the dominant character of black fur colour was crossed with a brown rat. If two of their offspring were then mated together what types of offspring, and in what phenotypic ratios, would you expect?

☐ (a) 75% black : 25% brown
☐ (b) 50% black : 50% brown
☐ (c) 25% black : 75% brown
☐ (d) 100% brown
☐ (e) 100% black

68 Two genetically different but pure-breeding flowers are crossed and the offspring are investigated to observe genetic variation. What is the correct scientific name to apply to the offspring?

☐ (a) The A1 generation
☐ (b) The F1 generation
☐ (c) The first generation
☐ (d) The daughter generation
☐ (e) The son generation

69 A rat homozygous for the dominant trait of black fur colour was crossed with a brown rat. Two of the resulting offspring were then

crossed. What is the correct scientific term to apply to the generation resulting from this cross?

☐ (a) Second
☐ (b) Daughter
☐ (c) F1
☐ (d) F2
☐ (e) F3

70 The allele for a purple flower is dominant to the allele for a blue flower in a certain species of plant. A homozygous purple-flowered plant was crossed with a blue-flowered plant to produce an F1 generation. If two of their resulting offspring were then crossed to produce an F2 generation, what ratio of phenotypes would you expect in the offspring of this second cross?

☐ (a) 75% blue : 25% purple
☐ (b) 50% blue : 50% purple
☐ (c) 25% blue : 75% purple
☐ (d) 100% blue
☐ (e) 100% purple

71 In peas, the allele for a smooth seed coat is dominant to that for a wrinkled seed coat. A plant grown from a homozygous smooth seed was crossed with a plant grown from a wrinkled seed, as shown in the following diagram. One of the plants grown from a seed from this first cross was then pollinated by the parent grown from a wrinkled seed. What would you expect to be the proportion of plants producing wrinkled seeds resulting from this second cross?

☐ (a) 100% plants produce wrinkled seeds
☐ (b) 75% plants produce wrinkled seeds
☐ (c) 50% plants produce wrinkled seeds
☐ (d) 25% plants produce wrinkled seeds
☐ (e) No plants produce wrinkled seeds

Q71

84

72 The allele for tongue rolling (T) in humans is dominant to the allele that results in an inability to tongue roll (t). A man who can roll his tongue marries a woman who cannot roll her tongue. If the first three children from this marriage can roll their tongues, what is the genotype or possible genotypes of their father?

☐ (a) TT or Tt
☐ (b) TT or tt
☐ (c) Tt or tt
☐ (d) tt
☐ (e) TT

73 The gene that causes haemophilia is recessive and sex-linked. If a man who does not suffer from the disease marries a woman who is a carrier of the disease, what percentage of their daughters would you expect to suffer from the disease?

☐ (a) 100%
☐ (b) 75%
☐ (c) 50%
☐ (d) 25%
☐ (e) 0%

74 The gene that causes haemophilia is recessive and carried on the X-chromosome, as shown in the following diagram. If a man who is not a haemophiliac marries a woman who is a carrier of the disease, what percentage of their sons would you expect to suffer from the disease?

☐ (a) 100%
☐ (b) 75%
☐ (c) 50%
☐ (d) 25%
☐ (e) 0%

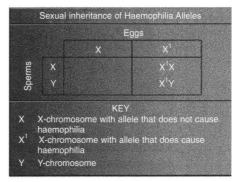

Q74

Scientific uses of genetics *(Single and Double Awards)*

Knowledge of genetics enables scientists to control the genetic make-up of organisms so that farmers use only the most productive animals and plants. This is not a new idea. For thousands of years, farmers have chosen the best seed from which to grow the next year's crops. This is called selective breeding.

Modern genetic engineering changes the genes in an organism. GM (Genetically Modified) plants have been produced that are resistant to weedkillers. Different bacteria have been produced that can, for example, convert an old newspaper into sugar or produce human insulin. Once an organism has been genetically modified, it is important to grow as many identical ones as possible. This is cloning. On 12 April 1988, genetically engineered mice used for cancer research became the first animals to be patented!

 KEY FACTS

• **Asexual reproduction** This produces new individuals with exactly the same genetic information as the parent. This is because the new individuals are produced by mitosis. Any individual produced by asexual reproduction is called a clone. There are many natural and artificial ways in which this can happen. Clones and selective breeding can greatly reduce the range of different alleles in a population. This can greatly reduce the potential to produce different varieties at any future time. There are important economic, social, ethical and practical considerations to be made when artificial techniques are used for reproduction.

• **Tissue cultures** These are used to make new identical plants from small groups of cells.

• **Cuttings from plants** These are used to produce large numbers of genetically identical plants. As the genetic material within each cutting is produced by mitosis, cuttings can be transplanted to produce identical offspring.

• **Selective breeding** This occurs when a farmer chooses the individuals he wants to breed from to produce the next generation. His choice is determined by productivity and maybe also by resistance to disease, so he is looking for individuals with characteristics such as lean meat, or high milk or grain yields.

• **Genetic engineering** This is the process by which genes are cut out of one cell and transferred to a bacterial cell, which then produces the protein coded for that gene. The protein is then purified and used. Large quantities of proteins can be produced in this way for use in the manufacture of drugs and hormones such as insulin, which is used to treat diabetes.

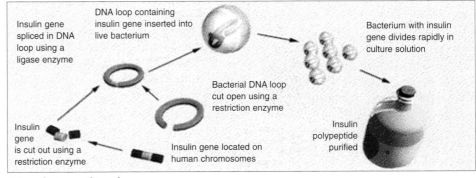

Manufacture of insulin

QUESTIONS

75 Mr White grafted a prepared stem, called a scion, from his favourite apple tree in December on to a crab-apple root (stock), as shown in the following diagram. He bound it firmly with tape and covered the join with melted wax. It grew that summer. Why did Mr White graft the apple tree?

- ☐ (a) To improve the quality of the apples
- ☐ (b) To produce bigger apples
- ☐ (c) To produce smaller apples
- ☐ (d) To produce more apples
- ☐ (e) To produce more of his favourite apples

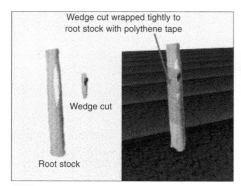

Wedge cut wrapped tightly to root stock with polythene tape

Wedge cut

Root stock

Q75

76 Andrew cut a section of woody stem from his favourite blackcurrant plant in winter. He trimmed and inserted it firmly in a prepared bed of compost, as shown in the following diagram. He covered it with a cloth and watered it occasionally. It grew and produced lovely fruit. What were the fruit like?

- ☐ (a) Identical to his favourite blackcurrant plant
- ☐ (b) Sweeter than the parent plant
- ☐ (c) Bigger than the parent plant
- ☐ (d) Less sweet
- ☐ (e) Smaller

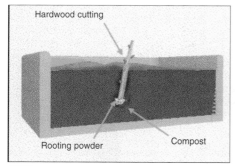

Hardwood cutting

Rooting powder

Compost

Q76

77 Which of the organisms in the following photographs have been modified by the selective breeding of farmers, so that they are quite different from their distant ancestors?

- ☐ (a) Cattle
- ☐ (b) Cereals
- ☐ (c) Pigs
- ☐ (d) Sheep
- ☐ (e) All four organisms

Q77

78 True ☐ of false ☐ ?
Selective breeding has been used by farmers for centuries to increase their yields.

79 True ☐ or false ☐ ?
Selective breeding is only good because it reduces variation.

80 Lu Kee, a chinese yak farmer, decides to use artificial selection to increase the yield of yak fleece. Which of the following does he intend to do?

- ☐ (a) Breed together only those yaks most attracted to artificial foods
- ☐ (b) Breed together only those yaks that possess the most wool
- ☐ (c) Breed together only those yaks that select each other as mates
- ☐ (d) Breed together any of the yaks by using artificial insemination
- ☐ (e) Breed only those yaks that will hybridise with sheep

81 Which of the statements about selective breeding are true? X: It increases the yields of many plants and animals. Y: It reduces the genetic variability of the selected animals. Z: It has been used by humans for at least 5,000 years.

- ☐ (a) X, Y and Z
- ☐ (b) X and Y
- ☐ (c) X and Z
- ☐ (d) Y and Z
- ☐ (e) X only

82 Selective breeding is an ancient way of improving the quality of domestic animals and plants. Which of the following would not be used to improve the milk yield in dairy cattle?

- ☐ (a) Allowing only those cows with high milk yield to produce milk in future years
- ☐ (b) Allowing only those cows with high milk yield to breed in future years
- ☐ (c) Artificial insemination using a bull known to produce daughters with high milk yield
- ☐ (d) Hybridisation of two good milker breeds to try to increase variation in milk yield
- ☐ (e) Using databases to select any appropriate sperm or eggs from all over the world

Higher Level only

83 Why is it important that the great majority of inheritable genetic information is carried on the cell chromosomes rather than elsewhere in the cell?

- ☐ (a) Because this arrangement makes the science of genetics easier as we always know where the genes are located
- ☐ (b) Because this arrangement makes genetic control of the cell easier with the chromosomes in the centre
- ☐ (c) Because this arrangement allows the genes to be easily altered
- ☐ (d) Because chromosomes are one of the few parts of a cell to be passed down reliably between generations
- ☐ (e) Because when cells divide the genes have to be split equally between two cells

84 Which of the following best defines the term 'genetic engineering'?

- ☐ (a) A change in the genetic make-up of an organism due to human intervention
- ☐ (b) A change in the genetic make-up of an organism due to human pollution
- ☐ (c) A change in the genetic make-up of an organism due to natural selection
- ☐ (d) A change in the genetic make-up of an organism due to sexual reproduction
- ☐ (e) A change in the genetic make-up of an organism due to spontaneous mutation

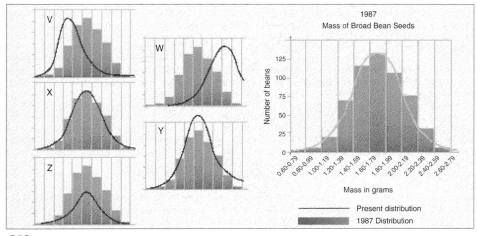

Q85

85 The large graph in the diagram above shows the normal distribution curve for a crop of broad beans produced in 1987. In 1988, a selective breeding programme began to increase the mass of broad bean seeds and therefore the crop yield. Which of the smaller graphs, V, W, X, Y or Z, might show the distribution of bean mass today, if the programme was a success?

☐ (a) V
☐ (b) W
☐ (c) X
☐ (d) Y
☐ (e) Z

86 Before 1982, the only way of obtaining the hormone insulin for human diabetics was to extract animal insulin from slaughtered pigs or cattle, but since 1982 diabetics have used genetically engineered insulin. Which of the following describes one advantage of the engineered insulin?

☐ (a) Insulin from other animals does not fulfil the same function as in humans
☐ (b) It can act as a source of energy to the diabetic
☐ (c) It is more easily available in third-world countries where pigs and cows are rare
☐ (d) It is identical to human insulin, and so cannot trigger an allergic reaction
☐ (e) It is widely available, even outside of agricultural communities

87 Diabetics, who need to inject insulin, may use a version of hormone genetically engineered to be identical to the human hormone but made by bacteria. Where would genetic engineers have found the code needed to produce the correct sequence of amino acids for this protein?

☐ (a) Within the cell cytoplasm in human ribosomes
☐ (b) Within chromosomes inside the nuclei of human cells
☐ (c) Within rough endoplasmic reticulum in human cells
☐ (d) Within smooth endoplasmic reticulum in human cells
☐ (e) Within the membrane that surrounds the human nucleus

88 In the genetic engineering of human insulin, what happens to the loop of bacterial DNA once the human insulin gene has been inserted?

☐ (a) It is replicated thousands of times by the application of ligases
☐ (b) It is genetically fingerprinted to make it suitable for human use
☐ (c) It is inserted into a bacterium where it will be treated as bacterial DNA
☐ (d) It is inserted, by injection, into the arm of a human diabetic patient
☐ (e) It is placed in a sterile petri dish, containing a nutrient agar, to grow

89 Once the human insulin gene has been inserted into a bacterium, how is it that such a large amount of insulin can be produced so quickly?

☐ (a) Each and every bacteria cell produces a very large quantity of insulin
☐ (b) The bacteria make a smaller and simpler version of the human insulin molecule
☐ (c) The bacterium makes the hormone in a totally different way to a human cell
☐ (d) The bacteria use catalysts even more effective than enzymes to make insulin
☐ (e) The bacterial population grows rapidly into thousands of cells producing insulin

90 How can genetic engineering be used to protect plants against viral attack?

☐ (a) By isolating a gene for a hard external shell and inserting it in the plant chromosome
☐ (b) By isolating a gene that makes an anti-viral chemical and inserting it into the plant DNA
☐ (c) By inserting a gene for the manufacture of T-lymphocytes into the plant chromosome
☐ (d) By genetically engineering all possible viruses so that they do not infect plants
☐ (e) By manufacturing vaccines against plant diseases and innoculating the plants

91 Which of the following would not produce insect-resistant crop plants?

☐ (a) Crossing the crop plant with ancestral types that have strong pest resistance
☐ (b) Designing a new gene that codes for a pesticide and inserting it into a crop plant
☐ (c) Dosing generations of crops with pesticide and letting natural selection take its course
☐ (d) Injecting foreign genes that allow insect-resistance in other organisms
☐ (e) The selective breeding of crop plants that show signs of pest-resistance

92 Which of the following factors need not be considered by scientists who work to change the genotypes of organisms in the laboratory?

☐ (a) Engineered organisms, once released into the wild, might transfer, via viruses, their engineered genes to wild species
☐ (b) Genes inserted into organisms in which they did not evolve might have some unforeseen consequences
☐ (c) Genetically engineered crop plants may hybridise naturally with a wild version of the plant to produce an unplanned weed species
☐ (d) Manufactured genes may have disastrous effects on the fitness of the new organism, yet still replace the original organism forever
☐ (e) The escape of newly created organisms from the laboratory before work is completed

93 How can you get two identical animals from a single embryo?

☐ (a) Immediately the egg cell has been fertilised, split it into two halves and each will develop into a distinct embryo
☐ (b) Fertilise the zygote a second time using sperm from a different father, after which two embryos will develop
☐ (c) When the zygote has just divided for the first time, separate the two new cells and both will develop into distinct embryos
☐ (d) When the embryo is 1 - 2 weeks old, expose it to a strong dose of X-rays and it will mutate into two distinct embryos
☐ (e) When the embryo is 1 - 2 weeks old, split it into two halves and each will develop into a distinct embryo

94 Which of the following is an advantage of cloning?

☐ (a) Being able to keep the organisms in a range of different habitats
☐ (b) Having a cheaper way of reproducing organisms
☐ (c) Having many organisms that are all exactly the same
☐ (d) Having many organisms that have identical genetic characteristics
☐ (e) Not having to keep organisms that are less than perfect

95 Which of the following is a disadvantage of using cloned plants as food-producing crops?

☐ (a) It increases the chances of genetic mutation in the crop
☐ (b) It increases the chances of attracting herbivores to the crop
☐ (c) It reduces the efficiency of mineral uptake by the crop
☐ (d) It reduces the ease of mechanised crop harvesting
☐ (e) It reduces the variety of alleles in a crop population

96 How might it be possible for a mare (a female horse) to give birth to a different species – a zebra foal?

☐ (a) A very young zebra embryo, fertilised out of its mother's body, is put into a mare's womb
☐ (b) A mare mates with a zebra, and there is a 50% chance a zebra foal will result
☐ (c) A mare is fertilised by a horse, but spends its pregnancy in a zebra herd
☐ (d) A mare mates consecutively, once with a horse and then once with a zebra
☐ (e) An ovum is taken from a female zebra, and fertilised in a laboratory with zebra sperm

97 One of the largest projects ever attempted in genetics is the production of a complete map of the human genes showing where they are sited on the 46 human chromosomes. Which of the following benefits would come from the use of such a complete map?

☐ (a) People would not need fortune-tellers; their future would be clear from their genes
☐ (b) Surgeons would know exactly where to operate in cases of accidental body injury
☐ (c) We could use the map to avoid all diseases, such as colds and influenza in winter
☐ (d) We could begin to understand the genetic cause of many serious genetic disorders
☐ (e) We could identify the sex of babies before birth, something we cannot do at present

98 Which of the following would be the best way of using domestic animals to improve the treatment of diabetics by genetic engineering?

☐ (a) Inserting the human insulin gene into a cow so it produces insulin in its milk

☐ (b) Inserting the human insulin gene into a cow so it produces insulin in its meat
☐ (c) Inserting the human insulin gene into a cow so it produces insulin in its blood
☐ (d) Inserting the human insulin gene into a cow so it produces glycogen in its milk
☐ (e) Inserting the human insulin gene into a cow so it produces extra glucose in its milk

99 Which of the following diseases might, eventually, be treated with gene therapy?

☐ (a) Acquired Immunodeficiency Syndrome
☐ (b) Coronary thrombosis
☐ (c) Cystic fibrosis
☐ (d) Influenza
☐ (e) Lung cancer

100 Improvements in the quality and quantity of products from animals have been achieved in many ways, both in the past and in the present. Which of the following is an ancient technique that has been used for hundreds of years to improve meat, milk, wool and other produce?

☐ (a) Chemical engineering of DNA
☐ (b) Implantation of embryos in surrogates
☐ (c) Practising artificial selection
☐ (d) Routine dosing with antibiotics
☐ (e) Supplements of growth hormones

101 Farmers select for breeding the cow that produces most milk, in the hope that her female offspring will also be productive. What is the name of this process?

☐ (a) Darwinian selection
☐ (b) Directed mutation
☐ (c) Natural selection
☐ (d) Selective breeding
☐ (e) Sexual selection

DNA *(Double Award only)*

KEY FACTS

• **DNA** This is the molecule carrying coded information that determines all the inherited characteristics. Chromosomes are made up of long molecules of DNA, which contain many thousands of genes.

Model of DNA

QUESTIONS

Higher Level only

102 What is the name of the molecule that contains the coded information that controls the order in which amino acids are assembled to produce a particular protein?

☐ (a) ADH
☐ (b) Auxin
☐ (c) DNA
☐ (d) Lipase
☐ (e) Protease

103 Which of the following is the way in which the coded information present in a DNA molecule is used by your body?

☐ (a) To control the order in which amino acids are assembled
☐ (b) To control the order in which fatty acids are assembled
☐ (c) To control the order in which mineral ions are assembled
☐ (d) To control the order in which simple sugars are assembled
☐ (e) To control the order in which vitamins are assembled

104 Which of the following statements are true?
X: Characteristics may sometimes be influenced by a single gene.
Y: Characteristics may sometimes be influenced by several genes.
Z: Genes are always made up from sections of a molecule called RNA.

☐ (a) X, Y and Z
☐ (b) X and Y
☐ (c) X and Z
☐ (d) Y and Z
☐ (e) X only

105 Which of the following is the best definition of a gene?

☐ (a) It is a length of protein that controls or influences one feature of an organism through its effect on DNA synthesis
☐ (b) It is a length of RNA that controls or influences one feature of an organism through its effect on DNA synthesis
☐ (c) It is a length of chromosome that controls or influences two features of an organism through its effect on alleles
☐ (d) It is a length of DNA that controls or influences the sex of the organism through its effect on the gonads
☐ (e) It is a length of DNA that controls or influences an organism through its effect on protein synthesis

106 In a molecule of DNA, which base is always hydrogen-bonded to thymine?

☐ (a) Adenine
☐ (b) Cytosine
☐ (c) Deoxyribose
☐ (d) Guanine
☐ (e) Uracil

107 In a molecule of DNA, which organic base is always hydrogen-bonded to guanine?

☐ (a) Adenine
☐ (b) Cytosine
☐ (c) Deoxyribose
☐ (d) Guanine
☐ (e) Uracil

108 From which of the following types of molecule is a gene made?

☐ (a) Cellulose
☐ (b) DNA
☐ (c) Lipids
☐ (d) Protein
☐ (e) RNA

Evolution *(Single and Double Awards)*

Fossils can be any type of hard evidence that proves an organism once existed. Usually, this is a rock shaped by the original organism as it slowly decayed. The oldest fossils are three billion years old. The theory of evolution is supported by a wide range of fossils that give us a glimpse into the past. When we can date fossils and detect the slight differences between them, we have evidence for evolution.

In a world without natural selection, each pair of animals or plants would need to produce two offspring that can themselves live to reproduce two more. However, all animals and plants have the ability to produce many more than just two offspring. Some will produce millions of offspring, but it is likely that most of these will die before they can reproduce. Natural selection states that any surviving offspring are those which are best suited to their environment.

KEY FACTS

• **The fossil record** This supports the theory of evolution, which states that all organisms have evolved from simple life forms that developed many millions of years ago. Fossils are the remains, found in rocks, of animals and plants that lived millions of years ago. By looking at fossils and comparing them to similar fossils from different times, as well as to similar organisms living today, we can learn how they have changed with time.

Fossil

•**Formation of fossils** Fossils can be formed in the following different ways: from the hard parts of animals and plants that do not decay easily, from parts of plants or animals that are replaced by minerals as they decay, and from parts of animals or plants that have not decayed because all the conditions for decay were not available.

• **Natural selection** Competition for food and resources, and the existence of predation and disease, mean that not all individuals survive to produce offspring. Some individuals may be more capable of surviving and producing offspring than others because they have characteristics best suited to the environment. The genes for those characteristics are then passed on to the next generation. This is called natural selection, which can lead to evolution of a species, as different characteristics become most suitable for a changing environment. However, if the environment changes faster than a species can adapt, the species may become extinct.

 QUESTIONS

109 Which of the following is not a way in which a fossil may be formed?

- ☐ (a) From parts of an organism that do not decay because of environmental conditions
- ☐ (b) From parts of an organism getting stuck in plant sap that eventually becomes amber
- ☐ (c) From the remains being slowly replaced by inorganic minerals as they decay
- ☐ (d) From soft parts of the organism being decomposed by bacteria
- ☐ (e) From resistant parts of an organism that do not easily decay

110 True ☐ or false ☐ ?
Fossils tell us about evolution.

111 Which of the following statements are true about fossils? X: They support the theory of evolution. Y: They are formed only from animal remains. Z: They can be formed from the hard parts of animals that do not decay easily.

- ☐ (a) X, Y and Z
- ☐ (b) X and Y
- ☐ (c) X and Z
- ☐ (d) Y and Z
- ☐ (e) X only

112 Put the following in the correct order (starting with the earliest event that leads to a fossil being formed): 1 – mud hardens to form sedimentary rock; 2 – tiny particles work their way into the animal's bones leading to the bone turning to rock; 3 – animal dies; 4 – animal covered in mud so decay impossible.

- ☐ (a) 3 then 4 then 2 then 1
- ☐ (b) 3 then 4 then 1 then 2
- ☐ (c) 3 then 4 then 1 and 2 at the same time
- ☐ (d) 4 then 3 then 2 then 1
- ☐ (e) 4 then 3 then 1 then 2

113 Which of the following does fossil evidence prove beyond doubt?

- ☐ (a) That Lamark's theory of evolution is correct
- ☐ (b) That Darwin's theory of evolution is correct
- ☐ (c) That evolution has occurred through natural selection
- ☐ (d) That mammoths existed, but are now extinct
- ☐ (e) That all animals were created at the same time

114 The following diagram shows the evolution of the horse limb. The sketch on the left is from a horse-type mammal that lived about 55 million years ago, whilst the one on the right is from the modern-day horse. What process is most likely to explain this evolution?

- ☐ (a) Artificial selection
- ☐ (b) Natural impressionism
- ☐ (c) Natural selection
- ☐ (d) Selective breeding
- ☐ (e) Variegation

Q114

115 Which of the following reasons explains why the fossil record is not complete?

- ☐ (a) Fossilisation only occurs very rarely
- ☐ (b) Many fossils have not yet been discovered
- ☐ (c) Once discovered, fossils are not always identified correctly
- ☐ (d) Some parts of a body may not be fossilised
- ☐ (e) They are all reasons

116 Which of the following statements about the fossil history of life on Earth is true?

- ☐ (a) They show how organisms have increased in complexity of structure through time
- ☐ (b) They show a steady decline in the number of species on Earth through time
- ☐ (c) They show that organisms decreased in complexity of structure through time
- ☐ (d) They show a decrease in the number of species of vertebrate through time
- ☐ (e) They show that the oldest forms of life on Earth were the decomposer organisms

117 If certain individuals in a population are better suited to their environment than others they will stand a better chance of survival and mating. Therefore, their better genes will be passed on to their offspring. What is this process known as?

- ☐ (a) Artificial selection
- ☐ (b) Natural selection
- ☐ (c) Reabsorption
- ☐ (d) Synapse
- ☐ (e) Ultrafiltration

Higher Level only

118 Which of the following, by causing the deaths of a large number of organisms, could be exerting natural selection?

- ☐ (a) Competition for food
- ☐ (b) Chromosome mutation
- ☐ (c) DNA replication
- ☐ (d) Genetic mutation
- ☐ (e) Protein synthesis

119 It was recently discovered that some foxes in a population have a slightly better sense of smell than others. What is the evolutionary importance of this?

- ☐ (a) That different foxes in a population are actually from many different species
- ☐ (b) That there is likely to be some variation in fox survival because of its ability to smell
- ☐ (c) That foxes have not yet evolved fully to the state where they can all smell equally well
- ☐ (d) That foxes raised in an environment with no strong smells develop better genes
- ☐ (e) That smell can be of no significance in the hunting of small mammal prey by foxes

120 Lofty the giraffe is born with a longer neck than his brothers. This difference still shows when he is an adult. Two of his brothers, Henry and Shorty, have short necks. Henry compensates by stretching to reach the top leaves of the trees. By continual exercise his neck becomes as long as Lofty's. Both Lofty and Henry mate with the same female. Which is most likely to produce calves with longer necks?

- ☐ (a) Henry
- ☐ (b) Lofty
- ☐ (c) Neither
- ☐ (d) Shorty
- ☐ (e) Both equally likely

121 Throughout the world there are hundreds of breeds of domesticated pig. Which of the following is the best explanation of how so many breeds have come to exist?

- ☐ (a) Each is the result of different environments and climates, acting on genetically identical pigs, affecting them as they grow to maturity
- ☐ (b) Each has become adapted both to local conditions through natural selection and the demands of humans through artificial selection
- ☐ (c) Each has arisen through a rapid process of mutation, occurring constantly and building up distinctive differences between breeds

- ☐ (d) In each part of the world humans need different things from pigs, and so each breed has been subject to artificial selection only
- ☐ (e) Wherever humans lived, they have found different breeds of natural pigs and have not altered these under domestication at all

122 True ☐ or false ☐ ?
Mutations can lead to inheritable variations, which can lead to evolution.

123 The peppered moth exists in two forms: a light-coloured form and a darker form (sometimes called a 'melanic' form). In a population of moths living in the countryside, well away from any town, approximately what percentage of the melanic form would you expect to find?

- ☐ (a) 2% melanic
- ☐ (b) 25% melanic
- ☐ (c) 50% melanic
- ☐ (d) 75% melanic
- ☐ (e) 98% melanic

124 The peppered moth exists in two colours: a light-coloured and a dark-coloured (melanic) form. At the beginning of the nineteenth century, the melanic form was extremely rare, yet by the end of the century it was very common in certain areas of the United Kingdom (UK). In which kinds of habitat would you expect the melanic moth to become more common?

- ☐ (a) Coastal habitats
- ☐ (b) Industrial habitats
- ☐ (c) Mountain habitats
- ☐ (d) Riverside habitats
- ☐ (e) Woodland habitats

125 At the beginning of the century the melanic (dark) form of the peppered moth made up the majority of the population in industrial areas of the UK, while in the countryside the light-coloured form of the moth was most common. If a survey were to be made, this year into populations of peppered moths in industrial and countryside areas, what do you think the results would be and why?

- ☐ (a) No change because the moth has evolved already and evolution cannot go backwards
- ☐ (b) The darker form is even more

common in the towns because evolution continues
- ☐ (c) The town populations are now 100% light- coloured because mutation has stopped
- ☐ (d) The percentage of light-coloured moths in towns has increased because of lower pollution
- ☐ (e) The percentage of dark-coloured moths in towns has increased because of higher pollution

126 What do biologists call the type of change in which the genetic composition of a population alters over long periods of time, such as the change from a light form of the peppered moth to a dark form during the industrial revolution (in parts of the UK)?

- ☐ (a) Absorptive change
- ☐ (b) Devolutionary change
- ☐ (c) Evaluationary change
- ☐ (d) Evolutionary change
- ☐ (e) Inflationary change

127 Which of the following statements about natural selection is not true?

- ☐ (a) Competition will lead to no deaths in the population
- ☐ (b) Disease will kill off some of the population
- ☐ (c) Individuals best suited to the environment survive and breed
- ☐ (d) Predation will kill off some of the population
- ☐ (e) The organisms within a species vary

128 A population of bacteria has been treated with penicillin in order to kill it off. There are, however, a few mutated bacteria that are resistant to the penicillin. Assuming the mutated bacteria can reproduce as well as the original bacteria, how would this affect future generations of the bacteria?

- ☐ (a) The mutated bacteria would mutate back to 'normal'
- ☐ (b) The mutated bacteria would remain a small percentage of the population
- ☐ (c) The population would settle at about 50% mutated, 50% normal bacteria
- ☐ (d) The whole population, normal and mutated, will die out
- ☐ (e) There will be a very high percentage of the mutated bacteria in the population

129 Charles Darwin first noticed that there are about a dozen different species of finches on the Galapagos Islands, even though the total area of the islands is quite small. Why are there so many?

☐ (a) The different islands all broke off from the mainland of South America, taking their own distinctive species of finch with them

☐ (b) A finch flock from South America was blown onto one of the islands, colonised other islands, and adapted differently to cope with different conditions

☐ (c) The human inhabitatants of the Galapagos Islands had domesticated the finches for their meat and selected for the differences on each island

☐ (d) The local volcanoes had caused such difficult conditions that mutations were very common, leading to differences in the finches

☐ (e) Each species of finch has been windblown to the Galapagos Islands, during occasional storms, from a different part of South America

Q129, 130

130 Scientists studying a species of seed-eating Galapagos finch witnessed an interesting episode. For two years rain did not fall on one of the islands, the small plants did not flower, so no fresh seeds were produced. Which of the following would you predict happened to the finch population?

☐ (a) The population size fell, the average body size of surviving finches increased, and the beak size of surviving finches increased

☐ (b) The population size fell, the average body size of surviving finches decreased, and the beak size of surviving finches increased

☐ (c) The population size fell, the average body size of surviving finches decreased, and the beak size of surviving finches decreased

☐ (d) The population size rose, the average body size of surviving finches decreased, and the beak size of surviving finches increased

☐ (e) The population size rose, the average body size of surviving finches decreased, and the beak size of surviving finches decreased

131 Which of the following could not cause the extinction of a species?

☐ (a) A new strain of disease
☐ (b) A new type of prey organism
☐ (c) Destruction of the environment
☐ (d) Increased pressure from predators
☐ (e) A new species of competitor

 ANSWERS

Variation

☐ **1** *(d)*
A typical insect has a body, which can be divided into a head, thorax and abdomen, three pairs of jointed legs attached to the thorax, and a hard exoskeleton. On many species of insect you would also find two pairs of wings attached to the thorax, two compound eyes, and a single pair of antennae situated towards the front of the head.

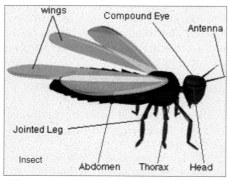

A1

☐ **2** *(b)*
Arachnids, a group of animals that includes spiders, scorpions and mites, live on land. They have four pairs of legs, no antennae, two body parts, and mouthparts with pincers.

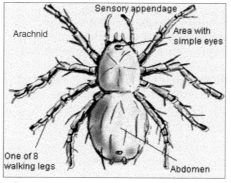

A2

☐ **3** *(a)*
A species is a group of organisms that are able to interbreed sexually to produce offspring, which can also reproduce. This definition excludes such familiar hybrids as the mule, a cross between a horse and a donkey, because the mule cannot produce fertile offspring.

A3

☐ **4** *(d)*
The frog's features are typical of amphibians: the adults have four legs (and can swim well), moist skin with no scales, and lungs, and they lay their eggs in water. The young amphibians, called tadpoles, live in water, have no legs, and breathe using gills. The tadpoles gradually metamorphose into adults as they grow legs, lose their tail, and develop lungs. Other examples of amphibians are toads, newts and salamanders.

☐ **5** *(b)*
Birds, such as the peregrine falcon, are clothed in feathers and have a beak, two legs and two wings. Most birds use their wings for flight although penguins, for example, use them for swimming, and some birds, such as the kiwi, never use them. Young birds always hatch from eggs, and, in general, the parents stay to incubate and feed their growing chicks.

☐ **6** *(a)*
Fish have no legs, spend their lives in water, have fins to help them swim, and are streamlined to ensure efficient movement through water. They use their gills to gain the oxygen for respiration from the water. There are a few species of extraordinary fish in some tropical habitats. For instance, the lungfish

found in Africa have developed simple lungs to help them stay out of water.

☐ 7 *(c)*
Mammals, such as the fox in the picture, possess four limbs and their bodies are covered with hair. They give birth to live young, and they care for their young by providing food, warmth and shelter. One aspect of this care unique to mammals is that the mother provides her young with milk from her mammary glands.

☐ 8 *(e)*
Reptiles, such as the grass snake, are 'cold blooded' and have a very dry, scaly skin for protection and for preventing water loss. The young hatch from eggs, or in some cases, as with vipers, are born live. Reptiles show less parental care for their young than either mammals or birds. Other examples of reptiles are lizards, tortoises, turtles and crocodiles.

☐ 9 *(e)*
A sperm is a male gamete produced by the testes and is considerably smaller than an ovum, which is a female gamete produced by the ovaries. A sperm can move while an ovum cannot. The chromosomes of both a sperm and an ovum are contained within the nucleus and not within the cytoplasm.

☐ 10 *(d)*
Fertilisation is defined as the moment the nucleus of the sperm fuses with the nucleus of the ovum.

☐ 11 *(a)*
An ejaculation contains a very large number of sperm but only one passes through the cell membrane of the ovum. Once one sperm has broken through the membrane, all other sperm's attempts to enter the ovum will fail. The nucleus of the successful sperm will fuse with the nucleus of the ovum: this is the moment of fertilisation.

☐ 12 *(c)*
Living organisms pass on information to their offspring's cells through their own sex cells, or gametes. Therefore, the young have similar characteristics to their parents. In humans, the male sex cells are sperm and the female sex cells are eggs.

☐ 13 *(c)*
Identical twins occur when one egg is fertilised by one sperm but, during early division, the embryo splits in two to give

two embryos. Non-identical twins, or fraternal twins, occur when two eggs are released by the woman and each is fertilised by a different sperm.

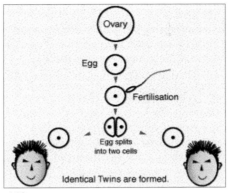
A13

☐ 14 *(d)*
Identical twins have the same inherited information, or genes. On the rare occasions when identical twins separated at birth and brought up in differing environmental conditions have been discovered and studied, it has been found that the environmental conditions have had an effect on each twin's inherited characteristics.

☐ 15 *(c)*
Vegetative reproduction is a type of asexual reproduction that occurs in plants and all the offspring are genetically identical to each other and to their parent. Many gardeners use this process when they grow new plants. One way of making a plant reproduce asexually is to use cuttings.

☐ 16 *(e)*
Sexual propagation is one method of plant reproduction. Pollen (the male sex cell) from one flower fuses with an egg cell from another similar flower to form a seed. Each sex cell contains half the genetic information from the parent. Hence the new plant receives half its genetic information from each parent.

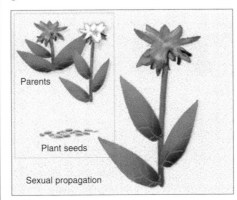
A16

☐ 17 *(d)*
Both the genetic make up, or genotype, of an organism and its environmental circumstances influence the final phenotype of the organism. No characteristic is ever influenced by only one or the other; each allele needs an environment in which to act, and each environmental factor needs cell organisation in order to have an effect. It is very common to say that certain things are 'determined' by genes, but this is incorrect.

☐ 18 *True*
Identical twins have exactly the same genetic information in all of their cells, because they are formed by a fertilised egg, or zygote, which splits into two individuals early on in cell development. Differences that might exist between identical twins can be caused by the environment's actions on them. Any mutations will be caused by the environment.

☐ 19 *(a)*
The birth weight of a baby is influenced by its genes, and the genetics of a baby is influenced by the genetic make-up of both parents. So both parents' genes are important factors in birth weight. If the mother smokes, or if her diet is poor during pregnancy, the birth weight of the baby can be reduced. The body temperature of the mother does not influence the birth weight, since all humans should have the same, or very similar, temperature.

☐ 20 *(a)*
Two factors influence the phenotype of an organism: inheritance and the environment. If organisms sexually reproduce, they generate much more phenotypic variation among their offspring than if they reproduce asexually. As a rule, a more variable environment will give rise to more variability in a population.

☐ 21 *(d)*
If a gene is changed or mutated, the characteristic controlled by that gene is also often altered. A more specific name for a change affecting just the single gene is 'gene mutation', not a 'chromosome mutation', which involves a whole chromosome, or complete segments of a chromosome.

☐ **22** *(c)*
The only factor in the list given that could cause genetic variations within a population is mutation – the spontaneous change of the genetic material due to physical or chemical damage. Mutation is the ultimate source of all genetic variation, as it is the only source of new alleles (though the process of sexual reproduction shuffles these basic variations into many millions of further combinations of alleles).

☐ **23** *(c)*
Mutation can be caused by radiation. Mutations can occur under natural conditions but are more common when the cells have undergone doses of radiation.

☐ **24** *(c)*
Visible light will not cause an increased rate of cell mutation. Ultra-violet light, gamma rays, x-rays, and some chemicals in cigarette smoke can, and often will, lead to the development of cancer.

☐ **25** *(d)*
Radiation is often used by research scientists, who are investigating the effects of mutations, because mutations are relatively common in situations where the cells have undergone doses of radiation.

☐ **26** *(c)*
Asexual reproduction, binary fission, and vegetative propagation are all examples of reproduction by mitosis, where the genetic information of the cell is copied exactly into the new cells. However, meiosis is a type of cell division where the chromosomes perform an elaborate series of movements and gene exchanges, to increase the genetic variety among the offspring. Half of the genes from the female parent are then combined with half from the reproductive partner.

☐ **27** *(b)*
Cancer is caused by cells that do not respond to their natural control mechanisms and so divide repeatedly and lose their original functions. A cancerous growth can be benign, which means the cells remain at the original site and can be removed by surgery, or it may be malignant and spread to other parts of the body. If malignant growths are caught early they may be surgically removed.

☐ **28** *(d)*
Exposure to ionising radiation increases the rate of mutation in human cells. The technique is used experimentally when

geneticists want to increase the rate of mutation in cell cultures. Mutation can cause cancer if the mutated genes lead to the uncontrolled growth of cells.

☐ **29** *(b)*
When offspring are produced by sexual reproduction, half the genetic information comes from the mother's gametes, eggs, and half from the father's gametes, sperm. Each of the parent's sex cells performed a kind of cell division called meiosis. During meiosis, one of each pair of chromosomes is chosen randomly to go into each sperm or egg. When these gametes combine in fertilisation, the offspring has a genotype produced from both parents.

Genetics

☐ **30** *(b)*
The gene is usually regarded as the smallest indivisible unit of inheritance. Most genes are located on chromosomes in the cell nucleus, and they influence the characteristics of an organism by acting with the organism's environment.

☐ **31** *(d)*
Members of the same family do not have identical alleles because sexual reproduction will have mixed the genetic material between the ancestors of the family so that, by descent, each person has only one quarter of their alleles in common with any one grandparent. Members of the same species, or family, should have the same sequences of genes on their chromosomes. Members of the same family may have identical alleles only if they are identical twins.

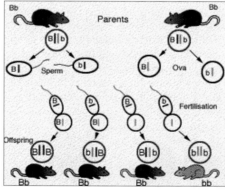

A31

☐ **32** *(a)*
A human cell contains 23 pairs of chromosomes, one of which is a pair of sex chromosomes that determines the sex of the owner. The sex chromosomes are either XX, in which case the two members of the pair appear identical and the individual is female, or XY, in which case the chromosomes look

different and the individual is male.

☐ **33** *(a)*
The individual is male as the one pair of sex chromosomes is XY. A Down's syndrome sufferer has three copies of chromosome number 21. Cystic fibrosis is caused by a gene mutation and would be undetectable in the kind of picture shown.

☐ **34** *True*
Gender in humans is controlled by one of the 23 pairs of chromosomes called the sex chromosomes. Males have an X- and a Y-chromosome, while females have two X-chromosomes. Because a female has two X-chromosomes, all her offspring will inherit an X-chromosome. Whether children are male or female depends on whether they inherit the X- or the Y-chromosome from their father.

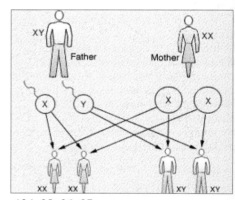

A34, 35, 36, 37

☐ **35** *(c)*
In mammals, the sex chromosomes of the male are XY, with the Y-chromosome appearing much smaller than the X-chromosome, while in the female the sex chromosomes are XX and both chromosomes look identical.

☐ **36** *(b)*
The gametes contain only one of a pair of sex chromosomes. The male gametes will contain either an X- or a Y-chromosome, while the female gametes will only ever contain an X-chromosome. Because the male gametes come in two varieties, when male and female gametes combine, there is a 50:50 chance of the resulting offspring being male or female so ensuring an even sex ratio at conception.

☐ **37** *(c)*
The gametes each contain half of each parent's chromosomes, so the male gametes will carry either the X- or the Y-chromosomes, while all gametes from the female will carry the X-chromosome. It is clear from the diagram given that

when gametes combine there is a 50% chance of a female offspring.

☐ **38** *(e)*
Every time a child is born the probability of it being a boy or girl is always 50%. The percentage remains 50%, no matter what the sex of any previously born children, unless Mr Brown is producing sperm that will only lead to girls being born, or Mrs Brown's reproductive system is killing the sperm that may lead to girls. Both these conditions are very rare.

☐ **39** *(b)*
Cystic fibrosis can be inherited, but it only develops when the recessive allele is passed on from both parents. The parents may not suffer from cystic fibrosis themselves. Its symptons include infection of the respiratory tract.

☐ **40** *(b)*
Huntington's chorea is a disorder of the nervous system and can be inherited from one parent who suffers from the disease.

☐ **41** *(c)*
Muscular dystrophy can be inherited. The cause of the disorder is carried in the genes of the parents, so it can be passed on to the child. The disease causes muscles to degenerate and they eventually become unable to contract.

☐ **42** *(b)*
Haemophilia can be inherited. The cause of the disorder is carried in the genes of the parents, so it can be passed on to the child.The disease prevents blood clotting quickly and causes extensive bruising and continual bleeding.

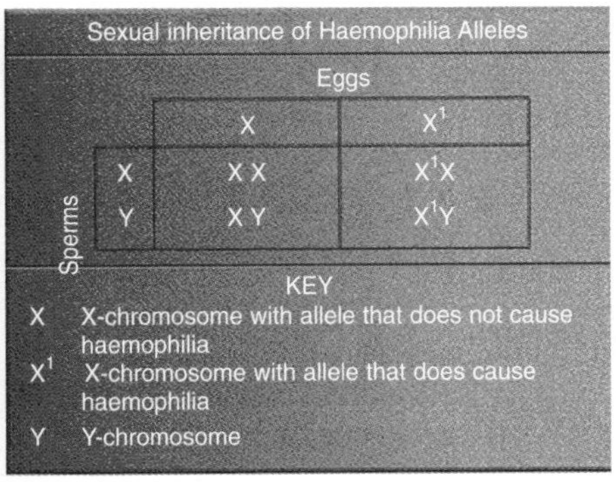
Sexual inheritance of Haemophilia Alleles
Eggs
X
X1
Sperms
X
Y
X X
X Y
X1X
X1Y
KEY
X X-chromosome with allele that does not cause haemophilia
X1 X-chromosome with allele that does cause haemophilia
Y Y-chromosome
A42

☐ **43** *(c)*
Sickle cell anaemia can be inherited. The cause of the disorder is carried in the genes of the parents, so it can be passed on to the child. When there is little oxygen around, red blood cells change to a sickle shape and these can block the blood capillaries, causing pain.

☐ **44** *(a)*
Cystic fibrosis is caused by a recessive gene located on an autosome – a chromosome that is not a sex chromosome. Huntington's disease is caused by a dominant gene on an autosome, and haemophilia is caused by a gene on the X-chromosome.

☐ **45** *(a)*
Cystic fibrosis is caused by a recessive gene located on an autosome, which is not a sex chromosome. Sufferers of the disease produce abnormally thick mucus because of a deficiency in a protein that pumps chloride ions across cell membranes. This mucus may block respiratory passages and parts of the gut. The lung congestion can be relieved by physiotherapy, and antibiotics are often taken to ward off infection. Unfortunately, many sufferers develop diabetes.

☐ **46** *(d)*
First described in 1872 by George Huntington, an American doctor, Huntingdon's disease causes terrible nervous degeneration. The onset of the disease occurs normally in the sufferer's thirties, and he or she will probably die within ten years. There is no known cure for this disease.

☐ **47** *(d)*
Albinism, cystic fibrosis, haemophilia and sickle cell anaemia are all medical conditions that are a direct result of genetic disorders and therefore can be passed on to the next generation. Rubella, often known as German measles, is an infectious disease passed from person to person by a virus.

☐ **48** *(a)*
Meningitis, measles, salmonella and influenza are all infectious diseases caused by micro-organisms that are 'caught' from other people. Colour blindness is a condition that can be inherited.

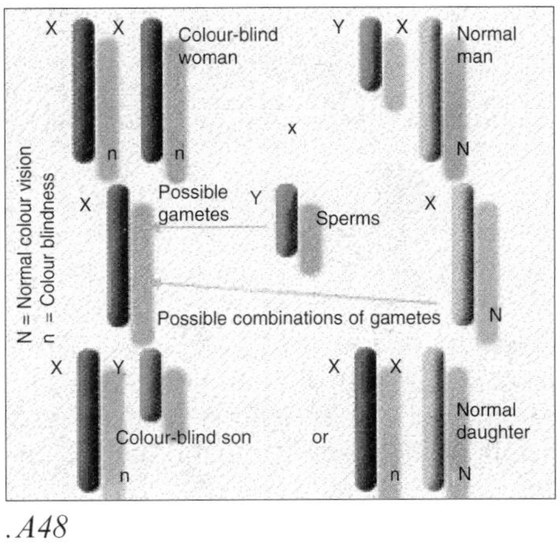
Colour-blind woman
Normal man
Possible gametes
Sperms
Possible combinations of gametes
Colour-blind son
or
Normal daughter
N = Normal colour vision
n = Colour blindness
.A48

☐ **49** *(a)*
Dominance is a term describing the relationship between different allelic forms of a gene. A body cell carries two alleles for each gene, and either one or both alleles may have a phenotypic effect. If one allele is inactivated by the other, so that it has no effect in the phenotype, then the inactivated allele is called 'recessive' and the other allele 'dominant'. When both alleles show effects, they are called incompletely dominant, or co-dominant.

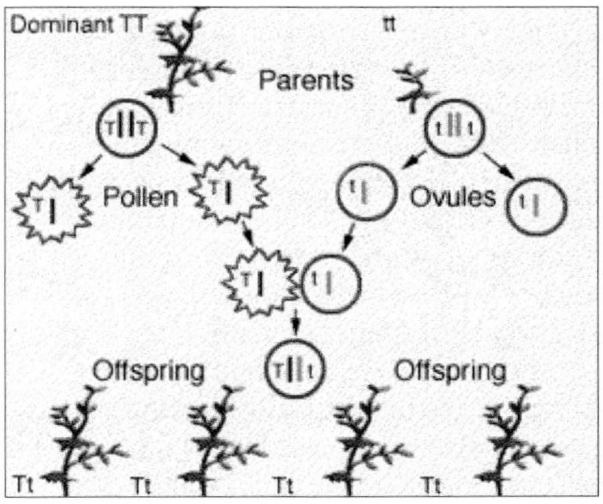
Dominant TT
tt
Parents
Pollen
Ovules
Offspring
Offspring
Tt
Tt
Tt
Tt
A49

☐ **50** *False*
It is recessive alleles that have to be present in pairs if they are to be expressed in a phenotype. Dominant alleles will be expressed even if there is only one of them in the pair and the other allele is different and recessive. For example, beetles that have short antennae, a dominant characteristic, may have one or two alleles for short antennae, but beetles that have long antennae must have two alleles for long antennae because it is a recessive trait.

☐ **51** *(c)*
When the allele is completely recessive, its effect in the phenotype will be masked if there is a different allele present. Such an allele will express itself in the phenotype only when the carrier is homozygous for the allele (homozygous recessive).

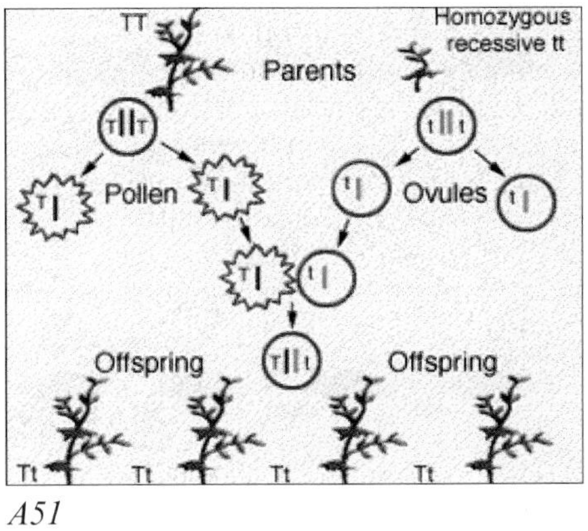
TT
Homozygous recessive tt
Parents
Pollen
Ovules
Offspring
Offspring
Tt
Tt
Tt
Tt
A51

☐ 52 (c)
A description of the specific alleles present in a cell or organism is termed the 'genotype'. We very rarely (probably never) give a full description of all the genes present in the nucleus, since we are normally interested only in one or a few of these genes. For example, saying that a particular person is Bb for eye-colour does not give a full description of the 200,000 alleles probably present in that person!

☐ 53 (b)
The genotype strongly influences the phenotype. For example, two alleles BB will produce a black coat colour phenotype in the rat, while bb will produce a brown coat. However, genes cannot determine the details of the phenotype alone, without interacting with all sorts of environmental factors, so both genes and environment always combine to produce phenotypes. For instance, in the example, it might be possible to prevent the BB black coat if we cut certain amino acids from the diet.

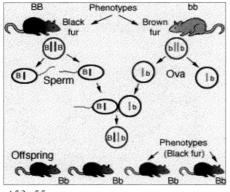

A53, 55

☐ 54 (d)
If two alleles controlling a characteristic are identical, the individual is known as being homozygous for that character, whereas if the alleles are different, the individual would be heterozygous for the character.

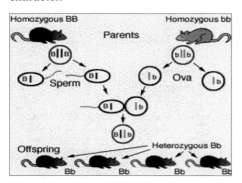

A54, 56

☐ 55 (d)
If two alleles controlling a characteristic are different, the individual is known as being heterozygous for that character, whereas if the genes were the same, the individual would be homozygous for the character.

☐ 56 (a)
We must always use a suitable symbol (usually a single letter) to represent a single gene, and different forms of that symbol to represent any different versions (alleles) of that gene. The convention for representing alleles is that if the allele is a dominant one, the capital form of the gene symbol should be used, whereas if the allele is a recessive form, the lower case form of the gene symbol should be used. For example, two alleles of a gene should never be referred to as B and D.

☐ 57 (b)
Each gene is always represented by one symbol, with alleles of that gene being represented by different versions of the symbol. The symbol chosen is up to the user, so it is perfectly acceptable to choose B or E, or even the words Eye or Brown to represent the eye colour gene. Dominant alleles are shown by the use of a capital letter, so EYE or B would denote brown eyes. Different symbols, for example B and G, must not represent alleles of the same gene.

☐ 58 (c)
The dominant gene is for a black coat, therefore the logical letter to pick to represent the dominant allele is B. Since there were both white and black offspring, the father cannot be homozygous (otherwise all babies would be black) so he must be heterozygous.

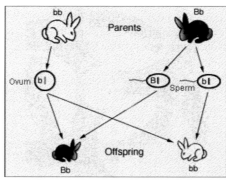

A58

☐ 59 (d)
As Bob cannot roll his tongue, Angus cannot be homozygous, so he must be heterozygous Tt. Although Bob was not

able to roll his tongue, Angus' and Joanna's future offspring may be able to roll their tongues.

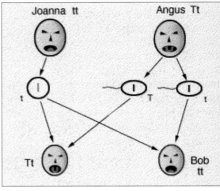

A59

☐ 60 (e)
Both parents have brown fur, so they must be homozygous for the brown allele, and they will have only the brown allele in their gametes. When these sex cells combine at fertilisation, the only possible result is that the offspring will also be homozygous recessive and so have brown fur.

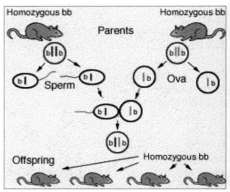

A60

☐ 61 (c)
As all the offspring had red flowers, and as the numbers of offspring in the experiment are very high (and therefore reliable), it is very likely that the prize plant is homozygous dominant (RR). However, the experiment would need to have been done on several occasions, with different plants, to be absolutely sure that this was not a 'freak' result.

☐ 62 (a)
Whenever two heterozygotes are crossed, the expected phenotype ratio of offspring is 3:1 (or 75%:25%) of the dominant trait to the recessive trait respectively. In this example we can expect 75% green (the dominant trait) and 25% yellow (the recessive trait) from the mating.

☐ **63** *(c)*
Whenever two heterozygotes (in this example Ff) are crossed, the expected ratio of offspring is 3:1 (or 75:25) of the dominant trait to the recessive trait respectively. Therefore the expert can expect 75% four-spined (the dominant trait) and 25% three-spined (the recessive trait) beetles from the cross he has carried out, which works out as 60 four-spined and 20 three-spined beetles. However, as this is all down to chance, he will probably not get exactly this number!

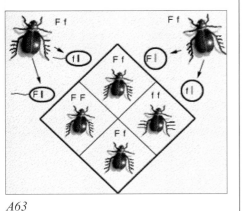

A63

☐ **64** *(d)*
If two homozygotes for the same trait are crossed (whether both parents are homozygous dominant or both are homozygous recessive), all the offspring will be of the same phenotype for that character as their parents.

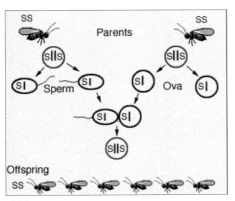

A64

☐ **65** *(c)*
We know that the parent with long antennae must be homozygous recessive (ss) in genotype, but at first sight the other parent might be either homozygous SS or heterozygous Ss. However, once they have mated, and we see that there are some offspring with long antennae, we know that the other parent must have been heterozygous. The phenotype ratio we would expect from a cross between ss and Ss is 50% long and 50% short.

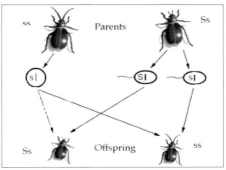

A65

☐ **66** *(b)*
Crossing a homozygous recessive mouse, with no tail, with an heterozygote will always deliver a 50:50 ratio in the offspring.

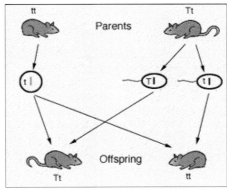

A66

☐ **67** *(a)*
All the offspring from the first cross will be heterozygous, and are properly called the 'F1' generation because they are the product of a cross between two different homozygous parents. When two of these heterozygote offspring are mated the expected ratio in their offspring (properly termed the 'F2' generation) is 75% of the dominant trait to 25% of the recessive trait. In this case, therefore, three black rats would be expected for every brown rat.

☐ **68** *(b)*
The term F1 was originally used by the 'discoverer' of genetics, Gregor Mendel, to label the heterozygous offspring that result from a mating of two homozygotes: one dominant and one recessive. When Mendel then crossed, or sometimes self-fertilised, these F1 individuals, he obtained what he called the F2 generation. These terms are sometimes used loosely nowadays, but genetics is a precise science and we should try to use these terms precisely.

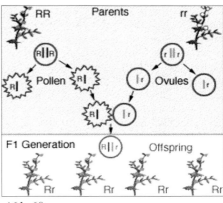

A61, 68

☐ **69** *(d)*
When Gregor Mendel crossed, or sometimes self-fertilised, the F1 heterozygous offspring, he obtained what he called the F2 generation.

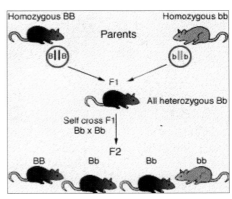

A69

☐ **70** *(c)*
All the offspring, the F1, from the first cross will be heterozygous. When you cross two heterozygotes, the expected ratio in their offspring is 75% of the dominant to 25% of the recessive phenotype. In this case, therefore, three purple-flowered plants would be expected for every plant with blue flowers.

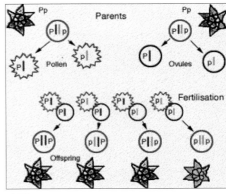

A70

□ 71 (c)

The first cross involved two different homozygous parents producing an F1 generation of all heterozygote offspring. The second mating is an example of a backcross or test cross, in other words a cross to a fully recessive individual (in this case the wrinkled seeded plant). It is likely half of the resulting offspring would be of each type, since the heterozygous F1 carries the recessive allele for wrinkledness.

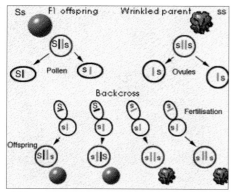

A71

□ 72 (a)

From such small samples of offspring, it is impossible to reach a definite conclusion about the father. Since he can roll his tongue he must be either TT or Tt, but either of these genotypes could have had three 'roller' children if he had married a homozygous recessive woman. It is more likely that the father is homozygous, but we can say no more than that.

□ 73 (e)

Neither the Y-chromosome nor the X-chromosome of the male carries the haemophilia allele. The woman does not suffer from the disease but does carry the haemophilia allele, so she must be heterozygous, and so we would expect 50% of their daughters to carry the recessive allele, and none to be sufferers.

Sexual inheritance of Haemophilia Alleles		
	Eggs	
	X	X¹
X	X X	X¹X
Y	X Y	X¹Y

(Sperms label on left side)

KEY	
X	X-chromosome with allele that does not cause haemophilia
X¹	X-chromosome with allele that does not cause haemophilia
Y	Y-chromosome

A73, 74

□ 74 (c)

As the diagram given shows, neither the X- nor the Y-chromosomes of the father will carry the allele that causes haemophilia. The woman is a carrier and so must be heterozygous for the allele on her two X-chromosomes. It is clear from the diagram that we would expect only 50% of their sons to suffer from the disease.

Scientific uses of genetics

□ 75 (e)

Grafting is asexual propagation (vegetative). An apple tree identical with the mature one can be produced. The apples will be identical. Many young plants can be produced readily and quickly using this inexpensive method.

□ 76 (a)

The hardwood cutting developed roots and grew. The young plant is identical with the parent plant, as no new genes have been introduced, so the fruit is exactly the same. This cheap and easy method of propogation enables us to take many cuttings from the same plant. The young plants are often called clones.

□ 77 (e)

Cereals, which are a form of Middle-Eastern grass, and farm animals have been selectively bred for centuries to bring out the desired characteristics and to dispose of the unwanted ones. For example, some cattle have been bred so that they produce as much milk as possible, and others so that they produce as much beef as possible.

□ 78 True

Selective breeding is when a farmer chooses to use only his most productive organisms to breed – the cows that produce the most milk, or the plants that produce the most seed. Any cows that produce little milk or the plants with less seed are not used for breeding. Farmers may have other criteria for choosing which organisms may breed, such as disease resistance or shorter stalks in corn.

.□ 79 False

Selective breeding is beneficial, but not just because it reduces variation. Selective breeding gives a farmer a more predictable crop and allows him to select which organisms to breed. However, if the farmer does use selective breeding, he is reducing the amount of variation in the population. If, for example, a disease strikes, most of the population might suffer.

□ 80 (b)

Artificial selection is the process that starts with farmers picking animals or plants with useful characteristics – sheep with a high wool yield, for example. These individuals are allowed to mate to produce the next generation, in the hope that the parents will pass the alleles for a high yield on to their offspring. This process is also known as selective breeding and has been carried out by farmers for thousands of years.

□ 81 (a)

Selective breeding offers advantages, such as greater milk yield per cow, or pigs producing leaner meat. We know this method has been used for thousands of years because ancient Egyptian illustrations depict domestic cats that must have been produced by selective breeding. One problem with any kind of selection, however, is that it inevitably reduces the amount of genetic variation in a population, making it more and more difficult to make further changes in the breed.

□ 82 (a)

A selective breeding programme involves many generations, often at least seven to ten, before an improved animal is achieved. The essential feature is that only the desirable attributes should be passed on, by allowing only cattle with those characteristics to breed. Whether you collect milk only from those selected animals is irrelevant. All the other alternatives listed are used in modern selective breeding.

□ 83 (d)

The chromosomes are manipulated in a careful and complicated way by the cell to ensure that all offspring receive their proper share of the genes in sexual reproduction. In asexual reproduction, the cell ensures that both new cells receive exact duplicates of its genetic material. On the other hand, most parts of a cell, for example the membrane, are not passed down reliably and precisely from parent to offspring.

□ 84 (a)

Genetic engineering is the alteration of the genetic makeup of cells by artificial or technological means. In principle, it has been possible only since the 1950s, when biologists began to understand the nature of the genetic material, but the actual practice of genetic engineering has had to wait for many techniques invented in the last 20 years and is still being developed.

☐ **85** *(b)*
If the selective breeding programme was successful, the average broad bean seed mass would have increased, and so the whole curve on the graph shifts to the right.

☐ **86** *(d)*
The main problem is that animal insulin is regarded by the human immune system as a foreign protein, and so the body may mount an immune reaction against the hormone. This means that after repeated injections, the hormone loses its effectiveness. Since genetically engineered hormones can use the human blueprint, there should be fewer problems.

☐ **87** *(b)*
To make 'artificial' human insulin, it is necessary to find the genetic code for insulin on the human chromosomes. This gene is 'cut out' of the chromosome using an enzyme, and the insulin gene is then spliced into bacterial DNA using another enzyme. The DNA loop is then put back into a bacterium, which divides rapidly producing millions of identical bacteria that all contain the insulin gene. The 'artificial' hormone is made.

☐ **88** *(c)*
The circular piece of DNA, known as a 'plasmid' and now containing a length of human DNA, is inserted back into a culture of bacterial cells. This culture will be put into conditions where the bacterial cells can grow and reproduce extremely rapidly. The ways in which the plasmid is inserted back into a bacterial cell are quite varied, but bacteria are much more willing than humans to accept foreign DNA into their cells.

☐ **89** *(e)*
The bacteria divide, by mitosis, very rapidly in their culture vessel, producing millions of identical bacteria, which possess the insulin gene and produce the hormone. With so many bacteria making insulin, a large amount is produced rapidly.

☐ **90** *(b)*
Anti-viral chemicals, such as the AZT used in the treatment of AIDS, could be manufactured within plant cells if a gene, or series of genes that manufacture the anti-viral chemical can be isolated and inserted into the plant chromosome. In a similar way, recent trials have involved inserting a gene for scorpion poison into a plant's DNA to provide a defence against caterpillars.

A90

☐ **91** *(c)*
Insect pests could develop resistance to an insecticide if sprayed for several years. Spraying would have some effect on the crop, but probably in the wrong direction, since the plants will rarely be exposed to insect attack and will not be selected to survive such attacks. All the other alternatives listed are becoming possible with biotechnology.

☐ **92** *(d)*
Geneticists must think hard about the ethical, social and safety issues concerning their work. Although genetic engineering has the potential to solve many of the world's problems, there is the possibility that something could go wrong with serious consequences. The alternatives given illustrate some of the things that might go wrong, but the answer is a nonsensical statement in the light of natural selection theory. If the new organism was unfit, then it would die out, and the new genes would die with it.

☐ **93** *(c)*
It is possible to remove an unfertilised egg and fertilise it in the laboratory. If we then take this fertilised egg and separate the two cells after the first division, two new embryos, which are genetically identical to each other, will result. This is what occurs naturally when identical twins are born. To develop, the embryos must be placed into a surrogate mother, who has been prepared to receive a fertilised egg. Both embryos do not have to go to the same surrogate mother.

☐ **94** *(d)*
Cloning produces genetically identical organisms; they will still vary slightly due to the environment in which they are kept. As the organisms will all be the same sex, other organisms will have to be kept if sexual reproduction is needed to produce variation at a later date. Cloning is not cheap, and as the organisms are all genetically identical, they are less likely to be able to live in a wide range of habitats.

☐ **95** *(e)*
The widespread use of a few clones reduces the number of different alleles in the population of a crop, so that very little genetic variety exists. The reduction may make it impossible for the species to be selectively bred, for an adequate variety of alleles might no longer exist. Cloned plants may also be equally susceptible to the same diseases. If a bacterium or fungus takes hold, then the entire crop might be wiped out.

☐ **96** *(a)*
If a zebra embryo is placed into a mare's womb, the embryo will construct a placenta and develop into a normal zebra; the horse will eventually give birth to a zebra. This technique can be used to help valuable or rare species, for many eggs can be fertilised from one animal and then implanted into substitute mothers, known as surrogates.

A96

☐ **97** *(d)*
The main use of a map of the 100,000 or so genes on the 46 human chromosomes would be to pinpoint the causes of inherited diseases. For instance, we could narrow down the genetic cause of cystic fibrosis once we knew its symptoms. We can already identify the sex of an embryo by looking at its sex chromosomes. None of the other three options listed make any sense.

☐ **98** *(a)*
In trials, domestic animals, such as cows and goats, have already received human genes enabling them to do things such as produce human insulin. If this is going to be a feasible way of manufacturing the hormone, it is most convenient to have the hormone produced in milk, since the cow does not then have to be sacrificed. Mechanisms for milking are well established, and the hormone is easily separated from the solution.

99 *(c)*
Cystic fibrosis and sickle cell anaemia are caused by alleles. If diseases such as these could be treated at a very young age, so that all afflicted cells receive the gene therapy, there may be the possibility of lifetime cures for some of these conditions. However, ethical, medical and financial problems would still exist.

100 *(c)*
Humans have practised selective breeding of domesticated animals for hundreds or even thousands of years, and must have used the technique without understanding any of the genetic principles that lie behind it. The other techniques mentioned have all originated in the late twentieth century.

101 *(d)*
Selective breeding is a process that allows only organisms with the most useful characteristics to reproduce. Those organisms with less useful characteristics are not used for breeding. Over many generations this has given us the great majority of our domestic animals and plants. The process is also known as 'artificial selection'.

DNA

102 *(c)*
Your DNA contains the coded information that has determined many of your characteristics. Half your DNA comes from your mother and the other half from your father. Your genes are made up of sections of DNA molecules.

103 *(a)*
The coded information present in DNA is responsible for joining together amino acids in the right order to make a protein.

104 *(b)*
Characteristics may sometimes be influenced simultaneously by many genes, which are sections of DNA molecules. The characteristics may show a continuous range of small variations within the population. If one variant proves to be advantageous to the others it may, over many generations, be naturally selected and become prevalent in the population.

105 *(e)*
A gene is a length of DNA that controls or influences one feature of an organism through its effect on protein synthesis. In humans, the DNA is attached to

special proteins that together make up a complicated structure called a chromosome, and sometimes one gene may affect more than a single characteristic. For example, the gene that is defective in the disease cystic fibrosis has many effects because this gene alters conditions in the lungs, pancreas, and elsewhere.

106 *(a)*
DNA has a double helical structure with the backbone of each helix being made up of pentose sugars alternating with phosphate groups. Bonded to the sugar is one of either cytosine, guanine, adenine or thymine, with the base on one chain bonding to a 'complementary' base on the opposite chain.

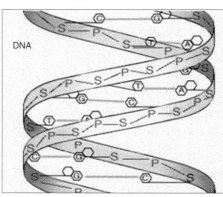

A102, 103, 106, 107, 108

107 *(b)*
Adenine bonds to thymine, and cytosine bonds to guanine.

108 *(b)*
Genes are the fundamental units of inheritance and are made of DNA molecules, located on chromosomes, in the nucleus of a cell.

Evolution

109 *(d)*
If the organism is decayed by bacteria, nothing will remain to be fossilised. Fossils are important because they provide us with knowledge of long-extinct species and provide us with ideas as to how evolution might have occurred.

110 *True*
Fossils are the preserved remains of organisms that lived a very long time ago and provide information about how organisms have evolved. For example, by looking at fossils of the likely ancestors of horses, we can see that horses have probably evolved from a smaller animal with shorter limbs and less-developed

sense organs, through a range of in-between stages to the larger animal we know today.

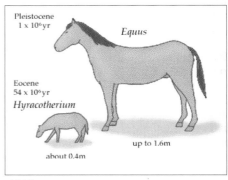

A110

111 *(c)*
Fossils can be formed in several ways including from the hard parts of animals that do not decay easily. They also support the theory of evolution by showing how organisms have changed, or evolved, over time. However, fossils are the 'remains' of plants and animals from many years ago, found in rocks.

112 *(c)*
There are two main features in the fossil formation described. Firstly, parts of the animal have not decayed as normal because one or more of the conditions for decay was missing (due to the fact the animal was buried in the mud). Secondly, when the bones did eventually start to break down, they were replaced by other materials.

113 *(d)*
The presence of fossils provides evidence for the theory of evolution through natural selection (Darwin's theory), but it does not prove the theory beyond doubt. However, fossils do show that mammoths once existed but, as they are no longer alive today, they became extinct.

114 *(c)*
The theory of natural selection states that the organism best suited to its environment will survive and pass its genes onto the next generation. For example, horses with a limb structure that enabled them to be strong, big and fast, and so best able to survive in the dry grassland environment where they now live, would be naturally selected.

115 *(e)*
There are several reasons why the fossil record is incomplete and it is, therefore, understandable that to 'trace' evolution is extremely difficult.

□ **116** *(a)*
Fossils show that life has evolved into modern species by a process of very slow change. From a simple ancestor, probably an autotrophic type of simple cell, organisms have developed an increasing complexity of body parts. The number of species present on Earth has increased and it is now thought to be about 30 million.

□ **117** *(b)*
Natural selection occurs when certain individuals in a population are better suited to their environment than others. Those individuals have a better chance of survival and mating. For example, if the length of neck varies in a giraffe population and there is a drought, as a result of which the only food left is on the highest branches of the acacia trees, the giraffes with shorter necks cannot reach the food and may die, while the giraffes with longer necks can reach the food and survive.

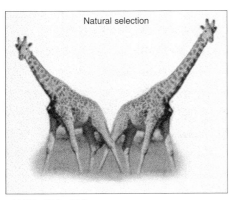

Natural selection

A117, 120, 122

□ **118** *(a)*
Competition for food, along with predation and disease, causes a large number of organisms to die. If an organism is born with a feature that gives it an advantage in either competing for food, avoiding predators, or coping with disease, then it is more likely to survive and have offspring that will carry the same advantage. This is natural selection, which is the most important mechanism of evolution.

□ **119** *(b)*
Variation will always exist in a population due to mutation and natural selection. For genetic reasons, there are always bound to be foxes with a better sense of smell than others, and these will be better adapted to some environments, because a good sense of smell increases the ability to sniff out prey. Such an ability might be especially useful in snowy winters.

□ **120** *(b)*
Since Lofty was born with a longer neck than his relatives, it is likely that this difference is inherited through his genes, and Lofty may therefore pass this on to his own calves. If a non-genetic change occurs to the body during an organism's lifetime, such as increased muscle or bone size through exercise, the changes cannot be passed to the genetic code and inherited. Therefore, Henry's long neck cannot be passed to his offspring.

□ **121** *(b)*
As humans migrated into new areas, he took his pigs with him. In those new areas the pigs would have been subject both to human's constant selective breeding for better pigs and, inevitably, to some natural selective forces from the local conditions, such as adapting to the climate and to the food available.

□ **122** *True*
Mutation might lead to evolution only if it is inheritable and useful. If a mutation is not inheritable then, whatever its benefit, it won't be passed on to the next generation. Inheritable variation means that some individuals survive better and produce more offspring, which inherit the useful variation, and these also survive better and produce more offspring. Gradually, more and more of the population carry the useful variation and evolution occurs.

□ **123** *(a)*
In a countryside area, the light-coloured trees on which the peppered moths like to rest during the day (such as silver birches) will be clean and white, so that the light-coloured moths will be well camouflaged. Birds, their main predators, will have difficulty finding them, and so the light forms will survive and leave many light offspring. The melanic moth will stand out clearly on a light bark and so be eaten by the birds, and, therefore, will not leave many dark offspring. Natural selection is at work.

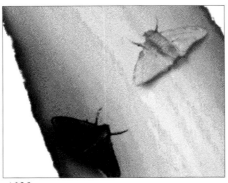

A123

□ **124** *(b)*
In an industrial area, during and after the industrial revolution, tree bark was often covered in soot, so any dark-coloured moths were well camouflaged and their bird predators could not find them. The light-coloured moths were easily seen on the sooty tree bark and the majority were eaten by birds before they could reproduce.

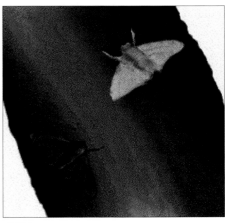

A124

□ **125** *(d)*
Recent laws controlling pollution, beginning with the Clean Air Act, have meant that soot has largely disappeared from tree bark in many industrial or urban areas, so that the dark moths are now easily seen by the birds. As the tree bark becomes lighter, natural selection has again favoured the light-coloured form.

□ **126** *(d)*
Evolution is the long-term genetic change of populations, reflected in the characters shown by those populations. Non-genetic changes are not usually regarded as evolutionary. For example, the average height of Englishmen has increased since Admiral Nelson's day due to a better quality of diet, and today we are becoming fatter on average with every passing year. Biologists believe that most evolution is caused by Darwin's mechanism of natural selection.

□ **127** *(a)*
Evolution occurs via natural selection. The theory of natural selection states that individuals within a species vary, so some individuals are less likely than others to die as a result of competition, predation or disease. These organisms are best suited to their environment so are more likely to survive, breed and pass their advantageous characteristics onto the next generation.

☐ **128** *(e)*

As the only bacteria surviving were the mutated penicillin-resistant ones, these are the bacteria that will survive to reproduce. In future generations, the population will be made up of the penicillin-resistant bacteria.

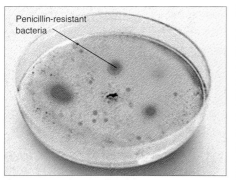

A128

☐ **129** *(b)*

While on the Galapagos Islands, Charles Darwin clarified some of his ideas on natural selection. The similarities between the different finches, he thought, pointed to a common ancestor, perhaps a flock of finches from Peru blown off course to one of the islands while migrating. These finches gradually colonised other islands and, because conditions on each island are slightly different, each new group of finches evolved slightly differently.

☐ **130** *(a)*

Normally, the finches would much rather eat small seeds that are easier to crack. With no new seeds being produced, the birds were forced to eat the larger seeds, and only the birds with larger bodies and larger beaks were able to do this. Many birds starved, so their population size decreased, and only large birds with large beaks were left. An additional interesting observation was that few females survived, because females are on average smaller than males.

☐ **131** *(b)*

Except for the introduction of a new prey species, all of the other factors listed could seriously deplete the number of organisms of a certain species, possibly leading to extinction. Any increase in the amount of food available to a population means that population numbers are likely to increase rather than decrease.

Living Things in their Environment
Adaptation, competition and predation *(Single and Double Awards)*

A community consists of all the different plants and animals living in an area. How many organisms there are and where those organisms are found in a habitat can be explained in terms of adaptation, competition and predation.

The relatively few plants or animals that survive natural selection will be those that are best adapted to their particular environment. This will mean that they can compete successfully with others of their own species and with other species. They will be able to avoid being eaten by other species because they can hide, out-run or fight off any predator.

KEY FACTS

• **Adaptation** Organisms are adapted to their environment because their appearance, behaviour, structure and way of living make them well-suited to survive in that environment. Different environments will demand different adaptations.

• **Competition** Organisms compete for resources, such as food and water, which are usually in short supply. Many organisms will die in the struggle for survival.

• **Predation** The population of prey will affect the population of predators and vice versa. If there are lots of prey, then the number of predators is likely to increase, which in turn will decrease the number of prey, and so on.

QUESTIONS

1 What will a plant growing in its natural habitat be affected by?

- ☐ (a) How much water there is
- ☐ (b) How much light there is
- ☐ (c) How much carbon dioxide there is
- ☐ (d) What the temperature is
- ☐ (e) All of these factors

2 Which of the following is the best definition of the word habitat?

- ☐ (a) The behaviours of an organism
- ☐ (b) The food supplies of an organism
- ☐ (c) The home of an organism
- ☐ (d) The population size of an organism
- ☐ (e) The mating habits of an organism

3 True ☐ or false ☐ ?
The place where an organism lives is called its environment.

4 Which of the following is the best definition of the word environment?

- ☐ (a) Only the living organisms in an area
- ☐ (b) Only the non-living features of an area
- ☐ (c) All living and non-living features of an area
- ☐ (d) All the pollution and destruction in an area
- ☐ (e) All the natural and good things in an area

5 True ☐ or false ☐ ?
All the organisms that live in a pond could be called a population.

6 Which of the following best defines the term population?

- ☐ (a) All the individuals of a particular species in the entire world
- ☐ (b) All the individuals that are able to breed in a particular population
- ☐ (c) All the individuals of a particular species living in a specified area
- ☐ (d) All the organisms, of all possible species, inhabiting a defined area
- ☐ (e) All the photosynthetic producer organisms inhabiting a defined area

7 Which of the following is a good definition of the word community as used in an ecological sense?

- ☐ (a) A set of individuals of one species that are genetically related and interact
- ☐ (b) A set of populations of many species living and interacting in an area
- ☐ (c) A set of ecosystems of one specific type scattered across many sites
- ☐ (d) A set of species of one trophic level that enter into competitive relationships
- ☐ (e) A set of species of many trophic levels that enter into predator-prey relationships

8 In species of desert cacti, leaves are often reduced to sharp spines. How might this help them survive in their desert environment?

- ☐ (a) Spines provide a way of capturing water during the cool night
- ☐ (b) Shadows of the spines shade most of the plant from the sun during the hot days
- ☐ (c) Spines collect carbon dioxide through tiny holes and transport it to the green stem
- ☐ (d) Spines protect the plant against hungry herbivores that might otherwise kill it
- ☐ (e) Spines protect the delicate stems from tumbleweeds rolling in the desert wind

9 Which of the following is an adaptation you might expect to find in a plant that lives in a very dry area, and is at risk of suffering excessive water loss, compared to a plant living in a cooler, damper habitat?

- ☐ (a) Fewer but longer roots
- ☐ (b) Increased number of leaves of the same size
- ☐ (c) Same number of leaves with larger surfaces
- ☐ (d) Thicker waxy cuticle covering the upper leaf surface
- ☐ (e) Thinner and taller stem holding leaves higher in the air

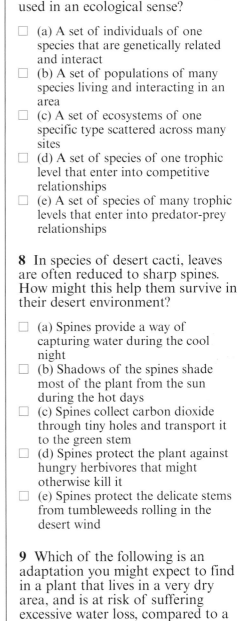

103

10 Which of the following is an adaptation you might expect to find in a plant that lives in a humid area compared to a species living in very dry conditions?

- ☐ (a) Heavily waxed surface to all leaves
- ☐ (b) Leaves reduced to spines or needles
- ☐ (c) Shallow but widespread roots
- ☐ (d) Stomata recessed in deep pits
- ☐ (e) Thinner leaves with large surface area

11 The following photograph shows a typical cactus. Which of the following is not an adaptation that helps it live in a desert?

- ☐ (a) No leaves, and so a lower surface area to avoid excess water loss
- ☐ (b) Thick, fleshy stem to reduce surface area and store water
- ☐ (c) Thick waxy coating to stems to avoid excess water loss
- ☐ (d) Catches animals on its spines and uses them as a source of nitrogen
- ☐ (e) Sharp spines for protection against desert animals

Q11

12 The following picture shows a mayfly nymph, which lives in a pond. Which of the following features is a clear adaptation to life in a pond?

- ☐ (a) Gills on the abdomen
- ☐ (b) Segmented body
- ☐ (c) Compound eyes
- ☐ (d) Two feelers
- ☐ (e) Six legs

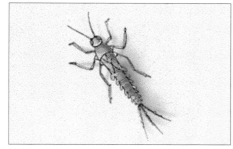

Q12

13 The following photograph shows a predatory insect that lives in freshwater ponds. Which of the following features is a clear adaptation to life in water?

- ☐ (a) Compound eyes
- ☐ (b) Long, hairy back legs
- ☐ (c) Segmented body
- ☐ (d) Sharp sucking mouthparts
- ☐ (e) Six jointed legs with claws

Q13

14 The following picture shows five animals that should be familiar, but which one would you never find in a pond unless it has fallen in accidentally?

- ☐ (a) V
- ☐ (b) W
- ☐ (c) X
- ☐ (d) Y
- ☐ (e) Z

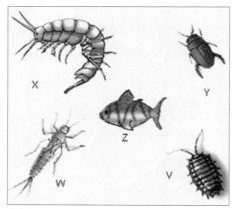

Q14

15 The following five sketches show some common animals that you may have seen in the wild. Which one would you find in a pond?

- ☐ (a) V
- ☐ (b) W
- ☐ (c) X
- ☐ (d) Y
- ☐ (e) Z

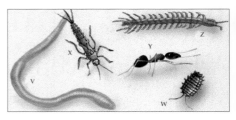

Q15

16 The following photograph shows two polar bears – mammals well adapted to life in the Arctic. Which of the following features is an adaptation to cold climates?

- ☐ (a) Ability to swim
- ☐ (b) Carnivorous habits
- ☐ (c) Good eyesight
- ☐ (d) Paired nostrils
- ☐ (e) Very large size

Q16, 17

17 The photograph above shows polar bears in the Arctic. Which of the following is not an adaptation of these animals?

- ☐ (a) They are kept warm by thick waterproof coats with several types of hairs
- ☐ (b) They are larger than other bears so their surface area to volume ratio is small
- ☐ (c) They can be shot only with a special hunter's licence in the USA and Canada
- ☐ (d) They have stiff bristles on their feet so that they can maintain their grip on icy surfaces
- ☐ (e) They have white fur so that seals cannot see them as the bears wait in ambush

18 The following photograph shows a fennec fox, which has an obvious feature that adapts it to life in a particular habitat. Which of the following is the correct habitat and reason for the adaptation?

☐ (a) It lives in deserts, where its large eyes enable it to see scarce prey easily

☐ (b) It lives in the Arctic, where its large size helps it to keep warm better

☐ (c) It lives in dry habitats, where its thick fat layer helps to hold more water

☐ (d) It lives in very cold places, where its large ears help to pick up what little heat is around more easily

☐ (e) It lives in very hot places, where its large ears help to get rid of heat more easily

Q18

19 One of the complicated things about ecological studies is that the environment of an area may change with the seasons. Which of these would be a good description of seasonal changes on a woodland floor, from winter to summer?

☐ (a) Days get longer, light levels increase, temperatures get higher

☐ (b) Days get longer, light levels get higher then lower, temperatures get higher

☐ (c) Days get shorter, light levels get higher, temperatures get lower

☐ (d) Days get longer, light levels get less, temperatures get higher

☐ (e) Days get longer, light levels get less then more, temperatures get higher

20 Which of the following adaptations are necessary in plants living in woodland in Britain?

☐ (a) An overwintering bulb, which looks like a spring onion, discouraging herbivores

☐ (b) A bright flower, which acts as a signal warning deer not to eat the poison leaves

☐ (c) A growing season finished by May, when the woodland floor becomes shaded by trees

☐ (d) Bright flowers to attract mammals, such as deer, that will eat and disperse the seeds

☐ (e) Deep roots because water is often very scarce in this type of habitat

21 Bluebells grow on a woodland floor, which can be shady. Which of the following describes how they are adapted to this environment?

☐ (a) Growth phase from early spring to late spring

☐ (b) Growth phase from early spring to autumn

☐ (c) Growth phase from summer to midwinter

☐ (d) High respiration and photosynthesis rates

☐ (e) Low respiration and photosynthesis rates

22 Why do many plants found on the floor of woodland have bulbs, corms, or other overwintering structures?

☐ (a) Leaves can withdraw into these structures on cold days and so survive

☐ (b) These organs anchor the plant much more firmly into the soil than would a root

☐ (c) These organs are their only method of reproduction

☐ (d) They act as a home for important nitrogen-fixing bacteria, which help the plant

☐ (e) They store food to allow very fast growth in spring, before the plants are shaded by trees

23 Competition occurs when one organism uses some of a limited resource, so that other organisms must then make do with less of that resource. Which of the following would not cause competition between two male polar bears?

☐ (a) Fertile female polar bears
☐ (b) Good fishing holes in the ice
☐ (c) Oxygen in the atmosphere
☐ (d) Suitable banks of snow for dens
☐ (e) Young seals unaware of danger

24 Which of the following are plants most likely to compete for?

☐ (a) Carbon dioxide
☐ (b) Food
☐ (c) Light
☐ (d) Nitrogen
☐ (e) Oxygen

25 If there is no change in the habitat in which a population of rabbits live, which of the following is the most likely to lead to greater competition for food?

☐ (a) An outbreak of myxomatosis

☐ (b) An increase in the rabbit population

☐ (c) An increase in the badger population

☐ (d) An increase in the population of foxes

☐ (e) Spraying the habitat with insecticide

26 A pair of breeding animals are introduced to an island. The animals have no predators on this island, but do have a plentiful food supply. What would you expect to happen to the numbers of this animal over the next few generations?

☐ (a) They would remain at two

☐ (b) They would increase to about 10, then remain stable

☐ (c) They would go up and down in a regular fashion

☐ (d) They would have died out by the fifth generation

☐ (e) There would be a population explosion

27 The following diagram shows a typical growth curve for a bacterial colony. What is going on at the time marked X on the diagram?

☐ (a) The colony is completely dead

☐ (b) There are more deaths than births

☐ (c) There are more births than deaths

☐ (d) Bacterial births and deaths are equal

☐ (e) Bacterial births and deaths are zero

Q27

28 The following diagram shows a population growth curve for a colony of rabbits. Which letter shows the part of the curve where the rate of growth is greatest?

☐ (a) V
☐ (b) W
☐ (c) X
☐ (d) Y
☐ (e) Z

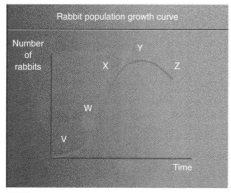

Q28

29 The following diagram shows a population growth curve for a rabbit colony. Which letter shows the part of the curve where the population is declining?

☐ (a) V
☐ (b) W
☐ (c) X
☐ (d) Y
☐ (e) Z

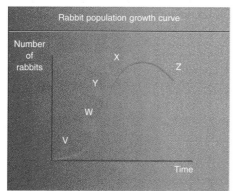

Q29

30 The following diagram shows a growth curve for a bacterial colony in a container of nutrient broth. Which letter shows the part of the curve where the population size is not increasing?

☐ (a) V
☐ (b) W
☐ (c) X
☐ (d) Y
☐ (e) Z

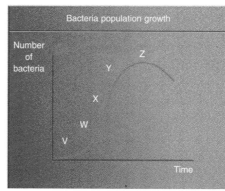

Q30

31 The photograph below shows a small floating pond plant, duckweed. This plant reproduces vegetatively by splitting in two once the plant reaches a certain size. Assuming that the number of individuals doubles each day, and it took 15 days to cover half the pond shown, how many more days will it take to cover the whole surface?

Q31

☐ (a) 1 more day
☐ (b) 2 more days
☐ (c) 15 more days
☐ (d) 20 more days
☐ (e) 30 more days

32 An experiment was set up to investigate the effects of overcrowding on cress seedlings. Damp filter paper was put in a dish and 200 cress seeds were randomly distributed across the filter paper, as shown in the following diagram. It was then left in a warm cupboard. After two days, 15 seeds had germinated. How might the experimental design be improved?

☐ (a) 100 seeds should have been put in the dish
☐ (b) 300 seeds should have been put in the dish
☐ (c) The dish should have been left for four days, not two
☐ (d) The seed numbers in several dishes should have been varied
☐ (e) Some seeds should have been put in the light

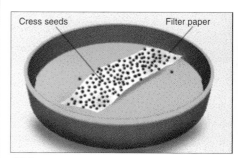

Q32

Human impact on the environment *(Single and Double Awards)*

All humans will affect the environment in which they live. The larger the population of humans and the higher their standard of living, the greater that effect is on the environment. Humans use land for housing, farming, industrial buildings, quarrying and dumping waste. They may pollute the surrounding environment by releasing sewage, fertilisers and toxic chemicals into water, by releasing gases into the air, and by using pesticides and herbicides on the land.

The list of how humans impact on the environment is endless: acid rain, oil spillage, nuclear waste, greenhouse effect, eutrophication and ozone. We also impact on a smaller scale in many ways. For example, if a balloon falls into the ocean, it can resemble a jelly fish and may be eaten, so causing the death of the animal concerned because it cannot be digested.

 ## KEY FACTS

• **Greenhouse effect** This warming of the Earth is being increased by deforestation, and by burning fossil fuels, which releases carbon dioxide into the atmosphere. A few degrees rise in the Earth's temperature will bring big changes to climate and sea levels.

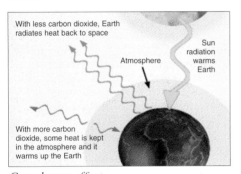

Greenhouse effect

• **Methane gas** This is produced by bacteria living in cattle's stomachs and in rice fields. Also, it increases the greenhouse effect.

• **Acid rain** This is partly caused by sulphur dioxide gas, released when fossil fuels are burnt.

• **Eutrophication** This is the rapid growth of algae caused by fertilisers and untreated sewage getting into water systems. As a result, many organisms die because oxygen is used up by the bacteria decaying the algae or raw sewage.

• **Depletion of the ozone layer** Widely used chemicals are reducing the shielding effect of the ozone layer, which leads to an ever increasing number of people suffering from skin cancer.

QUESTIONS

33 Which of the following is not a basic need of a human being?

- ☐ (a) Air
- ☐ (b) Computer
- ☐ (c) Nutrition
- ☐ (d) Shelter
- ☐ (e) Warmth

34 Which of the following is not a type of pollution?

- ☐ (a) Carbon monoxide from a car exhaust
- ☐ (b) Cow dung leaking from a storage tank
- ☐ (c) Fox droppings in a woodland
- ☐ (d) Paper litter in a school playground
- ☐ (e) Pneumatic drills on a building site

35 Which of the following would be the most likely cause if a town suddenly suffers an epidemic of bacterial disease?

- ☐ (a) Acid rain from the operation of two new coal-fired power stations
- ☐ (b) Agricultural fertilisers leaching and draining into the water supply
- ☐ (c) Radioactive gases emitted from a local reprocessing plant by accident
- ☐ (d) Sulphurous discharges from a steelworks draining into the local water supply
- ☐ (e) Untreated sewage in drinking water due to a breakdown in the local works

36 Which of the following human activities does not lead to land being lost to the animals and plants that originally lived there?

- ☐ (a) Building a new town on a green field site
- ☐ (b) Dumping waste in landfill sites
- ☐ (c) Establishing a new nature reserve
- ☐ (d) Growing a crop such as corn or wheat
- ☐ (e) Mining of a mineral such as gravel

37 Instead of throwing used things away, we are increasingly encouraged to recycle them. Which of the following is an example of recycling rather than re-use?

- ☐ (a) Keeping matchboxes as housing for your pet flea collection
- ☐ (b) Putting out the empty milk bottles for the milkman to collect
- ☐ (c) Taking empty wine bottles to the local bottle bank
- ☐ (d) Using empty jam jars, or similar containers, to put home-made jam in
- ☐ (e) Using the backs of old worksheets for rough notes in a lesson

38 The following photograph shows a recycling site. Which of the following is not always a benefit of recycling household waste?

- ☐ (a) It saves energy in the extraction of fresh supplies of raw materials
- ☐ (b) It saves money since raw materials do not have to be purchased
- ☐ (c) It saves natural landscapes since fewer have to be sacrificed to extract resources
- ☐ (d) It saves landfill dump space, which is otherwise filling up very quickly
- ☐ (e) It saves pollution, since there are fewer waste materials to leach into groundwater

Q38

39 Which of the following cannot be readily recycled?

- ☐ (a) Aluminium
- ☐ (b) Energy
- ☐ (c) Glass
- ☐ (d) Iron
- ☐ (e) Paper

40 Which of the following would be known as a renewable resource, in the sense that we can keep replacing it over the short or medium term?

- ☐ (a) Coal
- ☐ (b) Iron ore
- ☐ (c) Natural gas
- ☐ (d) Oil
- ☐ (e) Timber

41 In the last century, the human population has increased dramatically and so has the standard of living in many countries. Which of the following has been a consequence of these changes?

- ☐ (a) Less variety of industrial pollutants present
- ☐ (b) Less industrial waste produced
- ☐ (c) Less pollution of the environment
- ☐ (d) More non-renewable resources consumed
- ☐ (e) Less non-renewable resources consumed

42 The sign at the top of the next column is found near a reservoir in the Lake District, England, which supplies drinking water to Manchester. What is the main reason for the sign?

- ☐ (a) The water might become contaminated with dangerous germs by animals and swimmers
- ☐ (b) The water might become dirty and lose its attractive appearance for hikers
- ☐ (c) Swimmers, dogs and other animals might drown in the deep water
- ☐ (d) The fish in the water might become scared if people and other animals create noise
- ☐ (e) The visitors and swimmers might drink too much of the free water without paying

Q42

Higher Level only

43 Which of the following is not an advantage of sewage disposal?
- ☐ (a) Agricultural production is higher
- ☐ (b) Personal hygiene is much less trouble
- ☐ (c) Serious diseases are less common
- ☐ (d) Towns are more pleasant to inhabit
- ☐ (e) Vermin, such as rats, are less common

44 Sewage treatment is used to treat domestic and industrial wastes before they are released into rivers and seas. Which of the following is the most important reason for such treatment?

- ☐ (a) It adds increased oxygen into the water before it enters the rivers
- ☐ (b) It adds additional invertebrate food to the water before it enters rivers
- ☐ (c) It removes dangerous bacteria from the water before it enters the rivers
- ☐ (d) It removes organic matter that deoxygenates the water before it enters rivers
- ☐ (e) It removes toxic chemicals from the water before it enters the rivers

45 A common feature along many of our rivers is a set of steps that the water tumbles over, called a weir. What is the main purpose of a weir on a river?

- ☐ (a) To add sound to the total river experience
- ☐ (b) To discourage people from trying to swim
- ☐ (c) To oxygenate the river water by tumbling
- ☐ (d) To prevent upriver access to canoeists
- ☐ (e) To sample fish species for scientific studies

46 Which of the following structures are you likely to find immediately upstream of a river weir?

- ☐ (a) Factory producing heavy metal pollutants
- ☐ (b) Power station burning fossil fuels
- ☐ (c) Power station using nuclear fuels
- ☐ (d) Recreational centre with blue canoes
- ☐ (e) Sewage outlet from a treatment works

47 A number of changes occur in the river downstream from any sewage outflow. Which of the following would not be such a change?

- ☐ (a) Increase in the number of bacteria
- ☐ (b) Increase in the number of people fishing
- ☐ (c) Decrease in the number of fish
- ☐ (d) Decrease in the oxygen content of the water
- ☐ (e) No change in the number of water birds

48 Farmers frequently use fertilisers on their land. In wet climates, such as the UK, some of this is washed off into lakes, rivers and streams. Which of the following effects will not be caused by this leaching of fertiliser into rivers and streams?

- ☐ (a) A build up of foam on the water surface
- ☐ (b) A decrease in dissolved oxygen
- ☐ (c) Increased rate of bacterial growth
- ☐ (d) Increased growth of water plants
- ☐ (e) Death of fish and invertebrates

49 True ☐ or false ☐ ? Eutrophication might cause a river or a pond to run out of oxygen.

50 Which of the following could account for the fact that flooding in Bangladesh has become more common and more severe in recent years?

- ☐ (a) Damming of rivers in the uplands has increased the velocity of the water flow
- ☐ (b) Deforestation of hillsides has increased water run-off in the lowlands
- ☐ (c) Monsoon rainfall has increased over recent years as a result of global warming

(d) Soil erosion means that the soil cannot hold as much water as in previous years

(e) The water demands of the population are lower, leading to oversupply

51 The following photographs show two views of a nature reserve. Why were young trees removed from the grassland in the front of the photographs?

(a) The only way the management can raise funds is by selling the tree seedlings

(b) The trees may blow down in a gale and injure some of the nature reserve visitors

(c) The trees will shed their leaves in autumn and make the whole reserve untidy

(d) The open area is a valuable habitat and trees will drive away the more interesting species

(e) One important function of nature reserves is providing open areas to play frisbee

Q51

52 Which of the following is not due to acid rain on a community of plants?

(a) Increased growth rate of wood and twigs

(b) Poor root growth and development

(c) Poor flowering and fruiting success

(d) Stunted growth of the tops of conifer trees

(e) Yellowing and poor growth of the leaves

53 Which of the following pH values is typical of non-polluted rain?

(a) pH of 5
(b) pH of 6.5
(c) pH of 7.5
(d) pH of 8
(e) pH of 9

54 Which of the following gases is one of the causes of acid rain, a type of pollution that causes the kind of damage shown in the photograph?

(a) Carbon dioxide
(b) Carbon monoxide
(c) Methane
(d) Lead tetraethyl vapour
(e) Sulphur dioxide

Q54

55 True ☐ or false ☐ ?
Burning some fossil fuels releases a poisonous gas, sulphur dioxide.

56 Air pollution has been a problem through the 20th century. Many organisms are affected by this pollution, but some are affected more than others. There is one group of organisms that is particularly sensitive to air pollution, and which has been used to give a measure of the extent of air pollution. What is the name of this group?

(a) Birds of prey
(b) Deciduous trees
(c) Herbaceous plants
(d) Lichens
(e) Moths and butterflies

57 Which of the following may be damaged by air pollution?

(a) The alveoli
(b) The gaseous exchange surface in a fly
(c) The gaseous exchange surface in a bird
(d) The skin of an earthworm
(e) All the options

58 Which of the following components of car exhaust fumes is known to cause brain damage in young children?

(a) Carbon dioxide
(b) Carbon monoxide
(c) Lead tetraethyl
(d) Nitrogen oxides
(e) Water vapour

59 Which of the following polluting gases is not caused by car engines?

(a) Benzene
(b) Carbon dioxide
(c) Carbon monoxide
(d) Methane
(e) Nitrogen oxides

60 One important pollutant produced from vehicles is the greenhouse gas, carbon dioxide. Which of the following would not help in reducing this problem?

(a) Better public transport in cities
(b) Encouragement of car sharing schemes
(c) Imposition of lower speed limits
(d) Increased taxation on large engines
(e) Installation of more catalytic converters

61 There has been much environmental concern about the greenhouse effect, in which a build-up of certain gases in the atmosphere stops heat escaping from the Earth. Which of the following would not happen as a result of this global warming?

(a) Changing distribution of diseases
(b) Flooding of low-lying areas
(c) Increasing areas of dry desert
(d) Increased global rainfall
(e) Increased risks of skin cancer

62 Which of the following statements about greenhouse gases could be correct?

(a) Chlorofluorocarbon (CFC) levels have risen due to an increase in fumes from car exhausts

(b) Carbon dioxide levels have risen due to an increase in rice production

(c) Methane levels have risen due to an increase in rice production

(d) Methane levels have risen due to an increase in fumes from car exhausts

(e) Methane levels have risen due to an increase in deforestation

109

63 In the greenhouse effect, sunlight energy arrives at the Earth from the Sun, and warms both the atmosphere and the Earth's surface. Energy is then re-radiated back into space, but at longer wavelengths. The greenhouse gases in the atmosphere absorb some of this longer-wave energy, so warming the atmosphere. Which of the following combinations of gases are thought to be the major causes of the greenhouse effect?

☐ (a) CFCs and carbon dioxide
☐ (b) CFCs and methane
☐ (c) CFCs and sulphur dioxide
☐ (d) Methane and carbon dioxide
☐ (e) Sulphur dioxide and carbon dioxide

64 The following diagram shows a graph of changes in the carbon dioxide levels in the atmosphere since 1960. Which of the following could not be a possible reason for these changes?

☐ (a) Increased deforestation
☐ (b) Increased demand for electricity
☐ (c) Increased pollution of oceanic algae
☐ (d) Increased use of aerosol sprays
☐ (e) Increased use of the motor car

Q64, 65

65 The graph shows how the levels of atmospheric carbon dioxide have risen since 1960. In addition to the gradual rise, we can see that the levels fluctuate from season to season. To what are these seasonal changes due?

☐ (a) Increased output of carbon dioxide from animal respiration in winter
☐ (b) Increased uptake by photosynthesis of plants in summer
☐ (c) Decreased rate of both respiration and photosynthesis during winter
☐ (d) Decreased output of carbon dioxide from animal respiration in winter
☐ (e) Decreased uptake by photosynthesis in plants during summer

66 Which of the following is a greenhouse gas produced by animals or their waste?

☐ (a) Ammonia
☐ (b) Carbon monoxide
☐ (c) Hydrogen
☐ (d) Methane
☐ (e) Ozone

67 Which atmospheric gas has increased due to an increase in the number of rice-fields and cows in the world?

☐ (a) Carbon dioxide
☐ (b) Carbon monoxide
☐ (c) Methane
☐ (d) Nitrogen dioxide
☐ (e) Oxygen

68 Which of these pollutants does not cause the depletion of the atmospheric ozone?

☐ (a) Chlorofluorocarbons
☐ (b) Nitrogen
☐ (c) Nitrogen oxide
☐ (d) Nitrogen dioxide
☐ (e) Nitrous oxide

69 The following list includes several valid reasons given for why people may want to create nature reserves. Which of these is the reason for the creation of most of the reserves in the world?

☐ (a) Considerations of aesthetic beauty
☐ (b) Considerations of future economic value
☐ (c) Considerations of nature's ethical rights
☐ (d) Considerations of pollution monitoring
☐ (e) Considerations of rare species and habitats

70 Which of the following is a good argument for conserving hedgerows?

☐ (a) Hedges are a breeding ground for weeds and pests of crops
☐ (b) Hedges are a good place for game, such as partridges, to find cover
☐ (c) Hedges make harvesting and other farming operations more difficult
☐ (d) Hedges will shade crops at the edge of fields, reducing crop yields
☐ (e) Hedges will take up a lot of room, which crops might otherwise occupy

71 Which of the following is a main reason for the establishment of a National Park?

☐ (a) To conserve a particular rare wild flower
☐ (b) To maintain a large area of undeveloped land
☐ (c) To preserve a specialised and rare habitat
☐ (d) To provide an area for outdoor rambling
☐ (e) To restrict public access to a hunting site

Energy and nutrient transfer *(Double Award only)*

The German zoologist Karl Semper introduced the idea of food chains back in 1891. A food chain gives us an easy way of representing the feeding relationships between all of the organisms in one area. It also enables us to understand where our food comes from and how we might affect our environment if we destroy any one part of it. For example, an insecticide was used in Borneo to get rid of the mosquito that carried malaria. It worked. However, the insecticide also killed the natural predator of an insect that feeds on the thatched roofs of the houses. Before long, the thatched roofs collapsed! This shows the interrelationship between living organisms and the importance of food chains.

Some people, having read about energy transfer, decide that humans should all be vegetarians. Can you work out why they believe this?

However, an oak tree is very large and if we look at a pyramid of biomass, showing the mass of an oak tree that supports a number of insects and birds, then the pyramid shape is found again.

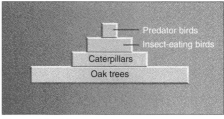

Pyramid of biomass

 ## KEY FACTS

• **A food chain** This summarises the feeding relationship between several different organisms in a habitat. The arrows in a food chain mean "is eaten by", for example:
grass → rabbits → fox

• **A pyramid of numbers** This is another way of simplifying most habitats, which contain a complicated range of plants and animals feeding off each other. If the numbers of organisms at each level are counted, a pyramid of numbers can be built. For example, there is usually more grass than rabbits, and more rabbits than foxes. Each type of organism is usually larger than what it eats and so has to eat several to get enough food. So a pyramid of numbers usually looks like a pyramid.

• **A pyramid of biomass** Sometimes the pyramid of numbers does not look like a pyramid, for example:
oak tree → insect → insect-eating birds (e.g. hawks)
In this example, the pyramid of numbers has an odd base as one oak tree supports many insects and birds.

• **Energy transfer** Energy is transferred through an ecosystem. Energy enters an ecosystem as light energy, which plants convert into food energy in photosynthesis. Plants are eaten by animals in the ecosystem, so transferring the food energy. At each level in a food chain, 90% of the energy is lost. Some of the energy is lost as heat, while some food cannot be digested and its energy is lost in waste materials. Birds and mammals always need to use energy to maintain high body temperatures, and so even more energy is lost.

 ## QUESTIONS

72 What type of living organism is at the start of almost every food chain?

- ☐ (a) Carnivores
- ☐ (b) Green plants
- ☐ (c) Herbivores
- ☐ (d) Insects
- ☐ (e) Mammals

73 Which of the following could properly be termed as an ecological 'producer'?

- ☐ (a) Cow
- ☐ (b) Lion
- ☐ (c) Locust
- ☐ (d) Man
- ☐ (e) Oak tree

74 True ☐ or false ☐ ?
In the following food chain, the algae are the primary consumers.

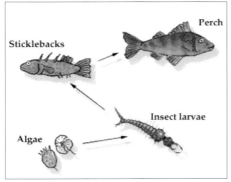

Q74

75 Apart from 'sheep', what other name might a biologist apply to the creatures shown in the following photograph?

- ☐ (a) Carnivore
- ☐ (b) Herbivore
- ☐ (c) Predator
- ☐ (d) Secondary consumer
- ☐ (e) Tertiary consumer

Q75, 76

76 The photograph above shows sheep grazing. What other term might an ecologist apply to these animals?

- ☐ (a) Omnivore
- ☐ (b) Predator
- ☐ (c) Primary consumer
- ☐ (d) Producer
- ☐ (e) Secondary consumer

77 Which of the following events would not allow an increase in the population of caterpillars on an oak tree?

☐ (a) Absence of caterpillar predators
☐ (b) Absence of fatal caterpillar diseases
☐ (c) Increasing population of a competitor
☐ (d) Large crop of oak leaves
☐ (e) Mild winter so that lots of eggs survived

78 Which of the following is the best definition of the word predator?

☐ (a) Eats only parts of plants, not killing them
☐ (b) Eats only parts of animals, not killing them
☐ (c) Eats dead animals, after others killed them
☐ (d) Eats only animals, after first killing them
☐ (e) Eats only its own species, after killing them

79 Which of the following ecological terms best describes the animal shown eating in the following photograph?

☐ (a) Consumer
☐ (b) Herbivore
☐ (c) Omnivore
☐ (d) Parasite
☐ (e) Producer

Q79

80 Which is the secondary consumer in the following food chain? Oak tree → Caterpillar → Robin → Hawk

☐ (a) Caterpillar
☐ (b) Hawk
☐ (c) Oak tree
☐ (d) Robin
☐ (e) Sunlight

81 Which of these organisms, in a food chain from a local stream, is a herbivore? Algae → Insect larvae → Stickleback → Perch

☐ (a) Algae
☐ (b) Insect larvae
☐ (c) Perch
☐ (d) Stickleback
☐ (e) Sunlight

82 A typical food web is shown in the following diagram. A diagram like this teaches us that living things interact with each other, and that changes to one population may affect many others. In this food web, which of the following do you think would happen if the rabbits became extinct due to myxomatosis disease?

☐ (a) Increase in the numbers of moles
☐ (b) Decrease in the number of slugs
☐ (c) Decrease in the biomass of cabbages
☐ (d) Decrease in the number of foxes
☐ (e) Decrease in the numbers of thrushes

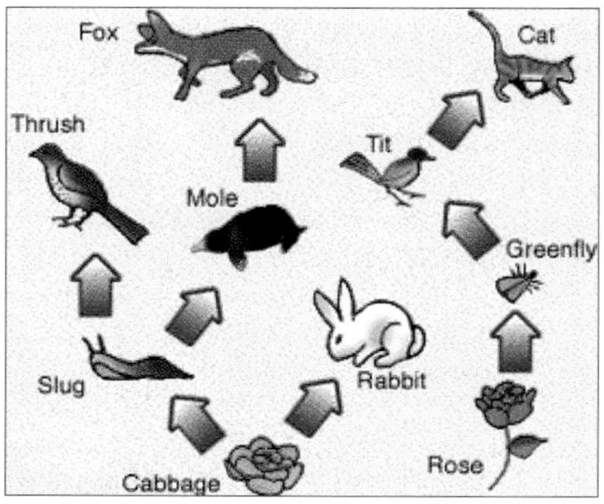

Q82, 83, 84, 85, 86, 87, 88

83 Which of the following species is a secondary consumer in the food web?

☐ (a) Fox
☐ (b) Greenfly
☐ (c) Mole
☐ (d) Rabbit
☐ (e) Slug

84 Which of the following pairs of species are both classed as carnivores in the food web?

☐ (a) Cat and rabbit
☐ (b) Fox and rabbit
☐ (c) Slug and greenfly
☐ (d) Tit and slug
☐ (e) Thrush and mole

85 Which of the following pairs of animals are both primary consumers in the ecosystem shown in the food web?

☐ (a) Greenfly and rabbit
☐ (b) Greenfly and tit
☐ (c) Mole and thrush
☐ (d) Slug and tit
☐ (e) Thrush and cat

86 Which of the following may accurately be called a food chain in the food web?

☐ (a) Cabbage → Slug → Mole → Fox
☐ (b) Cabbage → Slug → Thrush → Fox
☐ (c) Rose → Greenfly → Mole → Fox
☐ (d) Rose → Greenfly → Tit → Fox
☐ (e) Rose → Rabbit → Tit → Cat

87 In the food web, which of the following pairs would show a predator / prey relationship?

☐ (a) Greenfly and cat
☐ (b) Slug and mole
☐ (c) Slug and rabbit
☐ (d) Tit and mole
☐ (e) Thrush and fox

88 Which of the following organisms in the food web is a primary consumer?

☐ (a) Cabbage
☐ (b) Cat
☐ (c) Fox
☐ (d) Mole
☐ (e) Slug

89 In the following photographs you can see four species, which are known to feed on each other, and so form a food chain. Which of the following sequences is their correct order in the food chain, with producer organism listed first?

☐ (a) 1 - 2 - 3 - 4
☐ (b) 1 - 2 - 4 - 3
☐ (c) 2 - 1 - 4 - 3
☐ (d) 2 - 4 - 3 - 1
☐ (e) 3 - 4 - 2 - 1

Q80, 89

90 In the following photograph, black ants are seen taking honeydew from the abdomen of aphids on a rose bush. The honeydew is surplus plant sap that the aphids have sucked from the plant stem and, after extracting any protein, are now getting rid of. Which of the following ecological descriptions would you apply to the ants' level of feeding?

- ☐ (a) Primary consumers
- ☐ (b) Primary producers
- ☐ (c) Secondary consumers
- ☐ (d) Tertiary consumers
- ☐ (e) Tertiary producers

Q90

91 The sycamore leaves in the following photograph are covered in a shiny deposit, which is the excretion of a greenfly (the sycamore aphid). The aphids suck sugary sap from the phloem tubes in the plant, digest a little of the sugar and most of the protein, and excrete the remainder. To which trophic level do you think these greenfly belong?

- ☐ (a) Excretory consumers
- ☐ (b) Primary consumers
- ☐ (c) Primary producers
- ☐ (d) Secondary consumers
- ☐ (e) Secondary producers

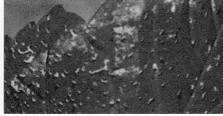

Q91

92 Which of the following terms would be the best description of the person eating the meal shown in the following photograph?

- ☐ (a) Herbivore
- ☐ (b) Omnivore
- ☐ (c) Predator
- ☐ (d) Primary consumer
- ☐ (e) Secondary consumer

Q92

93 To which of the following trophic levels do human vegetarians belong?

- ☐ (a) Carnivore
- ☐ (b) Predator
- ☐ (c) Primary consumer
- ☐ (d) Secondary consumer
- ☐ (e) Tertiary consumer

94 The following photograph shows a plant that has been eaten by a herbivorous insect. Why are green plants sometimes known as ecological producers?

- ☐ (a) Because they are eaten by the primary consumers
- ☐ (b) Because they produce oxygen for animal respiration
- ☐ (c) Because they produce substances of use to man's technology
- ☐ (d) Because they can make sugar from carbon dioxide and water
- ☐ (e) Because they die and produce good-quality soil

Q94

95 Which of the following statements is true of the pyramid of numbers shown in the following diagram?

- ☐ (a) There are more ladybirds than nettles
- ☐ (b) There are more blue tits than ladybirds
- ☐ (c) There are more blue tits than aphids
- ☐ (d) There are fewer ladybirds than nettles
- ☐ (e) There are fewer ladybirds than blue tits

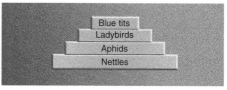

Q95

96 In many ecosystems the number of individual organisms at each trophic level decreases as you move up the food chain. However, to which of the following food chains does it clearly not apply?

- ☐ (a) Algae → Waterfleas → Sticklebacks
- ☐ (b) Duckweed → Ducks → Fox
- ☐ (c) Grass → Rabbit → Fox
- ☐ (d) Oak → Caterpillars → Thrushes
- ☐ (e) Wheat → Field mice → Owls

97 In the following pyramid, at which trophic level is the perch?

- ☐ (a) Level 1
- ☐ (b) Level 2
- ☐ (c) Level 3
- ☐ (d) Level 4
- ☐ (e) Level 5

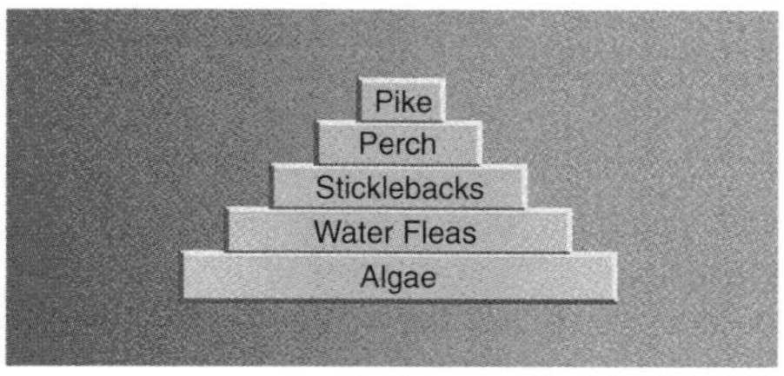

Q97

98 Which of the following statements can we say is definitely true of the pyramid of biomass shown in the following diagram?

- ☐ (a) All birds in this ecosystem eat either caterpillars or other birds
- ☐ (b) The mass of caterpillars is greater than the mass of their predators
- ☐ (c) The predator birds have larger bodies than insect-eating birds
- ☐ (d) The mass of predator birds is greater than the mass of insect-eating birds
- ☐ (e) The oak tree branches are going to break under the weight of consumers

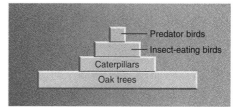

Q98

113

99 True ☐ or false ☐ ?
The following diagram of biomass could belong to most food chains.

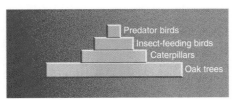

Q99

100 Many plant species grow on the floor of woodland. If an area of young woodland is allowed to grow without being cut, which of the following is likely to happen?

☐ (a) Community of the ground plants would decrease due to the decrease in light
☐ (b) Community of the ground plants would increase as the soil became richer
☐ (c) Community of the ground plants would decrease as the soil became poorer
☐ (d) Community of the ground plants would increase due to better soil quality
☐ (e) Community of the ground plants would not change over the next 100 years

101 The following diagram is a food web for the Antarctic Ocean. What is the source of energy for all the organisms in this web?

☐ (a) Krill shrimps
☐ (b) Iceberg meltwater
☐ (c) Mineral oil
☐ (d) Phytoplankton
☐ (e) Sunlight

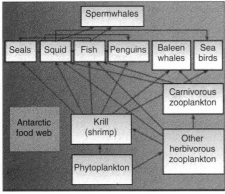

Q101

Higher Level only

102 As energy flows through an ecosystem some is lost at each trophic level. If the total energy in sunlight illuminating a pond was 1,000,000 kJ, approximately how much would be fixed in photosynthesis?

☐ (a) 1,000 kJ
☐ (b) 10,000 kJ
☐ (c) 50,000 kJ
☐ (d) 100,000 kJ
☐ (e) 500,000 kJ

103 If the total energy in sunlight illuminating a pond was 1,000,000 kJ, approximately how much would enter the primary consumers?

☐ (a) 100 kJ
☐ (b) 500 kJ
☐ (c) 1,000 kJ
☐ (d) 10,000 kJ
☐ (e) 1,000,000 kJ

104 If the total sunlight energy entering a pond was 1,000,000 kJ, how much energy would be found in the tissues of the first-level carnivores?

☐ (a) 1 kJ
☐ (b) 10 kJ
☐ (c) 100 kJ
☐ (d) 1,000 kJ
☐ (e) 10,000 kJ

105 Which of the following statements about the loss of energy in ecosystems is true? X: Energy is lost in an organism moving. Y: Energy is lost in mammals keeping a constant body temperature. Z: Most energy is lost in adult mammals producing gametes.

☐ (a) X, Y and Z
☐ (b) X and Y
☐ (c) X and Z
☐ (d) Y and Z
☐ (e) Y only

106 Green plants capture only about 1 - 3% of the solar energy that strikes their leaves. In what form is this small proportion of energy stored inside the plant?

☐ (a) In carbohydrates within the cytoplasm
☐ (b) In the cellulose cell walls
☐ (c) In chlorophyll in the chloroplasts
☐ (d) In DNA molecules in the chromosomes
☐ (e) In fat molecules in the membranes

107 Which of the following statements are clearly true? X: The removal of an organism from a food chain will affect the populations of others. Y: Longer food chains enable more energy to be available to top predators. Z: Energy is not lost between the trophic levels of a food chain.

☐ (a) X only
☐ (b) Y only
☐ (c) Z only
☐ (d) X and Y
☐ (e) Y and Z

108 Predator-prey cycles sometimes occur between two species in natural ecosystems. The following diagram shows some data from the capture of hares and their main predator, the lynx cat, in Canada. Under which of the following ecological conditions do you think it most likely to see predator and prey populations behaving in this way?

☐ (a) When the prey has many other predators and the predator has many other prey
☐ (b) When the prey has many other predators and the predator has few other prey
☐ (c) When the prey has few other predators and the predator has many other prey
☐ (d) When the prey has few other predators and the predator has no other prey
☐ (e) When the prey has no other predators and the predator has no other prey

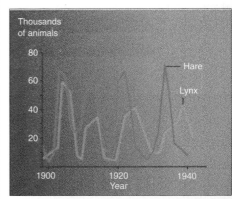

Q108

109 Which of the following statements about ecosystems are correct? X: The shorter the food chain, the more energy available to the top predator. Y: The greater the number of omnivores the more complicated the food web. Z: The size of organisms does not always increase up through the food chain.

- ☐ (a) X, Y and Z
- ☐ (b) X and Y
- ☐ (c) X and Z
- ☐ (d) Y and Z
- ☐ (e) X only

110 It is now known that the use of some pesticides, such as DDT, since the second world war had disastrous effects on the populations of predatory birds, like the peregrine falcon shown. Which of the following explains why their populations suffered?

- ☐ (a) Most predatory birds eat insect pests, and therefore ingest high doses of DDT
- ☐ (b) Predatory birds are 'top predators', and receive a concentrated dose of the DDT
- ☐ (c) Predatory birds are particularly susceptible to these substances, even in tiny doses
- ☐ (d) Predatory birds are highly strung, which means even a slight problem may be lethal
- ☐ (e) Predatory birds are very attracted to the smell of the pesticides when sprayed

Q110

Carbon and nitrogen cycles *(Double Award only)*

All organisms depend on the very thin layer of soil on the surface of the Earth, and the air above. It follows then that we must recycle all of the materials we are made from. Part of your body right now was probably part of a plant this morning, before you had breakfast! Part of your skin may well be part of an insect, or a bacterium, tonight. The carbon and nitrogen cycles describe in more detail how these two important elements are recycled continually between plants and animals.

 KEY FACTS

• **Decomposers** Life exists in a very thin layer of the Earth. Matter that is used for life must be recycled if life is to continue. Decay is the process that makes dead and waste material available for plants to grow. Microbes and other organisms are important in the decay of dead and waste materials, and so have a crucial part in the cycles of carbon and nitrogen. Bacteria and fungi are decomposers. These are very important organisms that break down dead organisms and waste materials.

• **Carbon dioxide** This gas is released by the respiration of the decomposers and can then be re-used by plants to turn into food in photosynthesis. This food is then available for animals to eat. Animals and plants also respire and release carbon dioxide.

• **Nitrates** Plants also need nitrates, which when combined with the sugars they have produced in photosynthesis, make amino acids and then proteins. Without decomposers and other bacteria in the soil, there would not be enough nitrates for plants to grow healthily. Some soil bacteria (nitrogen-fixing bacteria) convert nitrogen in the air into nitrates, which the plants can then use. Somes plants have special root nodules for these bacteria to live in. Waste materials are converted into ammonia, then nitrites and finally into nitrates by (nitrifying) bacteria in the soil. Other (denitrifying) bacteria return soil nitrates to the air as nitrogen.

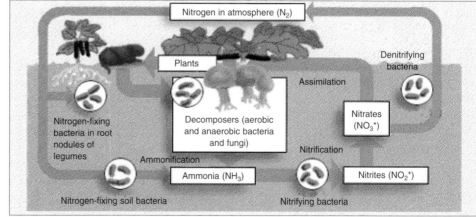
Nitrogen cycle

 QUESTIONS

111 True ☐ or false ☐ ?
We need to prevent all decay.

112 True ☐ or false ☐ ?
Micro-organisms are very important to all other living organisms.

113 Which of the following pairs of living organisms would help in the decay of leaves on a typical woodland floor?

- ☐ (a) Caterpillars and woodlice
- ☐ (b) Badgers and woodlice
- ☐ (c) Earthworms and woodlice
- ☐ (d) Earthworm and squirrel
- ☐ (e) Frogs and bacteria

114 Which of the following group of organisms is most likely to cause some unrefrigerated food going rotten?

- ☐ (a) Cockroaches
- ☐ (b) Fungi
- ☐ (c) Protozoans
- ☐ (d) Woodlice
- ☐ (e) Viruses

115 Which of these five types of waste is biodegradable?

- ☐ (a) Dumped washing machine
- ☐ (b) Empty glass drinks bottle
- ☐ (c) Old cardboard from greengrocers
- ☐ (d) Pieces of plastic car trim
- ☐ (e) Tin foil chewing gum wrapper

116 The fruits in the following photograph are decaying. Which of the following sets of environmental factors are necessary for decay?

- ☐ (a) Light, water, oxygen and microbes
- ☐ (b) Warmth, water and oxygen
- ☐ (c) Warmth, light, oxygen and microbes
- ☐ (d) Warmth, water, oxygen and microbes
- ☐ (e) Warmth, water and microbes

Q116

117 In the following photograph you can see the remains of a dead sheep. The main reason for the disappearance of most of a carcass is the process of decay. Decay requires certain conditions before it will happen. Which of the following is not needed for decay to take place?

- ☐ (a) A suitable temperature
- ☐ (b) The presence of animals
- ☐ (c) The presence of bacteria and fungi
- ☐ (d) The presence of moisture
- ☐ (e) The presence of oxygen

Q117

116

118 Decay or decomposition is a very important process in nature. Which of the following organisms is not involved in the breakdown of dead bodies and faeces?

- ☐ (a) Bacteria
- ☐ (b) Earthworm
- ☐ (c) Fungi
- ☐ (d) Oak tree
- ☐ (e) Woodlice

119 Which of the following is a micro-organism involved in the decay process?

- ☐ (a) Dung beetle
- ☐ (b) Earthworm
- ☐ (c) Fungus
- ☐ (d) Springtail
- ☐ (e) Woodlouse

120 Why are earthworms the gardener's best friend?

- ☐ (a) They chew up dead leaves, creating humus
- ☐ (b) They eat aphids
- ☐ (c) They prevent the drainage of water through the soil
- ☐ (d) They prevent the flow of air through the soil
- ☐ (e) They prevent the formation of humus

121 Mary placed a small piece of fresh soil on agar gel in a sterile petri dish. She covered the petri dish and incubated it at 25°C for a few days. What did she want to observe?

- ☐ (a) Humus
- ☐ (b) Plant roots
- ☐ (c) The earthworms
- ☐ (d) The micro-organisms
- ☐ (e) The particles of soil

Q121

122 Why will food rot if it is left lying around?

- ☐ (a) Because of the action of bacteria and fungi on the food
- ☐ (b) Because of the growth of viruses on the food

- ☐ (c) Food spontaneously breaks down with time
- ☐ (d) Insects feed on exposed food
- ☐ (e) Food reacts with air

123 What kinds of conditions encourage the growth of fungi on food?

- ☐ (a) Cold and dry with oxygen
- ☐ (b) Cold and moist without oxygen
- ☐ (c) Hot and moist with oxygen
- ☐ (d) Warm and dry without oxygen
- ☐ (e) Warm and moist with oxygen

124 Using sterile techniques, Mary placed two drops of fresh pasteurised milk on an agar plate, X, and two drops of stale pasteurised milk on another agar plate, Y. What differences, if any, would you expect between the two samples after two days' incubation at 20°C?

- ☐ (a) The agar in plate X turned white, Y remained unchanged
- ☐ (b) The agar in plate Y turned white, X remained unchanged
- ☐ (c) Plate X showed little or no growth of any organisms. Plate Y showed a significant growth of bacteria and fungi
- ☐ (d) Plate Y showed little or no growth of any organisms. Plate X showed a significant growth of bacteria and fungi
- ☐ (e) No differences between the two

Q124

125 How does refrigeration help to keep foods, like cheese and meat, fresh for a few days?

- ☐ (a) The cold air of the fridge kills the bacteria
- ☐ (b) The cold air slows down the activity of the bacteria and fungi
- ☐ (c) The cold air stops the activity of bacteria and fungi
- ☐ (d) The fridge keeps the bacteria out
- ☐ (e) The packaging of the food keeps the micro-organisms away from the food

126 The following diagram shows the carbon cycle in which the names of the processes involved have been replaced by the letters V to Z. Which letter represents photosynthesis?

- ☐ (a) V
- ☐ (b) W
- ☐ (c) X
- ☐ (d) Y
- ☐ (e) Z

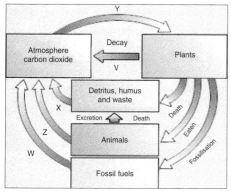

Q126

127 The following graphic shows the carbon cycle. What process has been replaced with the letter W?

- ☐ (a) Combustion
- ☐ (b) Feeding
- ☐ (c) Fossilisation
- ☐ (d) Photosynthesis
- ☐ (e) Respiration

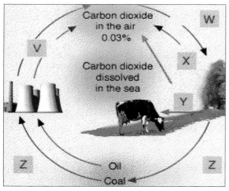

Q127, 128, 129, 130, 131, 132

128 In the graphic of the carbon cycle above, what process has been replaced with the letter V?

- ☐ (a) Combustion
- ☐ (b) Feeding
- ☐ (c) Fossilisation
- ☐ (d) Photosynthesis
- ☐ (e) Respiration

129 In the graphic of the carbon cycle, what process has been replaced with the letter X?

- ☐ (a) Combustion
- ☐ (b) Feeding
- ☐ (c) Fossilisation
- ☐ (d) Photosynthesis
- ☐ (e) Respiration

130 In the graphic of the carbon cycle, which letter represents the process of photosynthesis?

- ☐ (a) V
- ☐ (b) W
- ☐ (c) X
- ☐ (d) Y
- ☐ (e) Z

131 In the graphic of the carbon cycle, which letter represents the process of feeding?

- ☐ (a) V
- ☐ (b) W
- ☐ (c) X
- ☐ (d) Y
- ☐ (e) Z

132 In the graphic of the carbon cycle, which letter represents the process of respiration?

- ☐ (a) V
- ☐ (b) W
- ☐ (c) X
- ☐ (d) Y
- ☐ (e) Z

133 The following photograph shows fly agaric fungi. All fungi perform a very important process in the carbon cycle. Which of the following best describes that process?

- ☐ (a) Fungi convert carbon dioxide from the air and water from the soil into glucose sugars
- ☐ (b) Fungi convert carbon monoxide, a poisonous gas, into harmless carbon dioxide
- ☐ (c) Fungi decompose dead matter and release carbon dioxide back into the atmosphere
- ☐ (d) Fungi form delicious fruits that provide food for many animals on the forest floor
- ☐ (e) Fungi take carbon from the soil and make it into carbonates that can be used by plants

Q133

Higher Level only

134 The flow-chart below shows the nitrogen cycle, with the names of any organisms replaced by the letters V to Z. Which letter represents the denitrifier organisms?

- ☐ (a) V
- ☐ (b) W
- ☐ (c) X
- ☐ (d) Y
- ☐ (e) Z

135 In which natural cycle are the root nodules, found on the roots of plants in the pea family, important?

- ☐ (a) Carbon cycle
- ☐ (b) Nitrogen cycle
- ☐ (c) Phosphorus cycle
- ☐ (d) Sulphur cycle
- ☐ (e) Water cycle

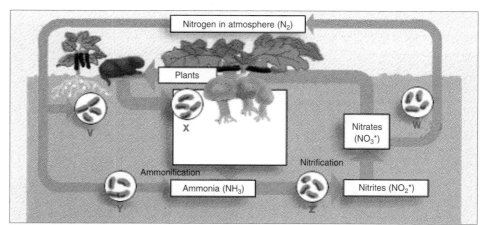

Q134

117

136 The following diagram shows a sketch of the nitrogen cycle. Which of the following would best replace the X on the diagram?

- [ ] (a) Absorbed by green plants
- [ ] (b) Excreted by green plants
- [ ] (c) Produced in photosynthesis by green plants
- [ ] (d) Produced by respiration in green plants
- [ ] (e) Taken in by plant bacteria

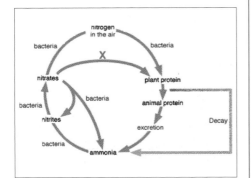

Q136

137 In industry, nitrogen is fixed in a process, called the Haber process, at pressures and temperatures much higher than any found in living cells. How then do the nitrogen-fixing bacteria in roots and soils convert nitrogen to nitrate?

- [ ] (a) Nodule bacteria gain their extraordinary powers from Gaia or Mother Earth
- [ ] (b) Nodules contain a special enzyme, called nitrogenase, which catalyses the process
- [ ] (c) Nodules start with a natural, rather than an unnatural, nitrogen gas
- [ ] (d) Nodules understand the power of heavenly bodies
- [ ] (e) Nodules use the sun's energy, well known to be much more powerful than heat energy

138 Green plants play a central role in the carbon cycle, by fixing the carbon dioxide from the atmosphere into carbohydrates. Only a few species play a similar role in the nitrogen cycle. Which of the following explains why?

- [ ] (a) Only plants with bulbs or corms fix nitrogen
- [ ] (b) Only plants which live in water fix nitrogen
- [ ] (c) Only plants with no chlorophyll fix nitrogen
- [ ] (d) Only plants with rhizomes fix nitrogen
- [ ] (e) Only plants with root nodules fix nitrogen

139 Which of the following crop plants are able to fix nitrogen from the atmosphere because they have nitrogen-fixing bacteria in their roots?

- [ ] (a) Barley
- [ ] (b) Cabbage
- [ ] (c) Peas
- [ ] (d) Radishes
- [ ] (e) Wheat

Food production *(Double Award only)*

To supply the entire human population with sufficient food we must produce that food in an efficient way. Science can help farmers to make the most of the land they have available and to improve the efficiency of energy transfer. This means interfering with the natural processes of food production. For example, we need to give plants the best conditions for growth by removing pests, weeds and diseases. We need to spread artificial fertilisers if the natural processes are not fast enough. Should we ask ourselves what we are doing to the natural environment? Or, should we be more concerned with feeding ourselves? There are positive and negative effects of managing food production.

 KEY FACTS

- **Fertilisers** Plants need nitrates and other minerals from the soil to grow healthily. A farmer can increase the growth rate of his plants by adding fertiliser to the soil. That way the plants use the light energy more efficiently to make food.

Fertiliser

Greenhouse

- **Greenhouses** Farmers can also increase the rate of plant growth by keeping plants in greenhouses, where the temperature can be controlled and extra carbon dioxide can be added to the air.

- **Chemical and biological pest control** This can be used to reduce the damage done by pests. Farmers try to reduce the competition from weeds by using herbicides, and the amount of crop damage from pests by using pesticides.

- **Animal control** Farmers can help animals to grow more efficiently by restricting their movement and keeping them away from predators. By keeping animals indoors and controlling the temperature, the farmer will reduce the amount of energy used by the animals for heat. Fish farms provide fish with the correct amount of food, and remove any disease or predators that might reduce the amount of fish produced. The fewer the number of links in a food chain, the less energy is lost to our surroundings and the more efficient our methods of food production.

QUESTIONS

Higher Level only

140 Which of the following is an example of pest management by biological control?

☐ (a) Breeding and releasing sterile male pests
☐ (b) Burning crop fields in winter to kill pupae
☐ (c) Planting crops in mixtures to confuse pests
☐ (d) Spraying with organochlorine pesticide
☐ (e) Spraying with pyrethrum, a 'natural' poison

141 The wheat crop in the following photograph is affected by an organism that causes parts of the plant to rot, and thread-like structures to appear around the stem and seeds. Which of the following would be the best treatment against this organism?

☐ (a) Spray with a bacteriocide
☐ (b) Spray with a fungicide
☐ (c) Spray with an herbicide
☐ (d) Spray with an insecticide
☐ (e) Spray with a wormicide

Q141

142 Farmers may use a lot of fertiliser on certain crops at some times, and it is often said by environmentalists that they should use less. Which of the following problems is not a result of using too much fertiliser?

☐ (a) Lack of oxygen causing death of fish in rivers
☐ (b) Deaths of predatory hawks and falcons
☐ (c) Deterioration of crumbly soil structure
☐ (d) Lowering of dissolved oxygen levels in rivers
☐ (e) Toxic levels of nitrate in drinking water

143 In the following sketch you can see the damage to a leaf caused by a caterpillar. Which of the following methods might control the caterpillar population?

☐ (a) Application of a bacteriocide
☐ (b) Application of a fungicide
☐ (c) Application of an herbicide
☐ (d) Application of an insecticide
☐ (e) Application of a rodenticide

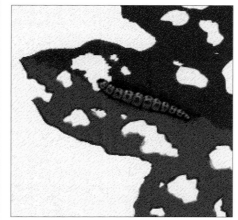

Q143

144 A greenhouse gardener has problems with a pest called the greenhouse whitefly, which sucks the sugar out of phloem tissues, and he is keen to use methods of biological control. Which of these methods should he not use?

☐ (a) Introduce an insect parasite of the whitefly into the greenhouse
☐ (b) Introduce an insect predator of the whitefly into the greenhouse
☐ (c) Introduce some whitefly infected with a fatal virus into the greenhouse
☐ (d) Spray with a natural pesticide, such as pyrethrum from chrysanthemum flowers
☐ (e) Use caged females to attract males onto an electrified landing platform

145 A greenhouse might have some of the following: U: A machine producing extra oxygen. V: A heater. W: Lights. X: A beehive. Y: A carbon dioxide machine. Z: An air humidifier. Which of the following combinations of these would you choose as the most useful for getting the most plant growth and fruit development?

☐ (a) U, V, W and X
☐ (b) U, V, W and Y
☐ (c) V, W, X and Y
☐ (d) V, W, X and Z
☐ (e) W, X, Y and Z

146 True ☐ or false ☐ ?
Increasing carbon dioxide concentration in a glasshouse will not increase crop yield.

147 Which of the following is not a way to increase the amount of a crop grown in a field?

☐ (a) Covering the growing crop with sheets of black polythene
☐ (b) Using artificial irrigation
☐ (c) Using herbicides
☐ (d) Using insecticides
☐ (e) Using mineral fertilisers

148 Which of the following would probably not increase production in crop fields?

☐ (a) Planting seeds much closer together
☐ (b) Using herbicides to kill weeds
☐ (c) Using inorganic fertilisers to deliver nitrate
☐ (d) Using irrigation to deliver water
☐ (e) Using selective breeding to improve strains

149 The following photographs show two very different habitats: a man-made crop field and an unfarmed alpine moorland. Which of the following is a reason why fertiliser is added regularly to the crop field, while the moorland manages without any fertiliser?

☐ (a) Crops need certain rare mineral elements that wild plants can do without
☐ (b) Crops need more minerals than the wild plants on the moor
☐ (c) Fertilisers protect the farmed crop against diseases caused by fungi and bacteria
☐ (d) Plants in the natural system do not need any minerals
☐ (e) Wild plants die and release their minerals, while crops are taken away from the field

Q149

150 Why is it sometimes said that we could increase human food supplies if we stopped farming animals, became vegetarian, and farmed only plants?

- ☐ (a) Animals, being higher up the food chain, involve the waste of energy between levels
- ☐ (b) Meat contains less energy per kilogram than plant foods
- ☐ (c) Meat contains far fewer vitamins than plant foods
- ☐ (d) More costly fertilisers have to be added to livestock farms
- ☐ (e) Plant foods are much more natural and their kilojoules contain more energy

151 Animal husbandry involves many techniques to increase both growth and profit, but which of the following is not used in this way?

- ☐ (a) Enriching the feed with protein
- ☐ (b) Intensive raising indoors in sheds
- ☐ (c) Irradiating the animals to kill diseases
- ☐ (d) Stimulating growth by adding hormones
- ☐ (e) Vaccination against diseases

152 One aspect of modern animal husbandry involves intensive production, but which of the following is not a widespread intensive method?

- ☐ (a) Beef cattle are kept in small pens
- ☐ (b) Chickens are kept at high densities
- ☐ (c) Farmed fish are kept at high densities

- ☐ (d) Pigs are kept in small indoor pens
- ☐ (e) Poultry are kept in small cages

153 Which of the following is not claimed as an advantage of intensive methods of modern animal farming?

- ☐ (a) Better disease control
- ☐ (b) Better protection from predators
- ☐ (c) Better-tasting meat
- ☐ (d) Savings in feed costs
- ☐ (e) Savings in the farm labour costs

154 Which of the following conditions is not controlled in the living environment of a battery hen?

- ☐ (a) Disease
- ☐ (b) Food
- ☐ (c) Living space
- ☐ (d) Oxygen
- ☐ (e) Temperature

155 Which of the following is not a management technique that could be used to ensure populations of cod and haddock remain high?

- ☐ (a) Less fishing allowed in breeding season
- ☐ (b) Less fishing allowed on breeding grounds
- ☐ (c) Limitations on the number of fish caught
- ☐ (d) Net size that catches small fish
- ☐ (e) Return to the sea of breeding adults

156 True ☐ or false ☐ ?
Fish farming (producing fish in small enclosed areas) is profitable for any type of fish.

157 Fish farming is an efficient way to produce protein, but it does cause problems for the surrounding environment. Which of the following is not an environmental problem associated with fish farming?

- ☐ (a) Farmed fish attack our native fish species and cause extinctions
- ☐ (b) Farmed fish might introduce new diseases to our wild populations
- ☐ (c) Fish food added to the water may cause eutrophication if it runs into rivers and lakes
- ☐ (d) Fish farms use antibiotics, which may select for resistant strains of wild bacteria
- ☐ (e) Fish farms use pesticide to control parasites, and these may pollute local waters

158 Overfishing around the world has led to a decline in the quantity of fish available. We catch too many young fish, which then do not live to reproduce. Which of the following measures would be most effective in ensuring that only mature fish are caught?

- ☐ (a) Allowing only nets of a certain minimum mesh (netting hole) size
- ☐ (b) Allowing vessels to catch only a limited weight of fish each year
- ☐ (c) Limiting the number of vessels allowed to fish an area of ocean
- ☐ (d) Limiting the number of days in the year on which fishing can occur
- ☐ (e) Limiting fishing to areas well away from the breeding areas of the fish

---

 ANSWERS

Adaptation, competition and predation

☐ **1** *(e)*
The four physical factors, temperature, water, light and carbon dioxide, will affect how well a plant can grow, or even if it can grow at all. All four affect the rate of photosynthesis, and therefore how quickly the plant can make its food.

☐ **2** *(c)*
The habitat of an organism is a description of the place in which it lives. For example, a blackbird's habitat is suburban gardens, a heron's habitat is the waterside, and a limpet mollusc's habitat is the rocky seashore. Some

animals are not fussy in their choice of habitat, the starling, for example, while others are extremely choosy, like the californian condor.

☐ **3** *False*
The place where an organism lives is called its habitat. For example, a squirrel's habitat is a woodland, or a water scorpion's habitat is a pond. The environment is the word used to describe the conditions of the habitat – the temperature, how wet or dry it is, how light or dark it is, and so on.

☐ **4** *(c)*
The word environment means total surroundings and includes all factors that affect living organisms as they exist in the world. Included in a proper description of the environment of a

particular species of tree would be the type of soil, the names of its competitor plants, the brightness of sunlight, and the names of any poisons in the atmosphere.

A4

☐ **5** *False*

All the organisms that live in a pond, or any other habitat, are called a community. A population is used to describe all the individuals of one species in a pond. For example, we might refer to the population of water scorpions, or the population of great diving beetles.

A5

☐ **6** *(c)*

Populations are all the individuals of a particular species living in a specified area. It is accurate to talk about the population of blackbirds in your local park, but not accurate to talk about the population of insects in the park, as there will be many species of insect in that habitat. The proper term would be the community of insects.

☐ **7** *(b)*

A community is the entire collection of living things in a specified area. This usually includes many different species, though the complexity of a community can vary greatly. For instance, a desert lake may contain only half a dozen species, whereas a similar area of coral reef in the Red Sea may contain hundreds. The community does not include the inorganic resources, such as minerals. These are part of an ecosystem.

☐ **8** *(d)*

Plants that live in deserts, or other hostile environments, must be very careful to avoid injury and attack from herbivores, since the slightest damage could cause great water loss, which would lead to death. A cactus photosynthesises using its green stem, and the leaves are modified into spines to offer some protection.

☐ **9** *(d)*

Plants, such as cacti, have evolved a variety of mechanisms to avoid excessive water loss. They have a thicker waterproof cuticle covering the surfaces, few or no leaves, shiny surfaces that reflect light and heat, thick stems to store water, shallow, far-reaching roots to pick up any rainfall, and stomata located in deep pits. These mechanisms allow desert plants to survive. Most grow extremely slowly for long periods of time. Large cacti may be very old.

A8, 9, 10, 11

☐ **10** *(e)*

Features that are typical of plants, such as desert cacti that try to avoid water loss at all costs, are sunken stomata to protect the leaf interior from dry air, waxy needles to reduce evaporation, and widespread roots to gather rain quickly after the occasional storm. However, very thin but wide leaves are typical of plants found in humid areas, like the cheese plants found in the humid tropics.

☐ **11** *(d)*

Carnivorous plants capture animals to supplement their supply of nitrogen. Most carnivorous plants live in swampy habitats where there are few mineral ions. All other features listed are true of most cacti.

☐ **12** *(a)*

The gills, positioned underneath the abdomen of a mayfly nymph, are arranged so that the animal can get oxygen from the water rather than from the air. Although all the other features listed are vital for the life of this animal, they are not special adaptations to pond life.

☐ **13** *(b)*

The long, bristle-covered back legs are specially designed so that the insect can swim just under the water surface, rather like the flattened oars a rower uses to move a boat. Although all the other alternatives listed are vital for the life of this animal, they are not special adaptations to pond life.

☐ **14** *(a)*

The woodlouse, although liking damp places, is not a pond creature but a creature found on land. All the other animals are pond-living.

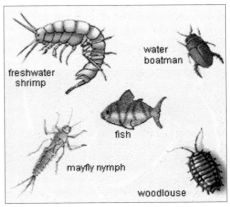

A14

☐ **15** *(c)*

Only the mayfly spends its life in a pond or a stream. The picture shows the mayfly at a young stage. All the other animals are found only on land.

A15

☐ **16** *(e)*

A large animal has a smaller surface area, in relation to body mass, than a small animal, and therefore loses internal heat less quickly. This explains why animals of the same species become larger the closer they live to the poles. Although all the other features listed are true of polar bears, and useful to their lives, only a large size is a clear adaptation to life in the cold.

☐ **17** *(c)*

Adaptations are features of living organisms, evolved by natural selection, that aid the survival and reproduction of those living organisms. A polar bear has thick fur, a thick layer of fat under its skin, hairy feet and white camouflage so its prey cannot see it approaching. All these are adaptations that have evolved over millions of years, but the fact that hunters need a licence is not an adaptation.

☐ **18** *(e)*

A fennec fox lives in very hot places so it has especially large ears that help to lose heat.

121

☐ **19** *(b)*
From winter to summer, there is an increase in daylength from the shortest day (December 21) to the longest (June 21) and the temperature gradually rises. The light intensity increases as spring approaches, but when leaves start to appear on the trees, the light intensity may decline again.

A19, 22

☐ **20** *(c)*
Many woodland plants have a growing season that is finished by late spring or early summer. This allows them to grow before the leaves on the trees block out too much of the light.

☐ **21** *(a)*
Many plants on the woodland floor have phases of growth that are very short. For example, bluebells appear above the ground in early spring and grow quickly before the trees have grown leaves. So, these so-called shade plants avoid too much competition for light with the tall trees. For the rest of the year, shade plants exist as bulbs or equivalent organs.

A20, 21

☐ **22** *(e)*
The woodland plants often finish their life-cycle before the trees even begin to open their leaves after winter; in this way, the plants avoid competition for light with the taller trees. The bulb, or

corm, helps in this by allowing them to rapidly grow in the spring without having to wait for ideal growing conditions.

☐ **23** *(c)*
All the resources listed, except for oxygen, could easily be involved in competition between male polar bears; if the bears are not successful in this competition then their ability either to survive or to reproduce will be lessened. However, one bear using oxygen will not reduce the amount of oxygen available to another bear. In other words, oxygen is not a limiting ecological factor for the bears because it is not in short supply.

☐ **24** *(c)*
Oxygen and carbon dioxide are plentiful in the air. Plants produce their own food and do not compete for mates, so they are most likely to compete for light. In order to obtain the clear space they need to get the light necessary for photo-synthesis, plants may employ one or more of several strategies, such as growing up very quickly to shade out competitors, or producing toxins that slow growth in other plants.

A24

☐ **25** *(b)*
An increase in the rabbit population would lead to more rabbits competing for the same amount of food resource. Badgers are omnivorous so they may eat some of the food that rabbits eat. However, competition within a species is always greater than competition between species because organisms of the same species have the same needs, whilst the needs of two different species may be similar but not the same.

☐ **26** *(e)*
With no predators and plenty of food, there is little reason for any of the animals to die, and so there will be a population explosion. This will continue until the food supply starts to run out, which may not be for many years, and

by then the animals may have changed the structure of life on the island forever. A situation similar to this occurred when rabbits were first released (accidentally) into the wild in Australia.

☐ **27** *(b)*
Population growth is a balance of the rates of birth and death. If death-rate equals birth-rate there is no change, if death-rate is greater than birth-rate the population will decline, and if birth-rate is greater than death-rate the population will grow. At point X, death-rate is greater than birth-rate, so the population is declining, perhaps as a result of food running out.

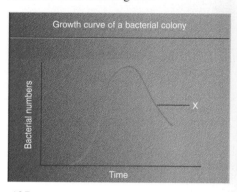

A27

☐ **28** *(b)*
Population growth has four phases. At first the population grows slowly because there are not many rabbits to reproduce (phase V). Then population growth becomes rapid as there are more individuals to reproduce, and these rabbits are not limited by food supplies or other competition (phase W). As resources, such as food, become scarce due to the increased population numbers, rabbits die and growth slows down (phase X). The rate of growth reaches a balance when birth-rate equals death-rate (phase Y). If food is not increased the population may decline (phase Z).

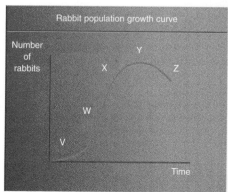

A28

□ 29 *(e)*
The gradient of a population curve at any point represents the rate of growth of the population at that time. In phase V, you can see that the population is growing slowly because the curve there is not steep, whereas at phase W, the curve is much steeper as the growth rate is higher. The gradient is negative at point Z, where the death-rate is greater than the birth-rate.

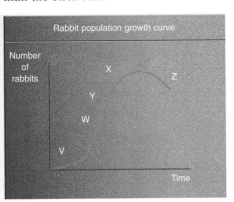

A29

□ 30 *(e)*
At point Z, the bacterial population is in a temporary equilibrium, or balance, where the numbers of births and deaths per hour are equal. The gradient of the curve at this point is zero, which shows that there is no overall growth of the population, even though bacterial cells are being created and die every minute.

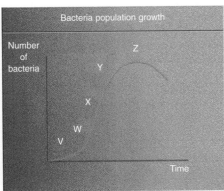

A30

□ 31 *(a)*
If half the pond is covered in 15 days and each duckweed produces a new plant every day, then only one more day is needed before the pond is totally covered.

□ 32 *(d)*
The experiment had the aim of investigating the effects of overcrowding yet, without other dishes germinated at different densities, we have no idea as to whether this dish has germinated at a high or low rate. The experimental design might be improved by setting up

five dishes with seed densities of 10, 50, 100, 200 and 400 seeds. All dishes should, of course, be exactly equal in all other respects – in other words, all other factors should be controlled.

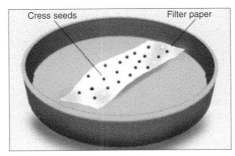

A32

Human impact on environment

□ 33 *(b)*
The five basic survival needs of a human being are nutrition, water, warmth, shelter and air. It is simply inconvenient to live without a computer!

□ 34 *(c)*
A simple definition of pollution is 'any substance in the wrong place at the wrong time', so that many pollutants are perfectly useful substances in the right circumstances. Litter might be called landscape pollution, carbon monoxide is air pollution, the storage tank causes water pollution by releasing too much organic matter into the stream and starving it of oxygen, and the drills cause noise pollution.

□ 35 *(e)*
Only the discharge of untreated sewage is likely to lead to more bacterial diseases, although some of the other alternatives listed might lead to different health problems.

A35

□ 36 *(c)*
The establishment of a nature reserve probably has the aim of preserving the original species. The other four projects listed all have direct effects on the land, which might damage the animal and

plant populations, and should be considered before the activity goes ahead.

□ 37 *(c)*
Melting down old glass to make different items is recycling, rather than re-use. The other alternatives listed are examples of the re-use of manufactured items, with no reprocessing or remanufacture. In many ways, re-use is better than recycling, because less energy is needed to make the item fit for its next use.

□ 38 *(b)*
Recycling has many advantages, but it is also a sad truth that many recycling schemes do not make money. For example, it is much cheaper to buy 1,000 new plastic bags than to take the time and energy to recycle 1,000 paper bags. Nevertheless, money may not be the deciding factor in whether we recycle or not.

□ 39 *(b)*
Once used in some kind of useful process, such as powering an aeroplane, energy is converted into a form (usually a low temperature heat) from which it cannot easily be re-used. All the other items listed are materials that are recyclable.

□ 40 *(e)*
Wood can be produced indefinitely by planting more trees and allowing them to grow, but all the other alternatives listed may eventually run out at the present rates of use.

A40

□ 41 *(d)*
The dramatic increase of the human population and the standard of living have led to a much greater use of raw materials – including non-renewable resources – a greater production of waste, and an increase in the amount of pollution. Some people are of the opinion that this situation will lead to an ecological crisis.

☐ **42** *(a)*
The most likely problem with drinking water supplies is that they might become contaminated with bacteria and viruses. Some of these contaminants might cause diseases in the drinking water, which is then carried to large cities. People or dogs defecating into the reservoir might cause serious health problems and even deaths.

☐ **43** *(a)*
Agricultural production will not rise because of a good sewage system. In fact, since human sewage is used to fertilise fields in many parts of the world, artificial fertilisers would be needed. The other alternatives listed remind us of how important a good sewage system is to our way of life.

A43

☐ **44** *(d)*
Sewage disposal removes most of the organic material, which would otherwise fertilise the freshwater rivers and cause algae to grow extremely rapidly. Once this happens, the algae shade the slow-growing rooted plants, and the bacteria living on their decomposing bodies use up any dissolved oxygen in the river. Fish then die through a lack of oxygen.

☐ **45** *(c)*
Oxygen is not very soluble in water, and freshwater is very easily made anaerobic by the addition of sewage or other organic waste from farms. A weir helps to add oxygen to the water from the air, maintaining populations of aerobic bacteria that will continue to digest organic material to carbon dioxide and water.

☐ **46** *(e)*
Weirs are provided to add oxygen to the water so they are very often found immediately down river from sewage outfalls.

A45, 46

☐ **47** *(b)*
Addition of sewage to a river adds nutrients, which help the growth of algae. When algae die, they are decomposed by aerobic bacteria and this leads to a reduction of oxygen levels in the water. The lack of oxygen kills fish, and although this makes little difference to the populations of birds, certain detritivore animals, such as the Tubifex and bloodworms, which can live with very little oxygen, are encouraged to grow.

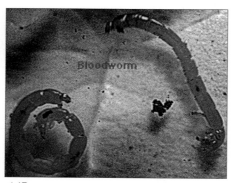
A47

☐ **48** *(a)*
The addition of fertiliser to water quickly leads to an increased growth rate of microscopic algal plants in the water, which then die and become food for bacteria. These aerobic bacteria consume the small amount of dissolved oxygen held in freshwater so animals, such as fish, die. Foam on the water is not caused by fertiliser but by polluting detergents.

A48

☐ **49** *True*
Eutrophication is the name for the excessive growth of algae, which may cause a river or pond to run out of oxygen. Nutrients in sewage and fertilisers may cause eutrophication.

☐ **50** *(b)*
The rivers running through Bangladesh rise to the north in mountainous Nepal. Due to extensive deforestation in Nepal, the soil and vegetation of the mountains now hold less water, and allow the rainfall to run off the mountains much more quickly after a storm. Bangladesh has always had to cope with flooding, but it has become more of a problem as the floods have become more severe.

☐ **51** *(d)*
The open habitat with its short turf allows different plant and animal species to live there. Most nature reserves are managed to maintain a variety of habitats within their boundaries. If one type of habitat was allowed to 'take over', this would lead to fewer species in the nature reserve. As a rough rule, untidy places have a higher conservation value than tidy places!

☐ **52** *(a)*
Acid rain is known to wash various minerals, especially magnesium, aluminium and calcium, out of the soil. Therefore, plants in a polluted community may show signs of several different mineral deficencies compounded by poor root health. The effect known as 'die back' of conifer trees is when the tips of the trunks fail to grow, stunting the height. There are no beneficial effects that might lead to an increased growth rate.

☐ **53** *(b)*
Even unpolluted rainfall is slightly acidic, because some atmospheric carbon dioxide will always dissolve in falling rain, making carbonic acid and a pH of less than 7. In acid rain, gases such as sulphur dioxide have also dissolved in the rain, sometimes lowering the rain pH to less than 4.

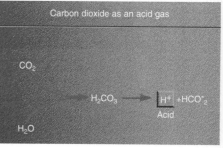
Carbon dioxide as an acid gas
CO_2
H_2O
$H_2CO_3 \rightarrow H^+ + HCO_2^-$
Acid
A53

☐ 54 *(e)*
Carbon dioxide, occurring naturally in the atmosphere, does cause even unpolluted rain to be slightly acidic. However, severe pollution is usually caused by the release of sulphur dioxide when fossil fuels are burnt in power stations, for example. The sulphur dioxide dissolves in rain to form sulphuric acid, which, when it falls in some parts of the world, may have a pH lower than 3. Plants cannot grow very well if there is sulphur dioxide in the air, and some are killed if exposed to certain levels of the gas.

A54

☐ 55 *True*
Sulphur dioxide is a poisonous gas released by burning fossil fuel. All organisms have moist tissues where the exchange of gases can take place, for example, an earthworm's skin or a human's lungs. When these tissues come into contact with sulphur dioxide, they become inflamed, and diseases such as bronchitis and asthma can be made worse.

☐ 56 *(d)*
Lichens are easily damaged by air pollution, particularly acid rain, which is caused by sulphurous fumes and smoky wastes. A survey of their abundance and diversity of species can give a very clear picture of the extent of air pollution in an area, without the need for lots of complicated and time-consuming physical and chemical tests. Such techniques, using biological characteristics to measure things, are known as bioassays.

A56

☐ 57 *(e)*
All the choices listed are gaseous exchange surfaces and so are very delicate. Air pollutants, on reaching these surfaces, may cause direct damage, or dissolve on the moist surface and then cause damage.

☐ 58 *(c)*
Lead tetraethyl compound is put into petrol to extract better performance from the car, and is called an anti-knocking agent. Unfortunately, this compound is not required at all by human metabolism and poisons certain enzymes in the brain, which can lead to problems with mental development.

☐ 59 *(d)*
Methane is given off from decomposing rubbish, rice fields and domestic herbivores, such as sheep and cattle. Vehicle exhausts and fuel systems may produce all the other polluting gases listed.

☐ 60 *(e)*
Any measure that cuts down car use, or increases the efficiency of car use in terms of passengers carried for each litre of fuel burned, will cut down the amount of carbon dioxide produced. Catalytic converters remove some toxic gases from car exhausts but mainly increase the amount of carbon dioxide emitted.

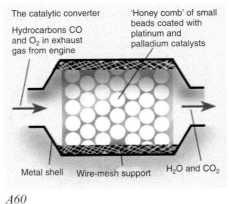

The catalytic converter

Hydrocarbons CO and O_2 in exhaust gas from engine

'Honey comb' of small beads coated with platinum and palladium catalysts

Metal shell   Wire-mesh support H_2O and CO_2

A60

☐ 61 *(e)*
The melting of ice, and the larger volume of a warmer sea, might cause the flooding of low areas. Tropical diseases might migrate northwards and, as warm air can hold more water, there might be an increase in rainfall. More parts of the world may become desert if the average temperature increases. However, the temperature changes predicted would have no effect on skin cancer rates, which instead might be increased by the thinning of the ozone layer in the atmosphere.

☐ 62 *(c)*
In the cultivation of rice, the waterlogged conditions encourage the production of methane (sometimes called marsh gas) by certain kinds of bacteria. There is a possibility that increasing rice production, during the past 50 years, may have increased atmospheric methane.

☐ 63 *(d)*
Sulphur dioxide is a major cause of acid rain, but does not cause the greenhouse effect. CFCs, or chlorofluorocarbons, are mainly a cause of increased skin cancer rates. They break down the ozone layer that protects us from the harmful ultra-violet light coming from the Sun. They do have a minor part to play as a greenhouse gas. The two gases causing most of the greenhouse effect are methane and carbon dioxide.

☐ 64 *(d)*
Using aerosol sprays may increase the levels of CFCs in the atmosphere, but not carbon dioxide. All the other factors listed could well lead to increasing carbon dioxide concentrations in the atmosphere, though proving the link would sometimes be very difficult.

☐ 65 *(b)*
Temperate regions show cycles of photosynthetic rate, with much more conversion of carbon dioxide to sugar during the summer than during the winter. A great deal of the photosynthetic increase will occur in the sea due to the activities of phytoplankton.

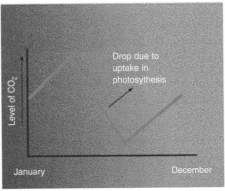

Level of CO_2

Drop due to uptake in photosythesis

January   December

A65

☐ 66 *(d)*
Methane is a greenhouse gas made during the fermentation of grass in the stomachs of herbivores, such as cows and sheep. From time to time, methane is belched back into the atmosphere.

□ 67 *(c)*
A large increase in the human population this century has led to more rice fields and cows, which may have caused an increase in the concentration of methane in the atmosphere. Bacteria in rice paddies produce methane when they metabolise, and cows make methane when they ferment food and excrete it by belching. There is cause for concern as methane is a greenhouse gas.

A67

□ 68 *(b)*
Ozone in the upper atmosphere prevents much of the harmful ultraviolet radiation from the Sun reaching the Earth. Depletion of ozone by CFCs and oxides of nitrogen lets more ultraviolet radiation reach the surface of the Earth and this, in turn, increases the likelihood of cataracts, mutations, and skin cancers. The notion of an ozone 'layer' is mistaken; it is a rare gas distributed thinly at high altitude.

□ 69 *(e)*
While there are many possible arguments for the conservation of parts of the Earth's surface, the one that is used most is the argument about endangered species or habitats. Whether concern is for rhinos in Africa or ospreys in Scotland, the strongest conservation argument depends upon our unwillingness to see organisms become extinct and their habitats decline.

□ 70 *(b)*
Hedges have become unpopular on farms during the last 50 years for some of the reasons listed. The government even gave grants for farmers to bulldoze hedges and increase field size. However, hedgerows' conservation value for game has always been appreciated, and many farmers have deliberately kept hedges to support their sport. This practice is part of conservation: using resources

sustainably and wisely for the mutual benefit of the human population and countryside.

A70

□ 71 *(b)*
The reason for setting up National Parks during the past 50 years is to maintain a large area of land that has been relatively unaffected and undeveloped by humans (even though humans may still be quite active in some of those areas, for example, by farming). Many of the other benefits listed follow on from the establishment of a park.

Energy and nutrient transfer

□ 72 *(b)*
Green plants are capable of producing their own food via photosynthesis, so animals rely upon one of these producer organisms for their food.

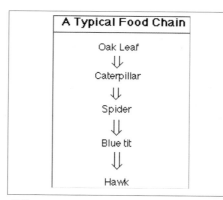

```
          A Typical Food Chain

                 Oak Leaf
                    ⇓
                Caterpillar
                    ⇓
                  Spider
                    ⇓
                 Blue tit
                    ⇓
                  Hawk
```

A72

□ 73 *(e)*
Green plants are called producers because they are capable of producing food molecules, such as glucose, from atmospheric carbon dioxide using the process of photosynthesis. Animals cannot do this and so are dependent on plants for their food either directly – by eating the plant itself – or indirectly, by eating another animal.

A73

□ 74 *False*
The algae are producers because they produce food by photosynthesis. The insect larvae are the primary consumers because they eat the producers; the sticklebacks are the secondary consumers because they eat the primary consumers, and the perch are the tertiary consumers because they eat the secondary consumers.

□ 75 *(b)*
The sheep is eating plant material, and this means that it must be a herbivore or an omnivore. Carnivores and predators, both also called secondary consumers or tertiary consumers, depending on the trophic level they occupy, eat other animals. Herbivores are also known as primary consumers, and are important for making the energy in plants available to the other consumers.

□ 76 *(c)*
Any organism that consumes vegetation is called a primary consumer. The vegetation they eat is called a producer because the plant produces its own food (glucose) by photosynthesis. If the sheep also ate some meat in its diet, it would be called an omnivore. A secondary consumer is an organism that eats primary consumers.

□ 77 *(c)*
Competition for limiting resources between two species may well reduce the birth rates of both species, so that both species of caterpillars, and their 'parent' moths, may eventually suffer population declines.

□ 78 *(d)*
Ecologists tend to use the word predator in several different senses. Some use the word to mean almost any kind of consumer except parasites, but the most commonly used meaning is 'an animal that first kills prey in order to eat it', for example, a lion.

☐ **79** *(a)*
The lion, like all animals, consumes another organism to gain energy and nutritious materials, and is therefore called an ecological consumer. More precisely, the lion is called a carnivore because it is eating another animal.

☐ **80** *(d)*
Secondary consumers eat the animals that eat the plants.

☐ **81** *(b)*
The word herbivore is used to describe animals that feed directly on plants. In the food chain shown, the only herbivores are the insect larvae. The algae are the producers, and the stickleback and the perch are carnivores.

☐ **82** *(a)*
Food webs show us the very complex ecological interactions in nature. In the food web diagram shown, if the rabbits begin to die, then there would be more food for the slugs, and so more food for the mole, the thrush and the fox. In a real food web, it may well be that the rabbits are also eaten by foxes, so the real outcome of this disease may be very different.

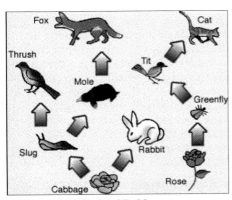

A82, 83, 84, 85, 86, 87, 88

☐ **83** *(c)*
A secondary consumer eats animals that feed on plants, and is therefore second in line for the food, or on the second trophic level. The mole, the thrush and the tit are all secondary consumers in the food web diagram.

☐ **84** *(e)*
Carnivores are animals that eat other animals so, out of the listed pairs, only the thrush and the mole, which both eat the slugs, are carnivores.

☐ **85** *(a)*
Primary consumers are the herbivorous animals that eat plants. Out of the organisms listed, only the rabbit and greenfly are both herbivores.

☐ **86** *(a)*
A food chain has to have a continuous series of links showing that energy and nutritious materials are passing, without interruption, between the producer and the highest-level consumer. The only series given that fulfils this condition is cabbage → slug → mole → fox.

☐ **87** *(b)*
Moles eat slugs, so they can be termed as predator and prey respectively.

☐ **88** *(e)*
In the food web diagram, slugs are the primary consumers eating green plants. Real slugs are sometimes omnivorous as they also eat animal material. A few slug species are totally carnivorous.

☐ **89** *(b)*
In the woodland system shown, the oak trees are the producers at the base of the food chain, the caterpillars are herbivores and feed on the leaves of the tree, the robin is an insect-eating bird, and the falcon feeds on birds.

☐ **90** *(a)*
The ants are effectively eating plant substances that have passed only through the aphid's gut and not entered the aphid's body. The ants are therefore primary consumers. At other times, ants are quite fierce carnivores so that, overall, the ant is classed as being an omnivore capable of feeding on several different trophic levels.

☐ **91** *(b)*
The trophic level is the level at which an organism feeds in the food chain. The very first level is the producer level, almost always occupied by green plants, and the next level, at which animals feed on plants, is known as the primary consumer level. Greenfly are therefore primary consumers.

☐ **92** *(b)*
The person is eating a meal that contains both plant (the green peppers and the wheat in the bread) and animal (the lobster) material, and is therefore best described as an omnivore.

☐ **93** *(c)*
Strict vegetarians eat only plant foods, and so are primary consumers along with herbivores. The majority of vegetarians would also consume milk or cheese, making them at least in part secondary consumers.

☐ **94** *(d)*
Plants are called producers because they can photosynthesise, and so produce sugars and starch from carbon dioxide and water. These molecules provide the basic materials for all other living organisms on Earth.

☐ **95** *(d)*
A pyramid of numbers shows the number of organisms at each feeding level in a food chain. In most number pyramids, the numbers of organisms becomes fewer as you go up the food chain, both because the predators tend to be larger creatures, and because the amount of useful energy gets less as it runs though the chain.

☐ **96** *(d)*
A single oak tree can support thousands of caterpillars, and these are then eaten by a few thrushes. The diagram of numbers in each trophic level of this food chain does not form a pyramid.

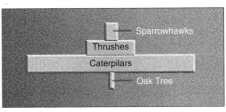

A96

☐ **97** *(d)*
A pyramid of numbers shows how the number of individual organisms varies between each level in a food chain. This diagram of numbers shows that there are less perch than sticklebacks, but more perch than pike. The perch are at trophic level four.

☐ **98** *(b)*
A pyramid of biomass tells us nothing definite about the body sizes, or mass, of the organisms in the pyramid. It does tell us something about the total biomass of living things at different trophic levels in a food web, but it tells us nothing about the other organisms in this ecosystem, which are not included in the diagram. The width of the bars does tell us that the biomass of caterpillars is greater than that of the insect-eating birds.

☐ **99** *True*
Diagrams of biomass tend to look like pyramids because at each level there is always waste. An oak tree, which has a very large biomass, can only support a smaller biomass of caterpillars, which only eat the leaves, and not the twigs or branches. Similarly, an insect-feeding bird will eat several caterpillars every day for many days, so the mass of caterpillars is more than that of the birds.

☐ **100** *(a)*
One of the most important ecological factors in woodland sites is the level of light getting to the woodland floor. As the woodland ages and the tree canopy thickens, light levels are reduced and only specialised shade-dwelling plants can live there. If woodland is managed, for example, by coppicing, there is usually a greater variety of plants.

☐ **101** *(e)*
Most ecosystems on Earth are powered by light energy from the Sun (a few very unusual ones are driven by a few species of chemosynthetic bacteria). Plants make sugars from carbon dioxide, water and sunlight in photosynthesis, and so are the only source of nutrients and energy for all other organisms in food chains.

☐ **102** *(b)*
Photosynthesis is usually about 1% efficient, with some exceptional species, such as sugarcane, able to fix about 5% of the sunlight illuminating the crop field. Of 1,000,000 kJ entering the pond, we would expect about 10,000 kJ of the energy to be converted to energy within carbohydrate molecules.

A102, 103

☐ **103** *(c)*
Photosynthesis is about 1% efficient, so 10,000 kJ of the original sunlight energy will be fixed in carbohydrates. Transfer between trophic levels, for example from plants to herbivores, is about 10% efficient, so this 10,000 kJ of plant carbohydrate is reduced to about 1,000 kJ of animal tissue at the herbivore trophic level.

☐ **104** *(c)*
Energy transfer from sunlight to plants is about 1% efficient, the transfer from plants to herbivores is about 10% efficient, and the transfer from herbivores to carnivores is also about 10% efficient. At the end of this chain

about 100 kJ will be found in the tissues of the first-level carnivores.

☐ **105** *(b)*
A mammal uses most of its energy in moving, or in maintaining its body temperature, and very little energy is used in making gametes.

☐ **106** *(a)*
The first product of photosynthesis is a simple sugar called glucose, and some of this sugar will be allowed to build up within the cytoplasm. When the level becomes too high, the glucose will be converted to another kind of carbohydrate called starch. A starch molecule is a chain of glucose molecules.

☐ **107** *(a)*
Energy is lost at each transfer between the trophic levels of a food chain, and so the shorter the chain, the more energy is available to the top predators. The agricultural application of this is that if we grow plants rather than raising animals that feed on the plants, we can harvest more energy from the land.

☐ **108** *(e)*
In predator-prey cycles, the numbers of predators are dependent upon the numbers of prey, and, simultaneously, the numbers of prey are linked to the number of predators, as many predators will kill many prey. The population of lynx will fall only when the population of hares has fallen and the lynx begin to die of starvation. If other predators and prey are present, the effect of each on the other will be weakened and cycles may not occur.

☐ **109** *(a)*
Energy is lost at every stage in a food chain. Omnivores complicate food webs by eating things at several different trophic levels, and producers can be much larger than any consumers.

☐ **110** *(b)*
Predatory birds, like the peregrine falcon, are at the peak of food chains, while pesticides like DDT enter the food chain much lower down at the level of the herbivorous invertebrates. The problem with these pesticides is that they cannot be eliminated from an animal's body, and so increasingly accumulate in the tissues as they ascend the food chain. Therefore, top predators, such as the falcons, may be exposed to an amount of DDT initially carried by thousands of insects.

A110

Carbon and nitrogen cycles

☐ **111** *False*
If food is 'off', it can make us ill so we do try to prevent our food decaying. However, decay is a very important process because it recycles the important resources that living things need to survive. If decay did not occur, important nutrients would remain locked up in dead bodies, which would not decompose and therefore take up lots of space.

☐ **112** *True*
Micro-organisms, such as bacteria and fungi, are very important to all other living organisms because they recycle dead and waste organic matter. If they did not, we would not be able to survive because important nutrients such as carbon would be locked up inside the dead and waste, and plants would not be able to make food for themselves and for the animals that eat them.

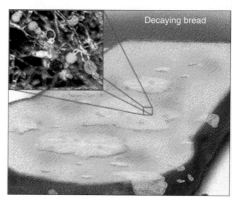

Decaying bread

A112, 114, 122

☐ **113** *(c)*
Earthworms and woodlice both eat dead leaves and break this material down when they egest it in their faeces. Fungi and bacteria can then work even faster on these faeces and complete the decomposition to simpler substances.

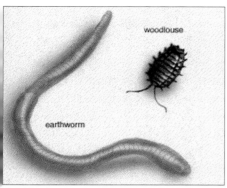

A113, 120

☐ **114** *(b)*
Microbes, chiefly fungi and bacteria, are largely responsible for the decay of food. Larger organisms may live where decay is happening, and they may be feeding on the food and breaking it up into smaller pieces, but they are not the cause of decomposition.

☐ **115** *(c)*
To be biodegradable, a material must be broken down by living organisms. Cardboard is pulped wood, so it can be broken down by fungi in any rubbish dump, but metals cannot be digested by organisms. Some plastics can be broken down by bacteria, but the process is very slow, and it is better to regard such materials as non-biodegradeable.

☐ **116** *(d)*
Decay relies on enzymes produced by micro-organisms. The temperature has to be high enough for these enzymes to work, and a moist environment is needed because the enzymes are working outside the bodies of the fungi or bacteria. In most cases, oxygen is also required as the microbes need to respire.

☐ **117** *(b)*
For decay to take place, bacteria and fungi are needed as well as the necessary conditions for their survival, which are warmth, oxygen and moisture. Animals (scavengers) may speed up the process by breaking down the material, but they are not essential for decay to happen.

☐ **118** *(d)*
Except for the oak tree, the organisms listed are involved in some way in the breakdown and recycling of dead organic matter. Worms and woodlice are detritivores that eat dead plant and animal matter and mince it into much smaller pieces, which emerge in their faeces. The micro-organisms, fungi and bacteria, breakdown relatively indigestible substances, such as cellulose and lignin.

☐ **119** *(c)*
Fungus is the only micro-organism on the list, but all the alternatives are involved in decay and decomposition in the widest sense. Along with bacteria, fungi are responsible for almost all the decomposition occurring in natural ecosystems.

☐ **120** *(a)*
Earthworms burrow through the soil constantly, improving aeration and drainage. They chew up and eat dead material, creating humus, and add their excretory products to the soil.

☐ **121** *(d)*
The population of micro-organisms in the soil grows because the agar provides all the nutrients the bacteria need, and the temperature, 25°C, is ideal for population growth. The petri dish should be covered to prevent bacterial spores escaping in large numbers.

A121

☐ **122** *(a)*
Most of our food is also suitable food for bacteria and fungi. The micro-organisms eat the food and cause it to rot. Sometimes the rotting food produces chemicals, which may be harmful to humans.

☐ **123** *(e)*
To preserve food, it must be stored where the conditions are unsuitable for the growth of fungi.

☐ **124** *(c)*
Food is spoiled due to the growth and activity of micro-organisms. This can be proven by showing that in stale food, such as the stale pasteurised milk on plate Y, there is a higher number of micro-organisms than in similar, fresh food, such as the fresh pasteurised milk on plate X.

A124

☐ **125** *(b)*
Cold temperatures will not kill micro-organisms, but a refrigerator at 4°C will slow down their activities. Colder temperatures of -20°C in a freezer will stop the activities of the micro-organisms, which is why the food lasts longer.

☐ **126** *(d)*
The movement of atmospheric carbon dioxide into plants happens in photosynthesis, when plants combine carbon dioxide with water to make carbohydrates.

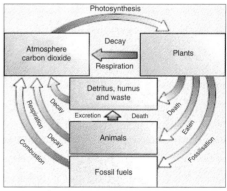

A126, 127, 128

☐ **127** *(d)*
Carbon, in the form of carbon dioxide, is taken out of the atmosphere by plants via the process of photosynthesis.

☐ **128** *(a)*
The carbon stored in fossil fuels has been there for millions of years. It is released into the atmosphere in the form of carbon dioxide via the process of combustion, or burning. We are burning large amounts of fossil fuels and so producing huge quantities of carbon dioxide. Carbon dioxide is a gas that contributes to the greenhouse effect. The greenhouse effect is therefore increasing due to the extra carbon dioxide from the combustion of fossil fuels.

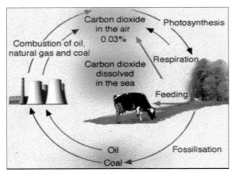

A129, 130, 131, 132

☐ **129** *(e)*
Respiration is the process by which all organisms gain the energy they need to survive. A waste product of respiration is carbon dioxide and this is released back into the atmosphere.

☐ **130** *(b)*
Photosynthesis is the process by which plants take carbon dioxide from the air and change it into sugars.

☐ **131** *(d)*
Carbon compounds, such as carbohydrates, fats or proteins, are vital to the survival of plants and animals. Animals take in the carbon they need by eating plants or other animals.

☐ **132** *(c)*
Respiration is the process that uses up carbohydrates in all organisms, producing energy and the waste product carbon dioxide.

☐ **133** *(c)*
Fungi are very important in decay, breaking down chemicals in dead bodies and putting them back into the ground. The fungi do this because they gain energy from the decomposition, in the same way as we gain energy from eating cornflakes, but their decomposition also recycles many essential chemicals. Unlike plants, fungi cannot convert carbon dioxide back into glucose.

☐ **134** *(b)*
Five groups of micro-organisms are involved in the five steps of the nitrogen cycle. The nitrogen-fixers convert nitrogen gas into ammonia. The nitrifiers are of two types: those that make ammonia into nitrite and those that make nitrite into nitrate. The ammonifiers release ammonia from dead material. The denitrifiers convert nitrate and ammonia into nitrogen gas, making the soil less fertile.

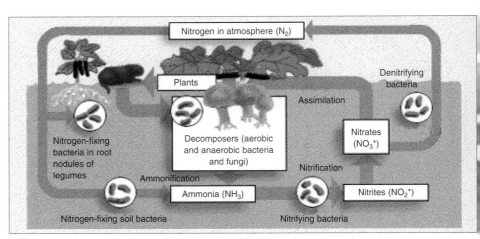

A134

☐ **135** *(b)*
In the root nodules, there are bacteria called Rhizobium, which can make gaseous nitrogen in the atmosphere into the nitrate and the ammonium that can be absorbed and assimilated by plants. This work is called nitrogen fixation and is one of the most important microbial activities on Earth.

☐ **136** *(a)*
The nitrates are dissolved in water in the soil and are absorbed by the plant's roots. They are transported around the plant and used to produce proteins vital to the plant's survival.

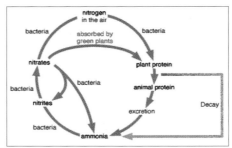

A136

☐ **137** *(b)*
Many reactions that occur in living organisms are very difficult to perform in the laboratory or in industry, and this is always due to the fact that living things contain many extraordinarily effective catalysts, called enzymes.

☐ **138** *(e)*
Some families of green plants, especially peas and beans, have special nitrogen-fixing bacteria within their roots as part of a symbiosis. The bacterium gets energy-rich sugars from the plant, and the plant gets nitrates from the bacterium.

☐ **139** *(c)*
Only a few plant families develop the root nodules that enable them to fix atmospheric nitrogen, and the legumes – peas and beans – are the most useful to the farmers. The legume family forms pod fruits, and also includes the clovers, the lupins, and the Acacia trees of the African semi-desert!

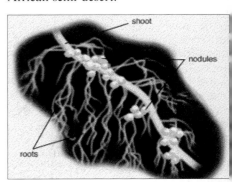

A135, 138, 139

Food production

☐ **140** *(a)*
The term biological control refers to the use of parasites and predators of a pest species to control the pest, so avoiding the use of chemical sprays. The 'sterile male' method swamps a population with artificially reared males that are unable to fertilise eggs.

☐ **141** *(b)*
The appearance of the threads and the rotting suggests that the crop has been affected by a fungus, so a fungicide is most likely to be useful. The term pesticide is often used as a general term for something that kills pests. However, it is usually applied to products that poison insects, while the term herbicide refers to weedkillers.

☐ **142** *(b)*
Overuse of fertilisers will not have an obvious effect on predatory bird populations, although they might have been affected, in the past, by pesticide

pollution. The escape of excess fertilisers into freshwater causes eutrophication, which will reduce oxygen levels and kill fish. Some public health authorities worry about 'blue baby' syndrome caused by nitrate in drinking water. Inorganic fertilisers, with no humus, do little to improve soil structure, aeration and drainage.

☐ **143** *(d)*
A fungicide kills fungi, a herbicide kills weeds, a bacteriocide kills bacteria, and a rodenticide kills rodents. The caterpillar is an immature insect and is successfully killed by an insecticide.

☐ **144** *(d)*
Chemical pesticides, even those extracted from a flower, do not count as biological control measures. The other methods listed could be used with varying success, but the most popular measure against the whitefly is to use a parasitic wasp, called Encarsia, which lays eggs in the fly. These eggs hatch into larvae, which eat the whitefly from the inside outwards.

☐ **145** *(c)*
There is no reason to have any extra oxygen in the atmosphere, and a humidifier is not really needed in a greenhouse if the plants are kept well-watered. However, a heater, lights, a beehive, and a carbon dioxide machine would all add to the productivity of the crop.

☐ **146** *False*
Carbon dioxide is a limiting factor of photosynthesis, especially in an enclosed area, so many greenhouses have a paraffin burner or a cylinder that releases carbon dioxide into the air. This increases the rate of photosynthesis, and the crop yield may increase by as much as 50%.

☐ **147** *(a)*
Artificial ecosystems are created in agriculture and horticulture. To increase production, farmers use fertilisers, herbicides, pesticides, fungicides, irrigation, selective breeding, and genetic engineering. Covering the growing crop with sheets of black polythene will not allow any light to reach the crop, which means the plants cannot photosynthesise and will eventually die.

☐ **148** *(a)*
Competition for resources occurs in artificial ecosystems, such as crop fields, just as it does in natural ecosystems. Any treatment, such as the use of herbicides, irrigation, selective breeding, and inorganic fertilisers, used to increase yield, should help to increase resources available to each plant. Planting seeds too close together will increase competition between seedlings so that yield will probably decline. Part of good farming is knowing how close seeds can safely be planted.

☐ **149** *(e)*
All plants need minerals, and all plants need basically the same set of mineral elements. However, crops would eventually do very badly if fertilisers were not added, because when a crop is harvested the minerals within it are taken away. In a natural system these minerals are put back by the decay of the dead plants. In addition, the farmer uses fertilisers to encourage his crops to grow faster than moorland plants.

☐ **150** *(a)*
Plants, such as a wheat crop, will harvest about 2% of the Sun's energy. If we eat this wheat, we ingest much of this energy, but if we feed the wheat to cattle, they will themselves lose about 90% of the wheat energy and pass on only about 10% to humans. So, we could produce more food energy if we farmed only plants.

☐ **151** *(c)*
Radiation is a way of killing bacteria very quickly and effectively. This technique is used on some food products in some countries but, so far, live animals are not deliberately bathed in radiation.

☐ **152** *(a)*
Intensive techniques for beef cattle are not common and it is unusual to keep them in pens, with the exception of veal production in which calves are penned and fed a special diet. In some areas, dairy cows spend a part of their day in stalls to minimise energy wasted in movement.

☐ **153** *(c)*
There are many economic advantages to keeping animals in intensive conditions, but no-one realistically claims that the products actually taste better. In fact, often free range products are thought to taste better.

☐ **154** *(d)*
The living environment of a battery hen is controlled so that the hen can spend the maximum amount of energy on laying eggs. The hen's living space is confined so that little energy is spent moving; the correct amount of food (no excess) is provided in front of the cage so that no energy is wasted searching for it; the temperature is controlled so that no energy has to be spent on maintaining the correct body temperature. Conditions to prevent disease from spreading are controlled as much as possible.

☐ **155** *(d)*
It is hard to imagine a net that would catch only small fish -- and if one could be invented, it would certainly have the effect of wiping out fish populations extremely quickly! Usually, the minimum size of net meshes is regulated so that only mature fish are caught, after they have had the chance to reproduce.

☐ **156** *False*
Fish farming works only for certain types of fish: those that grow well in confined conditions, that convert food into flesh at a high rate, and that are fairly resistant to disease. Fish farming can be expensive, so it is only worth it if people are willing to pay quite a lot for the fish produced in this way.

☐ **157** *(a)*
The fish that are usually farmed do not yet pose a danger to our native fish species, though we cannot rule out such problems if we farm other species in the future. All the other alternatives listed can cause difficulty, and our wild crayfish already suffer as a result of a disease introduced by an American farmed crayfish. Crayfish, of course, are not fish but freshwater crustaceans.

☐ **158** *(a)*
The most effective policy would be to outlaw the use of nets with very small holes, which catch even young, immature fish. Imposing a minimum mesh size (the distance between the threads of the net mesh) would allow small fish to escape the net and survive to breed. Within two to three years, the fishermen would have larger fish, and more of them to catch. However, until then they will catch very little – which illustrates one of the economic problems with this policy!

Quickfire Questions

Introduction

These questions are designed to give you a rapid way of identifying any major gaps in your knowledge of the syllabus. Most sections contain five foundation and higher level questions and five higher level only questions. Some sections only contain questions at one level.

On a separate piece of paper, write down your answers neatly and as fully as you can. Check your answers at the end of this section. If you have a wrong answer, you should go back to your own notes, or the key facts, to further revise all of that subject.

 QUESTIONS

LIFE PROCESSES

Cell activity and transport between cells

Single and Double Awards

1 MRS GREN is an easy way to remember the most important processes that all living things can do.
(a) What does the 'G' stand for?
(b) What does the 'N' stand for?
(c) What does the 'S' stand for?

2 Which word is missing from the following sequence?

Cell → Tissue → .... → Organ System → Organism

3 Name three structures that a plant and animal cell have in common.

4 What is the function of the cytoplasm in an animal cell?

5 Which process releases energy that a cell can then use?

Double Award and Higher Level only

6 What name is given to the random movement of particles that results in an even distribution of those particles throughout a solution?

7 Which process is able to transport molecules across a membrane from a region of low concentration to a region of high concentration of that molecule?

8 Which method for transporting substances across a membrane requires energy in a chemical form?

9 What is the definition of osmosis?

10 What do the villi in the intestine and the alveoli in the lungs have in common?

Organs working together and cell division

Single and Double Awards

11 What is the function of the nucleus in a cell?

12 Name one structure found in a nucleus.

13 Which cell is specialised by having a tail and being able to swim?

14 Which organ system removes waste urea, and excess salts and water from the body?

15 Which organ system includes the brain, the spinal cord, and the sense organs?

Higher Level only

16 Complete this sentence: Cells in the ovaries and testes divide using the process called ....

17 Which type of cell division produces cells with identical numbers of chromosomes to the original cell?

18 Which type of cell division produces gametes?

19 In which process do the cells actually divide twice?

20 Describe how fertilisation relates to the process of meiosis.

HUMANS AS ORGANISMS

Human diet and digestion

Single and Double Awards

1 What are the seven nutrients required in the basic diet of a human?

2 What is the effect of a lack of vitamin C in the diet?

3 What is the indigestible food that passes through the intestine, and makes up most of the faeces?

4 Which part of the digestive system contains a strongly acid liquid?

5 Which part of the digestive system absorbs most of the digested food?

Higher Level only

6 Where is bile made?

7 What is meant by the phrase: bile 'emulsifies' fats?

8 Which enzymes are used to break down fats?

9 What are fats broken down into?

10 Which large molecule is broken down into amino acids?

Human circulation and the composition and function of blood

Single and Double Awards

11 Which blood cells are responsible for carrying oxygen around the body?

12 Which blood cells help to defend the body against disease?

132

13 Name three substances transported in the plasma of the blood.

14 Which structures in the blood are described as tiny fragments of cells that help the blood to clot?

Double Award only

15 Complete the following sentences: Blood is pushed around the body by a .... called the heart. The blood leaves the heart through the .... When inside an organ, the blood vessels are very tiny and are called .... The blood is returned to the heart through the ....

16 What is meant by 'a double circulatory system'?

17 Which blood vessels have the thickest walls?

18 Where in the human circulatory system will the blood pressure be highest?

19 Explain why the circulatory system is sometimes referred to as the body's central heating system.

20 Which blood vessels are most likely to be carrying red blood cells in which the haemoglobin is being converted to oxyhaemoglobin?

Human breathing

Double Award only

21 Name the structures that air passes through as it enters the lungs.

22 Describe one way in which the surface of the lung is adapted to speed up the diffusion of oxygen into the blood.

23 Name the two sets of muscles that are used when you inhale.

24 Name the bones that are involved in breathing.

25 What happens to the pressure inside the lungs as you exhale?

Higher Level only

26 When inhaling, the muscles attached to the ribs contract. What happens to the ribcage when this happens?

27 What happens to the diaphragm when its muscles contract?

28 to 30 Complete the sentences: The two actions in questions **26** and **27** cause the volume in the thorax to become ....(**28**). Increasing the volume in the thorax causes the pressure to be ....(**29**). The result of this change in pressure is to cause ....(**30**).

Human respiration

Double Award only

31 Which cells in the body carry out the chemical process of respiration?

32 Why is respiration so important to a cell's activity?

33 Write a word equation for aerobic respiration.

34 State one use for the energy released during respiration.

35 Write a word equation for human anaerobic respiration.

Higher Level only

36 Which chemical causes muscles to feel very tired (fatigued)?

37 Why does a runner continue to breathe rapidly when resting after a race?

38 What happens to the lactic acid built up after exercise?

39 Aerobic respiration releases more energy than anaerobic respiration from the same amount of glucose. Is this statement true or false?

40 Give one characteristic that would indicate how fit an athlete is.

Human nervous system

Single and Double Awards

41 Name three main sense organs.

42 Name two stimuli to which the human skin is sensitive.

43 What connects the sense organs to the brain?

44 How does the message from the sense organ travel to the brain?

45 What is the advantage to an animal of having a nervous system?

Higher Level only

46 What is the function of a receptor?

47 The optic nerve carries nerve impulses from the eye to the brain. What type of nerve is this?

48 When the nerve impulse has entered the brain, there is a small gap between the end of the sensory neuron and the start of the next neuron. What is this gap called?

49 Describe how the nerve impulse is able to pass across this gap.

50 Complete the following list of terms that describe a reflex action: Stimulus ➔...........➔ Co-ordinator ➔...............➔ Response

Human eye

Single and Double Awards

51 Which part of the eye is sensitive to light?

52 What happens to the eye when you walk into a brightly lit room?

53 What is the tough, transparent outer coat of the eye called?

54 Which structure is attached to the lens?

55 What is the name of the nerve carrying impulses from the eye to the brain?

Higher Level only

56 How is the shape of the lens altered when focusing on an object close to the eye?

57 Explain why it is more relaxing to look at a distant object than one that is close to you.

58 Which structure in the eye, other than the lens, helps the lens to focus light?

59 What is the name of the two types of cell in the retina?

60 Which of these two types of cell is sensitive in dim light?

Human hormones

Single and Double Awards

61 How are hormones transported around the body?

62 Complete this sentence: Organs that produce hormones are called ....

63 Fill in the blank: Hormones will be carried to all organs in the body but will only have their effect on some of these organs. The organ that a particular hormone affects is called a .... organ.

64 Which two hormones are responsible for controlling blood sugar level?

65 A woman's monthly menstrual cycle is controlled by hormones. One of the functions of these hormones is to cause the thickening of the lining of the womb. Name the other function of these hormones.

Higher Level only

66 Name one sex hormone found in higher concentrations in men.

67 Name one sex hormone found in higher concentrations in women.

68 Which gland produces hormones that are able to control the production of other hormones?

69 Describe the effects of increased levels of adrenaline in the bloodstream.

70 Complete the following sentence. If blood sugar level is too high, ... is released from the .... into the blood.

Importance of homeostasis and excretion in the kidneys

Single and Double Awards

71 Describe what you understand by the term homeostasis.

72 Explain how sweating can help to keep the body's temperature at about 37°C.

73 How do the lungs help in the processes of homeostasis?

74 The kidneys help in the processes of homeostasis. Which waste product is removed by the kidneys?

75 On a hot, dry day a person will sweat a lot. Explain how this will affect the volume of urine produced by the kidneys.

Higher Level only

76 Explain how vasodilation and vasoconstriction of blood vessels in the skin can help to control body temperature.

77 Describe the differences between the blood entering the kidney in the renal artery and the blood leaving it in the renal vein.

78 There are two main processes in the kidney that are responsible for producing urine, which leaves the kidney and is sent to the bladder. What are these two main processes?

79 Describe how the pituitary gland is involved in controlling the water content of the blood of a person who has not been able to drink for a long time.

80 If a doctor suspects that a patient's kidneys are not working effectively, she may test the urine. Explain why the presence of red blood cells might indicate kidney failure.

Defence against disease

Single and Double Awards

81 Name two groups of microbes that might cause diseases.

82 Why are some diseases more likely to spread among people who live in crowded conditions?

83 The skin is a first line of defence against infection. What does the blood do if the skin is broken?

84 Describe one way in which the breathing organs can stop microbes entering the body.

85 Describe how the stomach can help to prevent illness.

86 Complete the following sentence: If microbes enter the body, they reproduce rapidly and produce .... that make us ill.

87 Once inside the body, the microbes can be attacked by which cells?

88 Describe two ways in which these cells can defend against microbes that have entered the body.

89 Explain why a person who has suffered from mumps is unlikely to suffer a second time from that disease.

90 Explain simply how a person can be artificially immunised against a disease.

Use and abuse of drugs

Single and Double Awards

91 Name a type of drug that can be used against an infection already present in the body.

92 Name a painkilling drug (analgesic).

93 Name a socially acceptable legal drug that can cause harm.

94 Name a group of drugs that can be bought legally, but are not socially acceptable and are very dangerous if used incorrectly.

95 Name two diseases that might be caused by smoking cigarettes.

96 Why is it so difficult to give up smoking once you have started?

97 What part of the body does a small amount of alcohol affect?

98 What can be the result of drinking small amounts of alcohol?

99 Which organ is affected by drinking large amounts of alcohol over a long period of time?

100 How might solvent abuse affect the body?

GREEN PLANTS AS ORGANISMS

Plant structure and plant nutrition

Double Award only

1 State the functions of the rooting system of a plant.

2 What is the function of chlorophyll in photosynthesis?

3 Write a word equation for photosynthesis.

4 Explain why plants produce more carbon dioxide than they use at night.

5 Carbon dioxide often acts as a limiting factor on the rate of photosynthesis. Explain what is meant by this statement.

Higher Level only

6 Sugars can be used for a range of purposes in a plant. How are sugars used to make cell walls?

7 Why is starch, rather than sugar, used for storage?

8 Sugars are composed of three elements: Carbon, Hydrogen and Oxygen. Which other element is required to make a protein?

9 What substance requires the mineral ion magnesium for its manufacture in plant cells?

10 After growing the same crop on the same land in his allotment for many years, Fred noticed that his beans had poor roots and younger purple leaves. Explain to Fred why he should not grow the same crop on the same land year after year.

Plant hormones

Double Award only

11 Complete this sentence: A plant shoot will grow towards the ....

12 Complete this sentence: A plant shoot will grow away from ....

13 Complete this sentence: A plant root will grow towards ....

14 Complete this sentence: A plant root will also grow towards ....

15 Complete this sentence: Plants produce .... to control growth.

16 Explain why a farmer does not need to worry about which way up a seed is planted.

17 Explain, briefly, how a plant responds to a stimulus through the 'unequal distribution of hormones'.

18 Describe how the use of a plant hormone might help humans to produce large numbers of identical plants quickly.

19 Describe how the use of a plant hormone might help a fruit farmer.

20 Describe how the use of a plant hormone might help humans to create a weed-free lawn.

Transport systems inside plants

Double Award only

21 Through which structures in a leaf does water vapour escape?

22 Which cells control the opening and closing of these structures?

23 What does a plant look like if it is short of water?

24 Which tissue transports water from the roots to the leaves?

25 Which tissue transports sugars from the leaves to the rest of the plant?

Higher Level only

26 What process enables the uptake of water by root hairs?

27 What process enables the uptake of mineral ions by root hairs?

28 Explain why a plant's leaves and stem droop if they are short of water.

29 Explain why plants lose water quickly on a hot day.

30 What other conditions will affect the rate of transpiration of water from the leaves of a plant?

VARIATION, INHERITANCE AND EVOLUTION

Variation

Single and Double Awards

1 Why do young plants and animals resemble their parents?

2 Identical twins have exactly the same set of alleles as each other. Explain why it is possible for parents to tell them apart.

3 What name is given to the change in an existing gene?

4 Which cells are involved in sexual reproduction but not in asexual reproduction?

5 Which type of reproduction, sexual or asexual, produces the greatest variation?

Higher Level only

6 Which type of cell division is used in asexual reproduction?

7 Which type of cell division creates cells with half the normal number of chromosomes?

8 Which type of cell division is used to produce clones?

9 State one possible cause of a mutation.

10 What are the possible consequences of a mutation in a sex cell (gamete)?

Genetics

Single and Double Awards

11 Which chromosome is present in a male human cell, but not in a female human cell?

12 Why are human sperm described as X or Y?

13 State the name of a genetic disease.

14 Describe one human characteristic that is affected both by the genes inherited from parents and the environment.

15 Describe one human characteristic that is affected only by the genes inherited from parents and is not usually changed by the environment.

Higher Level only

16 What term is used to describe an allele that has to be present on both chromosomes if it is to be expressed?

17 What name is given to an individual who has chromosomes with different alleles of a gene?

18 Give the name of a genetic disease that is caused when at least one parent must have the disorder.

19 A disease is caused by a recessive allele and both parents are heterozygous for that allele. What are the chances of any one child suffering from the disease?

20 A disease is caused by a dominant allele, when one of the parents is homozygous recessive and the other is heterozygous. What are the chances of any one child suffering from the disease?

Scientific uses of genetics

Single and Double Awards

21 What do you understand by the phrase 'artificial selection'?

22 A farmer wants to reduce the number of cows he is keeping. He doesn't want to lose money so he needs to breed cows that will each produce more milk. Describe how he should choose which cows to use for breeding.

23 State one reason for using artificial selection when breeding a crop plant.

24 A flower-grower notices that one of his geraniums has an unusual colour. How would he be able to produce more geraniums with the identical colour?

25 What term is used to describe a number of plants or animals produced by asexual reproduction?

Higher Level only

26 What do you understand by the term 'genetic engineering'?

27 Give one example of genetic engineering that involves using a human gene in a bacterium.

28 How is the product of this genetic engineering manufactured in large quantities?

29 Describe one example of a modern cloning technique.

30 Describe one disadvantage of the widespread use of cloning.

DNA

Double Award and Higher Level only

31 Describe the precise location of most of the DNA in a cell.

32 What is the relationship between a gene and DNA?

33 - 40 Fill in the spaces in the following paragraph: The DNA molecule is coiled to form a ....(**33**) DNA contains ....(**34**) information that determines inherited characteristics. This information is in the structure of the DNA molecule. It is therefore important that during mitosis the DNA molecule is perfectly ....(**35**). This information is used to order the sequence of amino acids when building ....(**36**). During genetic engineering, sections of DNA can be ....(**37**) of human cells. These sections of DNA are then transferred into a ....(**38**). The 'scissors' in genetic engineering are ....(**39**). The type of molecule most frequently genetically engineered is therefore a ....(**40**).

Evolution

Single and Double Awards

41 Describe how the remains of plants and animals can become fossils.

42 When comparing fossils it is important to be able to date the surrounding rocks. Explain why dating fossils is important to the study of evolution.

43 What do fossils tell us about evolution?

44 Study the following data and describe how the modern horse (Equus) evolved.

Age of fossil (millions of years)	Name of fossil	Number of toes on each leg
60	Eohippus	4
25	Merychippus	3
1	Equus	1

45 Describe one way in which Eohippus might have become extinct.

Higher Level only

46 Why should the widespread use of clones be a threat to evolution?

47 Individuals in a population vary. This is due to genetic and environmental causes. Which of these causes is most important in terms of evolution? Explain your answer.

48 Use the data in the table in question **44** to suggest why Equus was more successful than Merychippus.

49 Explain what is meant by 'survival of the fittest'.

50 Explain why it is important to evolution that a particular animal does not just survive, but survives and reproduces.

LIVING THINGS IN THEIR ENVIRONMENT

Adaptation, competition and predation

Single and Double Awards

1 What is meant by the term 'population'?

2 What is meant by the term 'community'?

3 Environmental factors can affect the size of a population. These environmental factors can be either physical or biological.

(a) Describe one physical factor that might affect a population of daisies.

(b) Describe one biological factor that might affect a population of daisies.

(c) Describe an adaptation that would allow daisies to be successful in a field of grass.

4 Each evening a biologist studied rabbits eating grass in a large field. Young rabbits were seen amongst the adults. Also in the field was a fox and often an owl. Both were on the lookout for young rabbits.

(a) What term would you use to describe the relationship between the fox and the owl?

(b) Explain what would happen to these animals if the farmer decided to plough up the field.

5 A keen gardener, Akram, planted seeds in trays in his greenhouse. He planted two different species. He used a different tray for each species and they grew very successfully. His neighbour, John, wanted to have an equally successful garden and so copied Akram. Unfortunately John was a little mean with the trays and used one large tray to grow his seeds. One species grew very successfully, but the other was very poor.

(a) Explain why John was less successful than Akram.

(b) Before planting his seeds Akram cleaned his greenhouse thoroughly with a disinfectant. Explain why he did this.

(c) Akram also checked each day for any pests in the greenhouse. Explain why he did this.

Human impact on the environment

Single and Double Awards

6 State one reason why humans produce more pollution today than we did 100 years ago.

7 Name two pollutants that can be produced by burning fossil fuels.

8 Describe one effect of acid rain.

9 State three ways in which humans reduce the amount of land available to wildlife.

10 Name a pollutant that can often be found dissolved in river water.

Higher Level only

11 Name two 'greenhouse gases'.

12 Describe how these gases raise the mean global temperature.

13 What are the likely effects of increases in the mean global temperature?

14 Describe two ways in which deforestation can make the greenhouse effect worse.

15 Choose one of the following situations and describe its cause and effects:
Raw sewage in a river
Chlorofluorocarbons in the upper atmosphere
Rabbits in Australia.

Energy and nutrient transfer

Double Award only

16 What does the arrow in a food chain represent?

17 Which type of organism does a food chain always begin with?

18 From where does this organism get its energy?

19 Which organism is the first consumer in the following food chain?
Dandelion → Snail → Thrush

20 What type of display shows the number of organisms at each level in a food chain?

Higher Level only

21 What type of display shows the mass of living material at each level in a food chain?

22 State one reason why the mass of material at each stage in a food chain is usually less than the previous stage.

23 Some energy is transferred at each stage to the next animal in the food chain. This provides food energy for that animal. However, most energy is 'lost'. What eventually happens to this 'lost' energy?

24 Why do food chains involving mammals and birds tend to 'lose' most energy?

25 Use your knowledge of pyramids of biomass to explain why birds of prey are only rarely seen.

Carbon and nitrogen cycles

Double Award only

26 Complete this sentence: All living things take materials from the environment for .... and to provide energy. These materials must be .... so that they can be used by other living things.

27 Describe two conditions needed for decay.

28 The carbon cycle describes one of the cycles that maintain a constant supply of materials for living things. What is the name of the process by which plants use carbon dioxide from the atmosphere?

29 Name two chemicals in plants and animals that contain carbon.

30 What is the name of the process by which plants, animals and bacteria return carbon dioxide to the atmosphere?

Higher Level only

31 The nitrogen cycle describes how nitrogen is recycled. In what form do plants absorb nitrogen from the soil?

32 Which molecule in a plant does this nitrogen help to construct?

33 How do animals get their nitrogen?

34 Dead plants and animals, and their wastes, are first broken down into which type of compound?

35 What is the name of the type of bacteria that convert these compounds into nitrates?

Food production

Double Award and Higher Level only

36 Explain why growing a food crop in a field can feed more people than if the same field were used for producing animals for meat.

37 Weeding can cost a lot of money. Explain why weeding a field where a crop is growing can still prove to be worthwhile.

38 Describe a cheaper way of achieving the same weed-free field of crops.

39 Explain why it might not be worthwhile growing a crop too close together.

40 Insect pests and disease are two ways in which plant crops are often reduced. State two different methods used to prevent pests and disease affecting crop production.

41 What is the disadvantage of intensive farming of plant crops?

42 Explain why most farm animals are herbivores.

43 Less than 5% of the energy fed to a bullock is returned as energy available to the human that eats its meat. How could this percentage be increased?

44 How does a greenhouse improve the productivity of a plant crop?

45 From your knowledge of how food energy is 'lost' in a food chain, explain why keeping fish might be a more profitable enterprise than keeping bullocks.

 ANSWERS

LIFE PROCESSES

Cell activity and transport between cells

1
(a) Growth
(b) Nutrition
(c) Sensitivity

2 Organ

3 Nucleus, cell membrane, cytoplasm

4 The cytoplasm is where most of the chemical reactions take place.

5 Respiration

6 Diffusion

7 Active transport

8 Active transport

9 Osmosis is the diffusion of water molecules from a region of high water concentration to a region of lower water concentration through a partially permeable membrane.

10 The villi and the alveoli are both exchange surfaces; they both have a large surface area; they both have a good blood supply; they both are moist; they both are one cell thick.

Organs working together and cell division

11 The nucleus controls the actions of the cell.

12 Chromosomes

13 Sperm

14 Urinary or excretory system

15 Nervous system

16 meiosis

17 Mitosis

18 Meiosis

19 Meiosis

20 Fertilisation restores the normal number of chromosomes from the half number in each gamete.

HUMANS AS ORGANISMS

Human diet and digestion

1 Carbohydrates, fats (lipids), proteins, vitamins, mineral ions (salts), dietary fibre, and water

2 Scurvy, which causes gums to swell and bleed, and teeth to loosen

3 Dietary fibre

4 Stomach

5 Small intestine (villi)

6 Liver

7 Bile breaks up large drops of fat into smaller droplets, increasing the surface area for enzyme activity.

8 Lipases

9 Fatty acids and glycerol

10 Protein

Human circulation and the composition and function of blood

11 Red blood cells

12 White blood cells

13 Any three of the following are correct: dissolved food substances, hormones, urea, carbon dioxide, and water.

14 Platelets

15 pump, arteries (aorta or pulmonary artery), capillaries, veins (vena cava or pulmonary vein)

16 The blood passes through the heart twice on one journey around the body.

17 Arteries (aorta)

☐ **18** The blood pressure is highest as the blood leaves the heart, that is, in the arteries near to the heart. (The blood in the aorta is at a higher pressure than in the pulmonary artery.)

☐ **19** Organs, for example, the liver, produce a lot of heat and as the circulatory system passes through them, the blood is warmed up. This heat is then carried to colder parts of the body, for example, the fingers.

☐ **20** Capillaries in the lungs

Human breathing

☐ **21** Nose or mouth, trachea (windpipe), bronchus, bronchioles, alveoli

☐ **22** Any one of the following is correct: large surface area, thin single layer of cells, moist surface, and capillaries.

☐ **23** Intercostal (rib) muscles and diaphragm muscles

☐ **24** Ribs

☐ **25** The pressure increases.

☐ **26** The ribcage is raised upwards and outwards.

☐ **27** The diaphragm flattens.

☐ **28** larger

☐ **29** reduced

☐ **30** air to rush in

Human respiration

☐ **31** All living cells carry out respiration.

☐ **32** Respiration provides a ready source of energy.

☐ **33** Glucose + Oxygen → Carbon dioxide + Water + Energy released

☐ **34** Any one of the following is correct: building larger molecules from smaller ones, active transport, muscle contraction, and maintaining a steady body temperature.

☐ **35** Glucose → Lactic acid + Energy released

☐ **36** Lactic acid

☐ **37** A runner breathes rapidly to repay the oxygen debt.

☐ **38** Lactic acid is oxidised to carbon dioxide and water.

☐ **39** True

☐ **40** Any one of the following is correct: slow heart beat (pulse), high tolerance of lactic acid, high heart output, high lung capacity, and short recovery period after exercise.

Human nervous system

☐ **41** Any three of the following are correct: eye, ear, nose, tongue and skin.

☐ **42** Any two of the following are correct: pressure, temperature change, and touch.

☐ **43** Nerves

☐ **44** The message from the sense organ travels to the brain by impulse or electrical impulse.

☐ **45** The nervous system enables the animal to react to its surroundings and to respond rapidly.

☐ **46** The receptor causes an impulse in a nerve cell, and changes a stimulus into a nerve impulse.

☐ **47** Sensory nerve

☐ **48** Synapse

☐ **49** A chemical (neurotransmitter) diffuses across the gap.

☐ **50** Receptor (or sensor), Effector

Human eye

☐ **51** Retina

☐ **52** The pupil becomes smaller due to the contraction of circular muscles in the iris.

☐ **53** Cornea

☐ **54** Suspensory ligaments

☐ **55** Optic nerve

☐ **56** When focusing on an object close to the eye, the ciliary muscles (body) contracts, and the suspensory ligaments slacken, so altering the lens to become more convex in shape.

☐ **57** When focusing on a distant object, the ciliary muscles are relaxed.

☐ **58** Cornea

☐ **59** Rods and cones

☐ **60** Rods

Human hormones

☐ **61** In the blood

☐ **62** (endocrine) glands

☐ **63** target

☐ **64** Insulin and glucagon

☐ **65** To release an egg from the ovary

☐ **66** Testosterone

☐ **67** Any one of the following is correct: oestrogen, progesterone, luteinising hormone, and follicle stimulating hormone.

☐ **68** Pituitary gland

☐ **69** Adrenalin prepares an animal for 'flight or fight'. It makes the animal more able to defend itself by increasing the flow of sugar into the bloodstream, opening the pupils wider, opening the bronchioles wider, increasing the flow of blood from the heart, and increasing the flow of blood to the muscles and the brain.

☐ **70** insulin, pancreas

Importance of homeostasis and excretion in the kidneys

☐ **71** Homeostasis is a term that describes how the body keeps a more or less constant internal body environment. This helps the chemical reactions to happen in ideal conditions.

72 Sweat evaporates from the skin and this helps to cool the skin.

73 Carbon dioxide is made during aerobic respiration and has to be removed from the body. The lungs excrete this waste gas.

74 Urea

75 When sweating increases, the volume of urine produced will decrease. This is because the formation of both sweat and urine uses water from the blood. To prevent the blood from losing too much water, the kidneys remove less. This means that the kidneys will produce less urine, but it will be more concentrated.

76 Vasodilation opens up the capillaries that flow close to the surface of the skin. The blood carries the heat to the surface where it is radiated away from the skin, so cooling the blood. Vasoconstriction closes these capillaries, helping to keep the heat in the blood. While this does not increase the temperature of the body, it does help to reduce heat loss.

77 The blood in the renal artery will contain more urea, more water, more mineral ions and more oxygen, and will have a higher pressure.

78 Ultrafiltration and reabsorption

79 If the water content of the blood is low, the pituitary gland releases the hormone ADH (anti-diuretic hormone). This increases the amount of water reabsorbed back into the blood from the urine, and so reduces water loss from the body in the urine. The urine becomes more concentrated.

80 Ultrafiltration in the Bowman's capsule should allow water and solutes, but not red blood cells, through to the kidney tubule.

Defence against disease

81 Any two of the following are correct: bacteria, viruses and fungi.

82 Diseases can be spread by coughing, sneezing or close contact. The closer you are to someone with a disease that is transmitted in this way, the more likely you are to catch that disease.

83 The blood clots and a scab begins to form.

84 Any one of the following is correct: the hairs in the nose filter the air, the mucus lines the bronchi that trap microbes, and the cilia or tiny hairs in the bronchi sweep the microbes out of the chest.

85 The stomach contains strong acid to kill microbes.

86 poisons or toxins

87 White blood cells

88 Any two of the following are correct: ingesting microbes, producing antibodies, and producing antitoxins.

89 Once the white blood cells have produced antibodies against a bacterium such as mumps, they can reproduce them again quickly before the bacterium has had a chance to multiply into large numbers.

90 Antigens, which have been killed or weakened, are injected into the blood. White blood cells learn how to produce the antibodies. When a living bacterium invades the body, the white cells already know how to produce the antibodies to kill the bacterium.

Use and abuse of drugs

91 Antibiotic, for example, penicillin or antibody serum

92 Aspirin or paracetamol

93 Alcohol or tobacco

94 Solvents

95 Any two of the following are correct: lung cancer, emphysema, and diseases of the heart and the blood vessels.

96 Drugs in tobacco are addictive.

97 Brain

98 Small amounts of alcohol can result in the slowing down of reaction time and the lack of self control.

99 Liver

100 Solvent abuse can cause damage to the lungs, liver and brain, and can also affect behaviour.

GREEN PLANTS AS ORGANISMS

Plant structure and plant nutrition

1 The rooting system anchors the plant in the ground, and absorbs water and nutrients (mineral ions).

2 Chlorophyll absorbs sunlight energy.

3 Carbon dioxide + Water + Light energy → Sugar (glucose) + Oxygen

4 Plant cells are always respiring and producing carbon dioxide. At night, they cannot use this carbon dioxide for photosynthesis because there is too little light. (Light is a limiting factor.)

5 Carbon dioxide is essential for photosynthesis. If there is no carbon dioxide, photosynthesis cannot happen no matter how much light or water is available.

6 Sugars are converted into cellulose for cell walls.

7 Starch is insoluble and therefore does not affect osmosis.

8 Nitrogen, which is usually absorbed into the roots as nitrates.

9 Chlorophyll

10 Growing the same crop in the same soil tends to deplete the soil of the particular mineral ions that the plant needs most. In this example, phosphates are the missing mineral ions, which makes them the limiting factor.

Plant hormones

11 light

12 the direction of gravity

13 water

□ **14** the direction of gravity

□ **15** hormones

□ **16** Shoots grow away from the direction of gravity, and roots grow towards the direction of gravity.

□ **17** The unequal distribution of hormones produces an uneven growth pattern. For example, the side of a shoot away from the light has more hormones and so grows faster. This causes the shoot to grow towards the light.

□ **18** Rooting powder encourages the growth of roots from cuttings.

□ **19** Seedless fruits are produced by applying hormones to unfertilised flowers; fruits can be ripened artificially by releasing an artificial hormone.

□ **20** Weeds in a lawn can be killed by applying a hormone weed killer.

Transport systems inside plants

□ **21** Stomata

□ **22** Guard cells

□ **23** Wilting

□ **24** Xylem

□ **25** Phloem

□ **26** Osmosis

□ **27** Active transport

□ **28** A lack of water in a plant's cells means a lack of turgidity and so the cells 'collapse' and the plant wilts.

□ **29** On a hot day, the air can hold more water vapour and so the damp leaf dries out more quickly. (There is a greater diffusion gradient between the inside and the outside of the leaf.)

□ **30** Humidity – high humidity will reduce the rate of transpiration; wind speed – high wind speed will increase the rate of transpiration; darkness – the stomata will be closed and transpiration will stop

VARIATION, INHERITANCE AND EVOLUTION

Variation

□ **1** The young plants and animals inherit genes from both parents.

□ **2** The children will grow up in slightly different environmental situations, and so will change according to those different environmental conditions.

□ **3** Mutation

□ **4** Sex cells and gametes (eggs and sperm)

□ **5** Sexual reproduction

□ **6** Mitosis

□ **7** Meiosis

□ **8** Mitosis

□ **9** Possible causes of mutation are the exposure to ionising radiation, such as gamma rays, ultra-violet rays and X-rays, and/or, to chemical mutagens, such as tobacco smoke.

□ **10** Mutations could be harmless, or they could affect the offspring by causing abnormal development or even death.

Genetics

□ **11** The Y-chromosome

□ **12** The X-chromosome and the Y-chromosome are separated before the sperm is made. Half of the sperm will have an X-chromosome and half will have a Y-chromosome.

□ **13** Any one of the following is correct: Huntington's chorea, cystic fibrosis, haemophilia, and sickle cell anaemia.

□ **14** Correct answers include height, weight and skin colour.

□ **15** Any one of the following is correct: eye colour, and hair type.

□ **16** Recessive

□ **17** Heterozygous

□ **18** Huntington's chorea

□ **19** One in four, or 25%

□ **20** One in two, or 50%

Scientific uses of genetics

□ **21** 'Artificial selection' means to choose plants or animals that have the desired characteristics, to use plants and animals to breed from, and to produce more plants or animals similar to the one originally chosen.

□ **22** The farmer should choose cows that produce a high yield of milk, choose a bull that is known to produce high yielding cows, and breed only from these.

□ **23** Any one of the following is correct: high yield, disease resistance, and the quality of the crop, for example, its flavouring, colouring, cooking, and keeping properties.

□ **24** Any one of the following is correct: by replanting cuttings, by grafting, and by cloning.

□ **25** Clone

□ **26** 'Genetic engineering' means to cut out the desired gene from one organism and insert it into the DNA of another organism.

□ **27** Human insulin production

□ **28** Bacteria are cultured in large quantities, and the product is removed.

□ **29** Either one of the following is correct: tissue culture – taking a small group of plant cells and growing them into an adult plant; embryo transplanting – taking embryonic cells before they become specialised and growing them into an adult animal.

□ **30** A reduction in the gene pool – a living organism may not have the range of genes required to survive any change in the environment in which it lives.

DNA

☐ **31** The chromosomes in the nucleus

☐ **32** The gene is a small section of the DNA.

☐ **33** double helix

☐ **34** coded

☐ **35** replicated or copied

☐ **36** proteins

☐ **37** cut out

☐ **38** recipient cell, bacterium, or new organism

☐ **39** enzymes

☐ **40** protein

Evolution

☐ **41** Some hard parts of animals do not decay; some living organisms decay very slowly and are gradually replaced by other materials so their shape remains; some living organisms do not decay at all because one or more of the conditions needed by the bacteria that cause decay are absent.

☐ **42** Dating the fossils allows the scientist to compare them in chronological order, so as to show how the organism may have evolved over time.

☐ **43** Fossils tell us how different organisms have changed since life developed on earth.

☐ **44** The number of toes on each leg has gradually reduced.

☐ **45** Eohippus might not have been able to run as quickly with four toes. You might think of another equally good idea, but it should use the information about the number of toes.

☐ **46** Clones have very little, if any, genetic variation, and so any change in the environment will mean that they cannot adapt genetically through natural selection.

☐ **47** Genetic causes are the most important because only genes are passed on to any future generation.

☐ **48** Equus has only one toe for each leg and so could probably run faster to escape predators. Again you might have another idea, but it should be supported by the data and linked to a way of surviving.

☐ **49** 'Survival of the fittest' means that individuals with the characteristics most suited to that environment will be most likely to survive and breed successfully.

☐ **50** Survival only benefits that particular individual. Breeding successfully passes those successful genes onto the next generation. Therefore, the survival of the genes could be considered more important than the survival of the individual, once that individual has reproduced.

LIVING THINGS IN THEIR ENVIRONMENT

Adaptation, competition and predation

☐ **1** 'Population' means the number of individuals of the same species present in a habitat.

☐ **2** 'Community' means the number of different species living together in a habitat.

☐ **3**
(a) Any one of the following is correct: light, water, nutrients and temperature.

(b) Any one of the following is correct: tall flowers, large leaves, and fast growth.

(c) Daisies are most likely to suffer from a lack of light, so any adaptation that would keep them in the light would help them to survive.

☐ **4**
(a) Competition

(b) The population of rabbits would decline due to a lack of food and so too would the population of foxes and owls, for the same reason.

☐ **5**
(a) John's plants were competing for light, nutrients, and/or water.

(b) Akram did this to prevent disease reducing his population of plants.

(c) Akram did this to prevent grazers from eating his plants.

Human impact on the environment

☐ **6** Either one of the following is correct: a higher population, and a higher standard of living.

☐ **7** Any two of the following are correct: carbon dioxide, carbon monoxide, sulphur dioxide, and nitrogen dioxide.

☐ **8** Any one of the following is correct: it damages trees, makes rivers and lakes acidic, and kills plants and small animals in the lakes.

☐ **9** Any three of the following are correct: building, quarrying, waste dumps, and farming.

☐ **10** Any one of the following is correct: sewage, phosphates and nitrates.

☐ **11** Carbon dioxide and methane

☐ **12** Light energy is allowed into the Earth's atmosphere, but the heat radiated by the Earth is trapped in the atmosphere.

☐ **13** Rising sea levels, and changes to the Earth's climate

☐ **14** Deforestation reduces the amount of carbon dioxide taken out of the atmosphere, and releases stored carbon dioxide when the wood burns or decays.

☐ **15**
Raw sewage in a river causes eutrophication – the death of animal life due to the excessive growth of bacteria decaying the sewage and so removing oxygen from the water. Chlorofluorocarbons in the upper atmosphere cause a reduction in the atmospheric ozone, which, therefore, lets in ultraviolet light, which can cause skin cancer.

Rabbits in Australia – imported from Europe – compete with the indigenous population, and, with no natural predators, there is no natural check on their population growth.

Energy and nutrient transfer

☐ **16** The arrow means 'is eaten by', and shows the direction of the food energy and materials.

☐ **17** Plant, or producer

☐ **18** Sunlight

☐ **19** Snail

☐ **20** Pyramid of numbers

☐ **21** Pyramid of biomass

☐ **22** Mass is lost as waste materials (to be consumed by decomposers and so recycled). Mass is also lost in respiration when supplying energy for living processes, such as movement, and maintaining a constant body temperature.

☐ **23** The 'lost' energy passes into the atmosphere as heat.

☐ **24** Birds and mammals have to maintain a constant temperature, which is usually higher than the environmental temperature, and so these organisms lose heat to the environment.

☐ **25** Birds of prey are the top carnivores placed at the very top of a pyramid of biomass, as they only eat other animals. For this reason, they are few in number and, therefore, are rarely seen.

Carbon and nitrogen cycles

☐ **26** growth, recycled

☐ **27** Any two of the following are correct: warmth, water and oxygen.

☐ **28** Photosynthesis

☐ **29** Any two of the following are correct: carbohydrates (for example, sugars), fats and proteins.

☐ **30** Respiration

☐ **31** As nitrates

☐ **32** Amino acids, or proteins

☐ **33** Animals get their nitrogen by eating plant, or other animal, protein.

☐ **34** Ammonium compounds

☐ **35** Nitrifying bacteria

Food production

☐ **36** Plants are lower down the food chain, and so there are fewer stages at which energy can be 'lost' from the chain.

☐ **37** Weeding reduces the competition from the plants not being harvested, and so allows the crop to grow more successfully.

☐ **38** The use of herbicides, or weedkillers

☐ **39** Competition between plants of the same species can reduce the yield of each plant. There will be a point at which the cost of the extra plants makes it unprofitable. A greater numbers of plants can also encourage disease, and the growing of plants close together will cause the disease to spread rapidly.

☐ **40** Chemical spraying, which uses pesticides and fungicides, and biological control, which uses natural predators

☐ **41** The disadvantage is the lack of opportunity for the natural plants and animals to survive, which leads to the destruction of the natural ecosystems.

☐ **42** Energy is lost at each transfer between the trophic levels of a food chain. Most farm animals are herbivores, because this reduces the number of stages in the food chain and, therefore, the energy 'lost'.

☐ **43** The percentage can be increased by reducing energy 'losses'. This can be done by reducing the movement of the bullock and keeping it in a warm environment.

☐ **44** A greenhouse increases the temperature, which helps to increase all the processes linked to the growth of the plant.

☐ **45** Fish are poikilothermic (cold blooded), and so they do not require heat to maintain their body temperature. Whereas, bullocks use energy to produce heat that will maintain their higher body temperature.

Success Guaranteed!

At Dorling Kindersley we believe that our Revision Guide books will help you achieve your full potential in your exams.

If you use this book as part of your study programme we believe that you will achieve a Grade C or higher in the relevant exam.

To back this claim, if you get a Grade D or lower* and meet the terms and conditions below, you will be eligible to claim a **FREE Dorling Kindersley book** to the same value of your choice.

Once your claim is verified we will send you a copy of **Dorling Kindersley's** catalogue with instructions for ordering your free book.

Please send claims (*following instructions below*) to:

Customer Support Manager
(GCSE Claims)
Dorling Kindersley Children's Marketing
9 Henrietta Street
Covent Garden
London WC2E 8PS

If you have any queries please write to the address above.

*or Scottish Standard Grade 4 or lower

TERMS and CONDITIONS

This guarantee applies only to students who achieve Grade D or lower (GCSE and Irish Junior Certificate) or Grade 4 or lower (Scottish Standard Grade). This guarantee is not extended to overseas syllabuses or students.
The student must have taken the relevant examination. (For students using Physics, Chemistry or Biology GCSE revision guides, the Single or Double Award Science and their equivalents in Scotland are covered.)
This guarantee applies only to students who have purchased a DK GCSE Revision Guide for use at home. Applications from schools will not be accepted. A claim must be made in writing to the address above no more than 30 days after the examination result is received. Students under the age of 18 must have their parent or guardian sign their claim as certification of the claim's authenticity.

The following documentation must be included with the claim:
Details of the date of your GCSE examination, the name and address of the school where you studied for the exam, and the grade achieved. A clearly legible copy of the examination certificate or official notification of your grade. **PLEASE DO NOT SEND ORIGINAL DOCUMENTS.** The original till receipt or invoice for the DK GCSE Revision Guide showing place and date of purchase, and price paid.
Photocopies of these items will not be accepted.